Britain's Imperial Histories

Other Books of Interest from St. Augustine's Press

Jeremy Black, *The Revolutionary War*

Jeremy Black, *Defoe's Britain*

Jeremy Black, *Smollett's Britain*

Jeremy Black, *The Importance of Being Poirot*

Jeremy Black, *The Age of Nightmare*

Jeremy Black, *In Fielding's Wake*

Jeremy Black, *The Civil War*

Chilton Williamson, Jr., *The Last Westerner*

Harvey Flaumenhaft, *The Framework of the Federalist: Visualizing the Structure of the Argumentation*

Daniel J. Mahoney, *The Other Solzhenitsyn: Telling the Truth about a Misunderstood Writer and Thinker*

Will Morrisey, *Shakespeare's Politic Comedy*

John von Heyking, *Comprehensive Judgment and Absolute Selflessness: Winston Churchill on Politics as Friendship*

Thomas F. Powers, *American Multiculturalism and the Anti-Discrimination Regime: The Challenge to Liberal Pluralism*

Gene Fendt, *Camus' Plague: Myth for Our World*

Jeffrey J. Langan (Translator), *The French Revolution Confronts Pius VI*

Nathan Lefler, *Tale of a Criminal Mind Gone Good*

Roger Scruton, *On Hunting*

Anne Drury Hall, *Where the Muses Still Haunt: The Second Reading*

Nalin Ranasinghe, *Shakespeare's Reformation: Christian Humanism and the Death of God*

Winston Churchill, *My Early Life*

Winston Churchill, *Savrola*

Winston Churchill, *The River War*

Britain's Imperial Histories

JEREMY BLACK

ST. AUGUSTINE'S PRESS
South Bend, Indiana

Manufactured in the United States of America.

1 2 3 4 5 6 30 29 28 27 26 25

Library of Congress Control Number: 2025939478

Paperback ISBN: 978-1-58731-087-4
Ebook ISBN: 978-1-58731-088-1

∞ The paper used in this publication meets the minimum requirements of the American National Standard for Information Sciences – Permanence of Paper for Printed Materials, ANSI Z39.48-1984.

St. Augustine's Press
www.staugustine.net

For
John Maurer

Table of Contents

PREFACE

"The approach is quite literally so last century given recent developments in the 'new imperial history' with a focus on culture, gender and race." Surprisingly, this was not the response of the Ukrainians when attacked by Russia in 2022, nor of South-Eastern Asian nations and Taiwan affected by Chinese territorial claims and pressure, nor those in the wider Middle East and North Africa assessing the geopolitical moves of a range of players from Turkey, Iran and the Houthis, to Israel, Egypt and the United Arab Emirates. In all these cases, imperialism was considered in terms of power, force and intimidation, and not "culture, gender and race." I found it amusing to be decried in those terms and again "like the kind of histories that were contemporaneous with the Beatles,"[1] for the inexorable dominance of force as an element in history is all-too-apparent, and, as a result, imperial history without at least a well-grounded understanding of military, political, diplomatic and economic factors and developments is seriously flawed. Indeed, in that light, mention of "literally so last century" might rather be directed to fashionable academic ideas about empire from its last third, as opposed to the realities felt around the world both then and now. There is an analogy with the emphasis in the same period in military history on "War and Society" as opposed to strategy, operations, tactics and effectiveness. Furthermore, it is mistaken to imagine that any work that was done in the era of the Beatles on the more military and political aspects of empires, British or other, was surely the last word.

"Welcome to the Free Territory of Trieste USA and UK come back!" is not the sign you expect, but in Trieste it is still (in 2024) prominently displayed in the second most important square, the Piazza della Borsa, a counterpoint to the nearby largest, the Piazza Unità d'Italia, which only got that name in 1919 after the loss of control of Austria under which it had been the Piazza Grande. Empires come and go. The particular reference is to the role of the two powers in protecting Zone A of the Free Territory of Trieste, an independent territory under the direct responsibility of the United Nations from 1947 to 1954. 5,000 British troops and 5,000 Americans were deployed under the Allied Military Government, until, in 1954, the Territory was divided between Italy and Yugoslavia, a decision confirmed by the 1975 Treaty of Osimo.

The victorious British in Trieste, as in Libya, Somalia, Germany and Austria in this period or the Americans in many places, notably Japan, were an aspect of military empire. In practice, empire took many different forms, some clashing, and in a variety of contingencies and conjunctures, and intersected with a range of issues and interests around the world. In a short book it is only possible to introduce a few, but a key point at the outset was that there was no one type of empire, no prototype. To many today, empire might seem obvious: governors with ostrich-feathers in their colonial garb ruling non-White peoples; but this scarcely describes the situation across time and place.

Moreover, linked to this, there was no one context, cause, course or consequence for empire and imperialism, whether in Britain or in those other areas affected. Nor was there a single set of assumptions in Britain, or elsewhere, about empire at the time or subsequently, and, correspondingly, no valid single definition of empire.

These points are relevant for the current discussion of empire, in terms of what allegedly "should" be discussed and how it "should" be presented. Much of the discussion is ahistorical and not grounded in an understanding of the particularities of the past. Moreover, by addressing (some) current concerns, the discussion tells us more about today than the past. Clearly, it is impossible to avoid a degree of retrospection, not least in the language employed, but there is a major difference between the effort to understand the past and that to condemn it, usually with both glibness and ignorance.

This book takes its place in a sequence of my writing on the British empire, particularly The British Seaborne Empire (2004) and, most recently, Imperial Legacies: The British Empire Around the World (2019). It is important to take note of recent research and, separately, I do not wish to repeat what I have already argued, but, equally, it is foolish to anticipate that earlier works should have been read, and, therefore, there is in the present title some summary of earlier work.

Throughout, I would like to thank those who have provided comments on earlier drafts and who have offered opportunities to travel and lecture, not least to speak at the Empire and Liberty Conference at the University of Chicago in 2005, to speak repeatedly for the University of Virginia and at the College of William and Mary, and to debate reparations for empire at the University of Pennsylvania in 2023. I found a debate between myself and Kehinde Andrews on Intelligence Squared on 8 April 2021 less helpful as I do not see Western Civilisation and the Enlightenment as inherently racist. I am particularly grateful to Bill Gibson, Malcolm Murfett, Thomas Otte, Steve Pfaff and Murray Pittock for their comments on earlier drafts. This book is dedicated to John Maurer of the Naval War College, a distinguished American historian of the Anglo-American relationship, with thanks for his long friendship, wisdom and humor.

LIST OF ABBREVIATIONS

Add	Additional Manuscripts
BL	London, British Library
EHR	English Historical Review
FO	Foreign Office Papers
HL	Huntington Library, San Marino California
IO	India Office Papers
MS	Mount Stuart, Bute papers, papers of John, 3rd Earl of Bute
NA	London, National Archives
SP	State Papers

1. INTRODUCTION: IMPERIAL ISSUES AND IDENTITIES

In September 2024, the three candidates to be the next Secretary General of the Commonwealth, candidates from Gambia, Ghana and Lesotho, called for "financial reparations" or "reparative justice," for slavery and colonialism. In response, the Prime Minister's official spokesman declared on 14 October 2024, "We do not pay reparations."

The argument very much spoke to present concerns and contexts. It drew on a limited understanding of enslavement, which in West Africa was carried out essentially by Africans and to their own profit, as well as that of the Arabs and Europeans who purchased the enslaved. Ironically, despite Nigeria, Gabon and Equatorial Guinea being oil-rich, there has been no pressure on them to pay reparations.

Nor, in the presentations by the candidates was there any addressing of the extent to which a former colony, Sudan, where slavery had been stamped out by the British, was, in 2024, in the midst of a humanitarian crisis linked to civil war. Moreover, after British rule had ended in 1956, Sudan had seen enslavement and other brutalities, notably relating to ethnic tensions, more especially in Darfur and in what became South Sudan.

The complexities of judgment in this and other issues will be much debated, and many will challenge my assessments and emphases, here and elsewhere in the book. The key point is that there is not one valid view, nor any monopoly of virtue or its absence. To argue for one correct view, in support, criticism or assessment of empire, British or other, scarcely captures the complexities of past or present,[1] and leads to serious ahistoricism, not that such criticism will impede the process one iota.

And so to the past, and the many experiences and views folded into that phrase. There were substantive issues at stake in the understanding, use and presentation of ideas of empire. Indeed, questions of goal and identity were very much part of the equations of empire, which was a concept, practice and term capable, both to contemporaries and subsequently, of a range of meanings and resonances and with variations accordingly to place and social rank, and with varied historical references.[2] Separately, as far as Britain is concerned, the use in some supposedly precise form, of the title of empire, as opposed for example to those of emperor/empress, state or country, is not terribly helpful, as, again, there was, and is, no fixed practice in discussing empire, nor an international body to determine validity.

This point is even more clearly seen if the other states that had this title are considered. Thus, in the nineteenth century, we have Haiti and Mexico as empires. Moreover, the relationship between multiple kingship and empire is complex: as the Habsburgs and Napoleon showed, multiple kingship did not mean an absence of imperial status, but, in many cases, there was no such formal status. It is of course possible to offer functional definitions of empires or imperialisms as alternatives to formal ones, but they also need to be handled with care and are open to debate.

So also with notions of certainty or just stability when assessing empire(s). Countering the idea of imperial stability, it is possible to draw attention to the repeated crises of empire, and to suggest an inherent instability for them based on challenges, both internal[3] and external. Indeed, the very processes of imperial formation could themselves encourage tendencies to dissolution irrespective of the nature of the practice of imperial control. This is indeed pertinent, although a similar point can be made about rulership and governance as a whole, whatever the level.

Moreover, from that perspective, empire could be a solution to problems, however short-term or precarious theses solutions. Instability in an area could encourage not only conquest by an empire and/or competition between them, but also alliance with an empire as a means of addressing problems and/or to create a new practice of mutual profit. This is a point that is underplayed in public discussion today, but can be seen still as relevant not least in seeking alliances.

Empire more generally was a strategy of adapting, and adapting to, rule and order. It was a strategy, by all parties, notably by the "imperializers" and the "imperialized," that was inherently subject to a recalibration of loyalty and acceptance. Empire was at once also both a "frontier" region, attitude or period, and a response to that, with the many senses of transnationalism important to the successful operation of this unstable relationship.

The term "Imperial Histories" in the title is deliberate, one relating not only to the number and range of views—on particular episodes[4] or more general themes and situations, present or past—but also to that of circumstances and attitudes. Furthermore, histories is an acceptance of the inherent diversity of scholarly (and other) views. These attitudes extended to the "empires of the imagination"[5] that were so significant.

In so far as imperialism can be separated from its contexts, there were quite varied contexts for empire, notably, but not only, political, economic and cultural ones. This diversity, in contexts, situations, and views, appears clearer if a chronological approach is adopted. This would be even more so if equal weight to the successive centuries was offered, so that the discussion of, say, the fourteenth century took as much space as that of the nineteenth, an approach that would definitely test those who see themselves as imperial historians. To do so, of course, is misleading because the numbers of those affected by empire in the nineteenth century was greater than in earlier centuries, both in absolute terms and, far more significantly, as a percentage of the world's population.

Nevertheless, it is pertinent to consider the long history of empire involving Britain prior to the sixteenth century, both Britain as the subject of the imperialism of "others" and as a creation and source of it, including with the oldest "colony," Ireland. To leave out this dimension is inappropriate as an understanding of the past, including of the development of attitudes and practices. Yet, adopting this approach very much challenges the current discussion of imperialism and much else in terms of "White Privilege."[6]

In assessing Britain, it is also appropriate to establish what was different or familiar in British imperialism in a Western European context by comparing it to other imperial powers. This was a practice long seen in discussing the British empire and notably both rise and fall, as with comparisons with Rome. Thus, in 1945, Alfred Landon, the unsuccessful Republican Presidential candidate in 1936, declared in a speech in

Topeka, "The British Empire is on the verge of breaking up just as did the Roman Empire and the Spanish Empire," and argued that the new Labor government's domestic policies were incompatible with the costs of great power status. Whether or not such views are held now, the comparisons provide a way in which the imperial past and its prospects were understood. Landon's point about the policies of the Attlee government also captured the sense that imperial history was a measure of the supposed health of a people.

It is also useful to assess Britain as an Asian imperial power alongside not only Russia but also non-European imperial powers, notably, but not only, China and India. In all cases, conquest could play a role but so also could adapting foreign rule into a practice of shared control. That adaptation was more significant than generally understood and notably so if, as in India, British imperialism was a stage in a longer sequence of empires. Indeed, the practice of shared control in and through adaptation contributes to the extent to which empire was often successful when not focused on what might be seen as a national quality and/or an alien tone.[7]

Across much of the world, Britain was constructing an informal empire that very much had the characteristic of an exchange network. Britain was at the center of the network and its key player, but the network worked through participation. It was a network that not only facilitated trade but cultural exchange of all kinds. It was a network that enriched Britain but also those who were part of the network. This is called platform economics by economists, meaning that empire brought participants onto a platform that enhanced the exchange opportunities of its members and was generally welfare enhancing across the network.

At the same time, that situation does not lessen the potential violence of empire, nor the extent to which adaptation can be seen in an unattractive light. Thus, the modernizing nature of the British empire has been qualified with the argument that it could be a conservative modernization, if not counter-revolutionary,[8] which is true in some lights and cases, but very much not so in others. At the same time, that very argument reflects the character of judgment, as both modernization and conservative are terms that, for many, carry would-be moral weight with them.

The notion of a British empire stemming from the British Isles (England, Scotland, Wales and Ireland) entailed, differently, but in an overlapping fashion, origins in terms of the suzerainty of the English Crown in the British Isles, dynastic links between England and Scotland, and the English conquest of Wales and Ireland, and their subsequent governance. In the sixteenth and seventeenth centuries, the establishment and securing of Protestantism was part of the equation. These elements provided both a territorial component to imperial ideology, explicit or otherwise, and a basis for a functional discussion of empire for this period.

At the same time, the scope and meaning of a functional definition and discussion of empire were far from clearcut. They could involve not only territorial rule but also authority or control over trade and the sea, as well as aspects of indirect and informal sway. In the ideological terms of the past, empire was generally an expression of sovereignty, but that definition is incomplete, as other aspects of control and/or influence could be involved. Moreover, subsequent discussion and definition can lead to a range of emphases on these factors.

It is also pertinent to ask how far, why and with what consequences understandings of empire varied in the past. and whether the explicit discussion of imperialism was tangential or more central. The degree to which the latter differed at any one time is also pertinent. The character of the imperial imagination then comes to the fore, with many key attitudes and assumptions notably xenophobic and nationalistic ones, as much directed against any foreign people or country as being relevant specifically to imperialism. This was certainly apparent in the cultural sphere, not that there was any homogeneity to it, a factor that challenges the attempt to provide a zeitgeist to empire. Thus, in his novel *David Copperfield* (1849–50), Charles Dickens presents the fictional character closest to Dickens himself. David is fired up in his imagination:

> "[I] had a greedy relish for a few volumes of Voyages and Travels … and for days and days I can remember to have gone about my region of our house, armed with the centerpiece out of an old set of boot-trees—the perfect realisation of Captain Somebody of the Royal British Navy, in danger of being beset by savages, and resolved to sell his life at a great price."[9]

So also for Bella Wilfer in Dickens' novel *Our Mutual Friend* (1864–5) who on the River Thames in London imagines:

> "all sorts of voyages for herself and Pa … now, Pa was going to China in that handsome three-masted ship, to bring home opium … and to bring home silks and shawls without end for the decoration of his charming daughter…. There would embark in that troop-ship … a mighty general … who wouldn't hear of going to victory, and she was destined to become the idol of all the red coats and blue jackets below and aloft. And then again: you saw that ship being towed out by a steam-tug? … She was going among the coral reefs and cocoa-nuts and all that sort of thing … to fetch a cargo of sweet-smelling woods…. The lovely woman who had purchased her and fitted her expressly for this voyage, being married to an Indian Prince, who was a Something-or-Other, and who wore Cashmere shawls all over himself, and diamonds and emeralds blazing in his turban, and was beautifully coffee-coloured and excessively devoted, though a little too jealous."[10]

In Dickens' novel *Edwin Drood* (1860), the protagonist plans to marry and "go engineering into the East," thus "to change the whole condition of an undeveloped country." However, in this novel, the Landless wards who arrive in Cloisterham (Dickens' term for Rochester) come from Ceylon (Sri Lanka) where their mother dies while they are young, leaving them to a cruel stepfather, Neville Landless, for whom there is a reference to the Tropics: "There is something of the tiger in his dark blood." In *David Copperfield*, Betsey Trotwood's husband, separated on the grounds of his incompatibility and cruelty:

> "went to India with his capital, and there, according to a wild legend in our family, he was once seen riding on an elephant, in company with a Baboon; but I think it must have been a Baboo—or a Begum."[11]

Empire, he shows, can be unsatisfactory and the source of unpleasant attitudes in England. David Copperfield finds "Jack Maldon not at all improved by India," and, instead, arrogant and callous toward the plight of others in England: "There's an account about the people being hungry and discontented down in the North, but they are always being hungry and discontented somewhere."[12]

Dickens was cautious about any assumption of superiority. Planning his periodical *Household Words*, he considered a piece that did not in the event appear: "A history of savages, showing the singular respects in which all savages are like each other; and those in which civilised men, under circumstances of difficulty, soonest become like savages."[13] The last, a theme of savagery within, presented imperialism as a frontier of personality in which feral personal traits could come to the fore. As Dickens correctly notes, with reference to parts of Africa, in his novel *A Tale of Two Cities* (1859), Londoners themselves had been "but newly released from the horror of being ogled through the windows, by the heads [of the executed] exposed on Temple Bar with an insensate brutality and ferocity worthy of Abyssinia or Ashantee."[14]

Dickens could also criticize those in favor of missionary work in Africa, as in his novel *Little Dorrit* (1857).[15] Mrs. Jellyby in the novel *Bleak House* (1852) is one of his comically horrid philanthropists:

> "She has devoted herself to an extensive variety of public subjects ... and is at present (until something else attracts her) devoted to the subject of Africa; with a view to the general cultivation of the coffee berry—and the natives—and the happy settlement, on the banks of the African rivers, of our super-abundant home population."[16]

Mrs. Jellyby is shown to be neglectful of her family, home and cooking, while Mr. Quale wants the natives taught "to turn pianoforte legs and establish an export trade."

In response to the difficult and costly victory over the Sikhs at Chillianwallah, Dickens wrote in 1849: "Indian news bad indeed. Sad things come of bloody war. If it were not for Elihu, I should be a peace and arbitration man" (Elihu Burritt being a somewhat foolish American pacifist). Dickens, however, had a personal commitment to the army. In 1863, his second son, Walter, who was serving in India with the army, but a disappointment to Dickens,[17] died of an aneurism. Of his other sons, Frank was sent to join the Bengal Mounted Police, while Henry served on the Africa station where the Royal Navy was principally involved in stopping illegal slave trading. His imperial connections contributed to Dickens' strong response at the time of criticism in Britain of Edward Eyre, Governor of Jamaica, who, in 1865, had very harshly suppressed the Morant Bay Rebellion (see chapter six). Other factors also played a role in Dickens' response, including anger at what he saw as a mismatch between the response to hardship abroad and at home, as well as his view that missionaries were humbugs:

> "The Jamaica insurrection is another hopeful piece of business. That platform—sympathy with the black—or the native, or the devil—afar off, and that platform indifference to our own countrymen at enormous odds in the midst of bloodshed and savagery, makes me stark wild. Only the other day, here was a meeting of jawbones of asses at Manchester, to censure the Jamaica Governor for his manner of putting down the insurrection! So we are badgered about New Zealanders and Hottentots, as if they were identical with men in clean shirts at Camberwell....[18] But for the blacks in Jamaica being over-impatient and before their time, the whites might have been exterminated."[19]

Drawing probably on this episode, Dickens referred to popular reports about imperial cruelty when he mocked the foolish reports about Neville Landless, the alleged murderer of Edwin Drood:

> "Before coming to England he had caused to be whipped to death sundry 'Natives'—nomadic persons, encamping now in Asia, now in Africa, now in the West Indies, and now at the North Pole—vaguely supposed in Cloisterham to be always black, always of great virtue ... and always reading tracts of the obscurest meaning, in broken English, but always accurately understanding them in the purest mother tongue."[20]

As was to be anticipated, Dickens offered a range of views and in a number of contexts, and quotation should not be selective. Crucially, neither virtue nor vice was national, imperial or foreign in Dickens' accounts. The same was the case for other writers.

In functional terms, and across the range of time and space, it is also appropriate to consider how far territorial, military, naval, political, settlement, commercial, religious, cultural, and other categories of empire aligned, overlapped, clashed and/or differed. There is also the question of how far the emphasis should be on formal or informal empire, rule or influence. These can be variously defined, and may be understood from a number of perspectives—notably, but not only, those of the "metropole" (Britain) and the "periphery" (the colonies). The conceptualization, methodology and historiography of empire are each up for debate.[21] All of these elements should be borne in mind in considering what follows, and in assessing the views offered here, as well as those provided by others.

2. IMPERIAL SUBJECTS

Imperialism for much of British history was a matter of "foreign" rule, however "foreign" is conceptualized. Apart from briefly in the 1290s, Britain was never conquered as a whole prior to the repeated triumphs of Parliamentary armies in 1644–52, and the latter extended to sway over the entire British Isles, which was not the case in the 1290s. Nevertheless, prior to that, large parts of Britain were frequently attacked from abroad and, indeed, conquered on numerous occasions. A series of foreign rulers came to the fore through invasion, beginning with the Romans and most latterly William III (r. 1689–1702). As with later British trans-oceanic imperialism, there was a process of adaptation, such that William III, unlike William I, "the Conqueror," in 1066, was often not presented in this light, nor the subsequent imposition of the rule of the monarchs of the Hanoverian dynasty (1714–1837) in Highland Scotland seen accordingly (at least outside the region). Yet, adaptation was part of the process by which the British were imperial subjects, a situation even more the case for Ireland.

Roman influence became a factor as a result of Julius Caesar's attacks in 55 and 54 BCE, but conquest as a significant and lasting project only began in 43 CE. Britain was the sole island attacked by Rome outside the far less tidal waters of the Mediterranean, and the invasions therefore were bold steps. Caesar claimed that they were necessary to end support for resistance to his conquest of Gaul (France). However, prefiguring a theme in later British imperialism, personal prestige and the dictates of politics in Rome were highly significant, as they also were for the Emperor Claudius' rapidly successful invasion in 43 CE. Caesar needed to show that the invasions were necessary for him to remain in control of the army, and he also wished to win glory. Yet, again showing the extent to which imperialism was part of a matrix of political factors, Caesar's expedition had not been followed up for decades due to a serious but eventually defeated rebellion in Gaul, civil war, and the higher priority of the German frontier.

Within four decades of Claudius' invasion, England, Wales and southern Scotland were conquered, but control of the last was to be short term, while Highland Scotland, other than very briefly, and Ireland (totally) remained outside the Roman orbit. Nevertheless, the control of the Romans, in duration, time and type, was far greater than any hitherto in the British Isles. Moreover, Roman rule helped establish what became a pattern in considering empire. This was very much seen in the long term with regard to the way in which British imperialists, notably in the nineteenth century, looked back to Rome as an exemplary imperial model. More significantly, the practice and ideas of Roman imperial rule in Europe, not least as carried forward by the Papacy, were to be an element affecting British, as well as European as a whole, notions of rulership into the sixteenth century. Indeed, this helps make discussion in terms of empire as if it is a fixed category and/or definition misleading. In practice, empire for long meant representations of rulership that drew on this echo, one sustained by the idea of a Western European imperial status that was begun by Charlemagne with his coronation by the Pope in Rome in 800, and that continued until the end of that empire (the Holy Roman Empire) in 1806 at the behest of the conquering Napoleon.

As introduced from the year 43 onward, Roman rule was similar in many respects to later British colonialism, in particular with some rulers accepting client status, notably Cogidubnus, the client ruler of the Atrebates of Surrey, Sussex and Hampshire, the remains of whose impressive palace at Fishborne can be visited. The settlement of people from elsewhere in the empire, many former soldiers, was matched by the Romanization of the native elite. Towns developed as centers of administration, trade and integration, and were linked by roads. The movement of goods and money encouraged both inter-regional contact and that with elsewhere in the empire. There were also religious and cultural changes. Roman cults spread, and if assimilation with native Celtic beliefs was important, the Druids were stamped out. When Christianity became the state religion in the fourth century, this brought more systematic cultural links between England and the Continent.

The end of Roman rule in Britain in the early fifth century was in many respects similar to the fall of the British empire in the twentieth. Rebellion by the subject population did not happen in the earlier instance, and was of limited significance in most colonies in the latter. Unreliability with the Roman case focused on the army, with commanders seeking a basis for power, as the self-proclaimed Constantine III did in 406. In the twentieth century, it was the local élites who were a source of pressure for change, whether autonomy or independence, a process that culminated in Southern Rhodesia (now Zimbabwe) in 1965 when the White settlers staged a takeover that was a rejection of imperial control. This was a resistance movement not generally seen in that light.

In both the case of the Roman empire and that of the British empire, external factors played a key role, although very differently so. The two world wars, which for Britain and its empire should be dated to 1914–18 and 1939–45, were to take this imperial presence to its greatest extent, but this also exhausted Britain, a process continued by the Cold War with the Soviet Union from 1946 to 1989. For Rome, defense against serious external attack from the 350s helped lead to a severing of the formal link with Rome a half-century later.

The subsequent conquest of England was not that by a single power, a process also not seen with the Roman empire more generally; and again with the fate of the later British empire which was divided among a large number of now-independent states. The imperial character of both Rome and Britain is thereby accentuated, rather than each being seen as part of a sequence as they were in particular areas—for example, Syria and northern India, respectively. The arrival and process of what is presented as post-imperial rule can seem normal and natural from the perspective of modern norms, but this approach underplays the extent of post-imperial violence, as in India in the late 1940s or Nigeria in the 1960s. So also with Anglo-Saxon conquest in the fifth, sixth and seventh centuries. This was highly disruptive, bringing Germanization, not least linguistically and with the interruption of Christianity, and the seizure of land by an invading élite so that the Romano-Britons fled or survived as slaves and peasants. There was more disruption than in much of the rest of the Western Roman empire, as towns, Latin and Christianity proved more lasting in most of the latter, and certainly in what became France, Italy and Spain. Furthermore, post-imperial England was more affected by conflict than had been the case under Roman rule, both because of the length of the period of Anglo-Saxon conquest and due to war between the Anglo-Saxon kingdoms (two overlapping processes).

There was to be a hierarchy among these kingdoms, with a Bretwalda ("wide ruler" or "over king"), but this proto-imperial position was made uneasy and unstable by continual conflict, with shifts, accordingly, from Kent to Northumbria, Mercia and Wessex, in turn, from the late sixth to the ninth centuries. Viking attacks from the 790s and conquest, in part, from the 850s, played a major role in weakening the identity and strength of English polities other than Wessex, which under Alfred (r. 871–99) eventually held off the Vikings. Viking settlement was seen especially in eastern England, although it is unclear how much of the population there continued to be Anglo-Saxon. The likelihood is that Viking immigration was extensive but patchy, while rapid acculturation ensured that the Viking and Anglo-Saxon populations were quickly co-assimilated. At the same time acculturation could be highly disruptive.

Tenth-century England underlined the ambiguities of imperialism, a situation that was to be differently seen in the following century when shared religion could ameliorate colonialization. Alfred presented himself as the champion of Christianity and all Anglo-Saxons against the pagan Vikings, which was an aspect of the revitalization of origin legends that was so important to the range of ideas that were available.[1] Moreover, under his heirs, Edward the Elder (899–924), Athelstan (924–39), and Edmund (939–46), the driving back of the Vikings was presented as a process of reconquest. Yet, in practice, it was as much one of imperial conquest, in which the rulers of Wessex brought modern England under their authority. There is a parallel with the later unifications of France, Germany and Italy that were perceived by contemporaries in part not as unification but as seizures of control through conquest, which was the experience, for example, of Languedoc, Bavaria and Naples respectively. The same might be said at present with the contrast between Ukrainian resistance and President Putin's attempt, in his eyes, to reunite Russia. "Imperialism at home" is a key background to the more common discussion of imperialism abroad. It is also one that complicates the attempt to use racism as an indicator of imperialist attitudes.

The understanding of authority and presentation of power are key elements in imperial policy, politics and pretension, and so also with tenth-century England. The legitimacy of the conquerors rested in part on the notion of reconquest, and was helped by the Viking adoption of Christianity, for that was an indicator of success and providential purpose in a culture in which Christianity was the context for ideology and provided much of the vocabulary. Athelstan employed the title *Rex totius Anglorum patriae*, while in 973 Edgar was crowned as king of the whole English nation.

This process involved a degree of imperial overlordship and was marked by ceremonial acts that represented and reaffirmed such overlordship. In 920, Wessex sources claimed that the rulers of Scotland, English Northumbria, Viking York, and the Strathclyde Britons, a list that captured ethnic variety, accepted Edward the Elder's lordship. Welsh princes attended Athelstan's court and were clearly regarded by the English as his subordinates (*subreguli*), while in 973 the king of Scots and other northern rulers allegedly submitted to Edgar at Chester. Under Edward the Confessor (1042–66), the royal titles of "King of the English" and "of Britain" were used indifferently, and Wales and Scotland were in part dependent.

The state-building of the "Old English" monarchy was therefore if not part of an "imperial project," at least configured in terms that functionally (not least to those outside Wessex) was imperial, and that also had elements of imperial purpose, in part due to the legacy of Rome. Albeit with differences in circumstances, the same was to be true of some of the states that succeeded the British empire. The "Old English" monarchy was affected by Roman ideas through the intermediaries of the Papacy/Church and the contemporary Western European Empire, particularly the influence of Carolingian ideology, that of the Frankish dynasty of Charlemagne and the subsequent Ottonian dynasty in Germany. Eadgyth, granddaughter of Alfred of Wessex, was married to Otto I. The notion of a Christian empire, expressed by Jonas of Orléans and Hincmar of Rheims, influenced Athelstan and Edgar. There was certainly a notion of kingship different from that of the amalgam of earlier kingdoms seen for example in Mercia under Offa (757–96), and that underlines the issues faced by precise definition. In practice, the power varied, being stronger in southern England. Alone among tenth-century rulers, Athelstan spent much time in Mercia. Other kings spent most of their time in the heartland shire of Wessex.

In 957–9, there was division over control of the country, Mercia and only recently-gained Northumbria rejecting allegiance to Eadwig in favor of his brother. In 1016, there was another short-term division, and again in 1035–7. The allegiance of Northumbria long remained precarious, and there was a degree of imperial control in terms of force and expropriation. The use of the term imperial power may appear inappropriate, but in journey terms, tenth-century England was more far-flung than modern states.

Renewed and stronger Viking invasion under King Swein I of Denmark (986–1014) was followed by his son, Cnut, becoming ruler of all England from 1016–35. After his older brother, Harald II, King of Denmark, died in about 1018, England became part of a powerful Scandinavian empire that included Norway from 1028 to 1035, while in 1031, after an invasion by Cnut, Malcolm II of Scotland submitted to him. (Malcolm III was to acknowledge the overlordship of William I and William II in 1072 and 1091, respectively.)

The experience of empire, again, depends on perspective. Cnut did not create any administrative structures to weld his extensive Anglo-Scandinavian empire together and sought to rule not as a foreign oppressor, but as a lord of both Danes and non-Danes. Underlining the difficulty of assessing what monarchical empire means, Cnut ruled a personal empire as the king of a number of kingdoms and who was also in effect seeking to enlarge one particular royal inheritance. In England, he adopted the practices of the "Old English" monarchy, including its support for the Church and its practice of legislating for the whole kingdom. From another perspective, Cnut introduced a number of Danes into the aristocracy, and created a new ruling group. Thus, the Earldom of Wessex was given to Godwin, an English protégé of Cnut, who married a Danish noblewoman, Gytha Thorkelsdóttir (sister of Cnut's brother-in-law), and gave Danish names to four of his six sons, including Harald, the Harald/Harold killed at Hastings in 1066.

The chance of Cnut creating a lasting imperial settlement was brought to a close in part because his sons died without heirs, Harthacnut in 1042, and also because of the failure of Viking attacks later in the century—notably by Harold Hardrada, King of Norway, in 1066, with subsequent attacks or threats of attack in 1069–70, 1075, and 1085–6. The house of Wessex had been restored with the childless Edward the Confessor in 1042, but his successor, Godwin's son Harald/Harold, was defeated and killed in an invasion of Duke William of Normandy, also in 1066.

This created a new context for imperialism to that of 1016, although there were also similarities.[2] While presenting himself as the rightful successor to Edward the Confessor, William pushed through major dispossession, the creation of a Norman ruling class with lands on both sides of the Channel and a Normanization of the Church such that all but one of the English bishops had been replaced by 1087. Opposition was harshly replaced, and the new order clearly expressed through numerous castles. Conquest meant an atmosphere of oppression and notably so in southern England that had long been under the House of Wessex.[3] Moreover, there was to be imperialism by this new dynasty in Britain, particularly in Wales and Cumbria, the latter occupied in 1092.

The character of Norman imperial rule can be differently evaluated, and the use of Norman French at Court and elsewhere must have meant that everyday experience was of an alien élite. Some of the changes that were seen would probably have occurred anyway, especially religious reform, while an Anglo-Norman identity was to be constructed in the early twelfth century with the celebration of aspects of the pre-Norman past, as in Geoffrey of Monmouth's *Historia Regum Britanniae* (c. 1135). Yet, this did not appreciably lessen the discontinuity and tension caused by the conquest, nor the subsequent impact of a long-term commitment to continental power politics as a result first of the Norman inheritance and then that from Anjou. This had significant consequences until the mid-fifteenth century. The *Anglo-Saxon Chronicle* presented the Norman government as predatory, and that situation and response owed much to successive rulers' need to support conflict on the continent, a situation repeatedly seen, as in the background to Magna Carta (1215) and the opposition to Henry III (1216–72).

Imperialism in the British Isles saw intervention in Ireland in 1171, the conquest of North Wales in the late thirteenth century, and an attempt to take over Scotland. The failure of the last was marked by the recognition of Scottish independence by the Treaty of Northampton in 1328,[4] only to revive in 1332 in a conflict that lasted until 1357 with Edward III backing Edward Balliol, whereas Robert's son David had to flee to France. The war saw English victories but also the development of a Scottish nationalism that in part was helped by the failure of successive English kings to build up a lasting faction of supportive Scottish nobles.[5]

This appears to be a one-way process in which England is presented as a unity, to succeed or fail accordingly. Yet, in practice, there was a close alignment with the divisions in English, Welsh, Scottish and Irish politics. As a consequence, there were cross-border links, such as between Welsh princes and opponents of John, Henry III and Henry IV, such as Simon de Montfort, and also between opponents of Henry II and John with the rulers of Scotland.[6]

As later with transoceanic imperialism, gains were consolidated by local alliances and by a military presence, including fortifications (as at Newcastle, Carlisle and Berwick). Looking toward the British decision to withdraw from much of Ireland in 1922, the earlier fate of Scotland was greatly affected by English commitments in France, especially in the 1290s and 1330s. In Wales, Ireland, Scotland and France, English success, albeit often short-term, rested in large part on politics—namely the ability to exploit divisions, as between the Bruces and the Balliols/Comyns in Scotland, and between the Armagnacs and the Burgundians in France. This anticipated British relations with both Native Americans and Indian rulers. In turn, the English/British imperial presence was weakened, if not undermined, when former allies changed sides—as with Philip III the Good, the Duke of Burgundy, by the Treaty of Arras in 1435—or became less important, as with the Indian princely rulers in the twentieth century.

From 1337 until 1453, there was a protracted effort to establish control of much of France. From the perspective of today, this was an attempt at control driven by personal monarchical claims to the French throne advanced from Edward III on, and a different form of imperialism to that in the British Isles. Indeed, Parliament insisted in 1340 and 1421 that the Crowns of England and France should remain separate and independent even if held by the same man. This was an answer to the issue that dynastic imperialism posed to English parliamentarianism. Henry V (1413–22) was recognized by the Treaty of Troyes of 1420 as the heir to Charles VI of France and as Regent in the meanwhile. Henry wished to be accepted by the French as ruler, the heir of St. Louis and not as a conqueror. The quest for the crown of France was an attempt to usurp, but also absorb, the leadership of Christendom in so far as it was held by the French.

This attempt crashed to failure under Henry VI (1422–61, 1470–1). He was crowned as King of France in 1431 in Notre Dame in Paris, but his position was under increasing pressure from the early 1430s, and was rapidly overthrown in the early 1450s. From 1453 until 1603, England was a unitary kingdom, although extended over Wales and part of Ireland. Calais was held until 1558 and the Channel Isles are still under the British Crown, while a claim to the French throne was advanced until 1802; but there would now need to be a new basis for imperialism.

3. THE SIXTEENTH CENTURY

English imperialism took on a new character as a result of the Protestant Reformation and its subsequent geopolitics. In England, the Reformation led to the assertion of an imperial theme for English monarchy as papal authority was challenged and in a very different context to the earlier rifts between kings and popes, notably John and Innocent III in 1208–13. All Church services were suspended and, in 1209, John was excommunicated. This reflected papal religious suzerainty, with powers of appeal and taxation owed to the papal court in Rome.

Henry VIII's acknowledgement, as "Supreme Head" on Earth, of jurisdiction over the Church under the Act of Supremacy of 1534 was accompanied by the statement that England was an empire, and, thus, jurisdictionally self-sufficient, with an imperial Crown allegedly descended from that of the Roman emperor Constantine, a figure of great symbolic potency. A crucial piece of legislation, the Act in Restraint of Appeals [to Rome] of 1533, declared "that this realm of England is an empire," and was the first claim of imperial status for the realm rather than the Crown.

The Reformation became confessional as well as being jurisdictional and this helped provide a sense of divine mandate. Protestant England was seen as God's New Israel, a Protestant people and state, with religious loyalty regarded as a defense of ruler, dynasty and state, and vice-versa. This process was brought to the fore for both clerics and laity. At the same time, the use of local men as officials in both Church and state helped in the grounding of change, a process seen in particular with Protestantism in Wales.

That France, Portugal and Spain remained Catholic lent a religious dimension to imperial competition, which was to be very important to the domestic understanding of empire, both then and subsequently. This situation also helped encourage the rethinking of territorial ambitions that was so important to England's changing role in the world.

Reformation divisions greatly increased a sense of anxiety about attack, notably when the major powers in Western Europe were aligned, as were Francis I of France and the Emperor Charles V (ruler of Spain, the Low Countries—Belgium and the Netherlands, and much else) in 1538, and as France and Spain threatened to be later in the century during the French Wars of Religion. In England, as in Scotland, the Reformation led to the conflation of a sense of national independence both with anti-Catholicism and with hostility to the major continental Catholic powers. As with other episodes in which national consciousness and a rhetoric of national interest were advanced, this conflation served a partisan purpose, for national consciousness was defined against domestic as much as foreign opponents, and this gave that consciousness a particular political force and urgency. Thus, Catholics could be presented as supporters of hostile foreign powers, and those same powers appeared more threatening precisely because of their apparent support within Britain, and uncertainty over the succession made the combination even more threatening. Empire rested ultimately on defense and this element was much to the fore. A chain of fortifications was constructed to defend southern England in the event of invasion, as others were to be built in the 1800s and the early 1940s. There was, however, no invasion: England was really protected by the Channel, growing its naval power, and great French interest in the Low Countries and Italy. These were key to English imperialism during the century, an imperialism as much about expeditions to France, the Low Countries, Spain and Portugal, as to Scotland and Ireland. Captured by Edward III in 1347, Calais remained an important forward-defense until taken by a French surprise attack in 1558. Henry VII (1485–1509), and in his early years Henry VIII (1509–47), had pursued their claim to the French throne, but, in capturing Boulogne in 1544, Henry VIII very much sought to impose English settlement and institutions, and brutally cleared existing settlers. The methods used were in part to be subsequently employed in Ireland, with English colonization again to the fore. Boulogne, however, was returned to France in 1550 at a period of English weakness.

England's changing role in the world was most strongly pressed in the British Isles, a traditional theme that underlines the problem with thinking of the transoceanic operations of the sixteenth century as if they marked a clearly new departure. The English played a major role in seeking to direct Scottish politics in 1547–60. Battles could be won—notably Flodden (1513) and Pinkie (1547)—but the English faced serious problems in locating and sustaining suitable allies in the complex mix of Scottish politics, and there were also significant military difficulties, not least logistical problems. England was far stronger than Scotland in population and financial resources, and had the English been able to maintain and support a permanent military presence in lowland Scotland, then the Scottish kingdom would have been gravely weakened. However, as Scotland did not yield the funds for its occupation, the impossibly high cost of maintaining enough garrisons would have fallen upon England. The center of English power was far to the south, and in sixteenth-century Scotland it was challenged by French intervention, which greatly affected the political and miliary equations of advantages. Scotland was not to be conquered by England until 1650–2 when France was distracted by civil war and while Scotland was weakened by acute divisions.

Wales was incorporated into the English kingdom—"incorporated, united and annexed to and with this his Realm of England"—by the Westminster Parliament's Laws in Wales Act of 1536 which were expanded by another Act in 1543. This allowed Welsh representation in Parliament, while English governmental and judicial practice was established in Wales.

The English also made a major attempt to increase power in Ireland. This attempt reflected the range of policies that can be encompassed in the term imperialism. In 1534, Thomas, Earl of Kildare rebelled, offering the overlordship to the pope or the Emperor Charles V, in place of the schismatic Henry, only to be defeated. In response, Henry was declared "Supreme Head" of the Irish Church by the Act of Supremacy passed by the Irish Parliament in 1537, and exchanged the title of Lord of Ireland for King, while Gaelic nobles were offered English law and charters for their lands, an attempt to incorporate them peacefully into the structure of governmental control. Such a conciliatory policy, however, faced formidable difficulties given the precarious nature of royal control over much of the island.

Under Henry's successors, this policy was replaced by that of the "plantation" of areas with English settlers, which potentially increased the security of the Crown's position but also heightened its unpopularity. As a reminder of the differing tones of imperialism, from the late 1560s English rule in Ireland became increasingly military in character and intention, leading to fresh attempts to extend and enforce control—notably at the expense of Gaelic Irish opposition, but also with little support from the Anglo-Irish.

Religion, not race, was the key dynamic of hostility. This is an element that tends to be underplayed in the modern account of imperialism as there is a far greater concern with race. However, in Ireland religious differences became more important, symbolizing, reflecting and strengthening a political rift, and the difference, if not hatred, fell between what were increasingly seen as conquerors and a subject population. Religious tension helped characterize imperial rule in Ireland. This was doubly important because policies and habits of authority developed there that were to be used in more distant English (later British) imperialism, while the Protestant aristocracy and gentry established there were to play a disproportionately large role in imperial rule.

The suppression of Irish resistance in a bitter conflict in 1593–1603 was a key episode in political history. For the first time, the entire island had been conquered, and this was followed by the imposition of English law and custom in Ulster (much of which subsequently became "Northern Ireland") and by the confiscation of much of it. Land was being allocated to English and Scottish settlers, Crown officials, the established (Protestant) Church, and, in return for financial support for the plantation, the City of London. The financial resources, enterprising energy and political connections of London were to be crucial to much of the dynamic of empire. Large portions of Antrim and Down in Ulster were granted as private plantations and settled largely by Scots. Across much of Ireland, the empire became a matter of the dispossession of native landowners, while in Ulster the native population as a whole saw their position deteriorate as large numbers of Protestants were settled.

Most of the history of the empire revolved around the situations of British Isles, for which such a description was only possible due to long-term imperialism. As with the later episodes that tend to attract more attention, a variety of factors were in play. These included the wish for land, the pursuit of commercial opportunity, the exigencies of defense, the concerns of security, religious consolidation, and imperial ideas that ranged from dynastic pretension to a sense of national destiny.

These factors were further expanded in scope by the interest in transoceanic opportunities that were enhanced by tension with Spain from the 1550s and, more particularly, 1570s, and war from 1585 to 1604. This led to a geopolitics that underlined the significance of Ireland as a possible basis for Spanish activity, but that also stretched to include concern about possible bases for Spanish invasion from the Low Countries to Cadiz, as well as an English ambition to seize Spanish wealth in the Caribbean, or, as with John Hawkins' shipping there of the enslaved from West Africa in 1562, 1564 and 1568, to gain wealth by trade. The last attempt to work outside the official Spanish licensing system was stopped by force.[1]

There was a major difference, however, between attacks on Spanish positions and trade, for example by Francis Drake on the Spanish silver route across the Panama isthmus in 1573, and, on the other hand, the seizure of positions. The latter was difficult, as it was hard to sustain control. Thus, the capture of Santo Domingo and Cartagena by Drake in 1585–6 yielded only transient gains—notably substantial ransoms from the two cities that, in fact, did not match the cost of the fleet. In 1598, George, 3rd Earl of Cumberland, captured the heavily-fortified San Juan, Puerto Rico, but he could not sustain a garrison there. More generally, aside from the strength of defenses, the Spaniards had an effective practice of grounding control in an integrated and profitable imperial system as well as Atlantic and Caribbean way-bases. England had none of these, but a model of success was created, and, as a strong recovered memory, was subsequently held up as the correct course for action, and notably so in periods of crisis in the 1620s, 1650s, 1720s and 1730s.

As a related process, there was the consideration and exploration of commercial and settlement prospects from Muscovy to North America, and from West Africa to the Indian Ocean. Publications such as Thomas Hariot's *A Brief and True Report of the New Found Land of Virginia* (1588) and Richard Hakluyt's *Principal Navigations, Voyages, Traffics and Discoveries of the English Nation* (1598–1600) encouraged such interest. John Dee's *General and Rare Memorials Pertaining to the Perfect*

Act of Navigation (1577) argued for England's position as an Atlantic power.

Yet, although knowledge was cumulative, the general effect was one of failure, from Martin Frobisher's mining in the late 1570s on Baffin Island of what he thought was gold only to discover it was iron pyrites, to the failure of the colony established on Roanoke Island in 1585, and that of the major Caribbean expedition of 1595–6 to seize any position. In contrast, in 1591, the first English ships arrived in the Indian Ocean. There was also the beginning of interest in the Pacific Ocean. Deteriorating relations with Spain led Sir Richard Grenville to plan for a Pacific expedition. He proposed in 1574 to enter the Pacific so as to seize Spanish treasure, found English colonies and sail the South Pacific, and thus approached the Privy Council with a:

> "Supplication for a new navigation, permission to seek rich and unknown lands, to discover and annex all or any lands, islands, and countries beyond the Equinoxial, or where the Pole Antarctic hath any elevation above the horizon."

Initial support, however, was followed by rejection in 1575 at a time of attempting to ease relations with Spain. On his subsequent circumnavigation, Francis Drake landed in 1579 on what is now northern California, which he claimed as New Albion but there was no lasting consequence (bar the name Drake's Bay). As so often happens, the emphasis for imperialism can be on growth or failure.

There was certainly an increase in interest and an accumulation of knowledge. Thus, trade with West Africa developed from the 1550s. Most English voyages there were for pepper, hides, wax, and ivory, and in search of gold rather than slaves. English trade with West Africa did not focus on slaves until the mid-seventeenth century. The English met with firm resistance in this trade with West Africa from the Portuguese.

Exploration further afield left echoes in print and in the theater. In Shakespeare's play *The Merry Wives of Windsor*, published in 1602 but written five years earlier, Sir John Falstaff contemplates the appeal and wealth of the two women he mistakenly thinks desire him: "[S]he is a region in Guiana, all gold and bounty. I will be cheater to them both, and they shall be exchequers to me: they shall be my East and West Indies, and I will trade to them both." In this, Shakespeare draws upon Sir Walter Raleigh's exploration of modern Venezuela in 1595, exploration that had led to his *The Discovery of the Large, Rich and Beautiful Empire of Guiana* (1596). Alongside other accounts of the Americas, this book influenced the background to Shakespeare's *The Tempest* (1611). Searching for El Dorado, Raleigh claimed to have found gold in the Orinoco Valley in modern Venezuela. He continued to be committed to his quest, for example sending out ships in 1596 and 1597, a quest that helped maintain interest in the region. In the 1610s, Raleigh focused on the issue even though in 1604 peace had been negotiated with Spain, who claimed the area. Against Raleigh's orders, a detachment of the expedition he organized in 1617 attacked the Spaniards, ignoring James I's insistence that he was not to do so; and it did not find any gold mines. Because of Spanish demands for his punishment, Raleigh was beheaded in 1618.

A very different account of the wider world to that by Raleigh was offered in Othello (1603–4) in which the protagonist describes his earlier travels offering an account of Africa in which, drawing on Classical and medieval ideas, the inhabitants were not equally human. He had seen:

> "… the Cannibals that each other eat,
> The Anthropophagi, and men whose heads
> Do grow beneath their shoulders." (I.iii)

Racism is to the fore in Shakespeare's earlier *Titus Andronicus* (1592–4), in which Aaron, a Moor, the black servant and lover of Tamora, the Queen of the Goths and new Empress of Rome, proposes repeated deadly crimes. Aaron is a far more dangerous, vicious and crude character than Othello, and lacks the tragic status and dramatic complexity of the latter. Earlier in the play, cruelty of a different type is revealed when Tamora seeks the death of the baby she has had by Aaron. The nurse declares the baby is:

> "Our empress' shame, and stately Rome's disgrace!
> … A joyless, dismal, black, and sorrowful issue:

Here is the babe, as loathsome as a toad
among the fairest breeders of our clime:
The empress sends it thee, thy stamp, thy seal,
And bids thee christen it with thy dagger's point."

Aaron refuses, and declares:

"Coal-black is better than another hue,
In that it scorns to bear another hue;
For all the water in the ocean
Can never turn the swan's black legs to white,
Although she leave them hourly in the flood." (IV.ii)
He kills the nurse, the killing being almost casual.

Transoceanic interest and attempts were pregnant for future achievements. The key element, however, was that England was focused more on imperialism in the British Isles than further afield. Furthermore, the English empire was very much smaller than those of Portugal and Spain, which from 1580 to 1640 were linked in a personal union. One was to follow between England and Scotland in 1603, but unlike that between Portugal and Spain—and, even more, Poland and Sweden—this, despite repeated difficulties, was to last and play a major role in what became British imperial history, not least if understood, as it should be, to include the British Isles.

4. THE SEVENTEENTH CENTURY

By the end of the seventeenth century, England was the leading maritime power in the world and, as also the foremost imperial power on the eastern seaboard of North America and a major one in the West Indies, ruled the principal empire in the North Atlantic. Moreover, there was a presence elsewhere, notably in India and West Africa, but, in each of those cases, England was not the dominant imperial power. Indeed, far from it. This helps explain the North Atlantic focus of interest and concern as far as contemporaries were concerned.

To the forefront, however, was imperialism in the British Isles, a situation that represented a prime continuity, and one that is generally underplayed by modern English commentators; although the perspective is very different in both Scotland and Ireland. Thus, what the English term the English Civil Wars and date to 1642–6 and 1648 were in fact a broader series of conflicts in the British Isles from 1639 to 1652. Similarly, the "Glorious Revolution," which is generally dated by the English to 1688 or 1688–9 and located in England, was in fact the launchpad for a civil war across the British Isles that ended in 1692, and then having resumed with successive Jacobite attempts and risings, definitively in 1746.

These conflicts were important to the development of empire both in the British Isles and overseas, and also to the self-image of the British state in terms of Protestantism, liberty, limited government, commerce, prosperity and a commitment to the values of change. In the British Isles, there was harsh conquest and brutal expropriation, but also the creation of a new ruling class, with a key cooperation developing between Scottish and English élites, although it did not really come to fruition until the eighteenth century. The history of the empire in the seventeenth century is therefore primarily the history of the British Isles.

Alongside this being a continuation, there was also a new geopolitical context. Hitherto concern about Scotland had largely been a factor of Anglo-French animosity, with Scottish rulers looking to France, while, in the sixteenth century worries about Ireland owed much to the possibility of Spanish exploitation. While these factors were not absent in the seventeenth century and, indeed, became far more significant from 1689, the key element earlier on was the struggle between Royalists and opponents, a struggle seen across the British Isles and one that looked toward elements in the tension between Jacobites and their opponents. Neither struggle was inherently about empire. However, the nature of a British imperial presence as a factor in the political and ecclesiastical governance and policies of the constituent parts of the British Isles played a significant role, not least as an enabler of English-based solutions.

Charles I (1625–49) sought to be the maker of empire in this respect—notably by pushing Scotland into a dependent political and ecclesiastical position. Whereas his father, James I of England (1603–25), James VI of Scotland (1567–1625), had tried to avoid war, Charles was involved in unsuccessful conflicts with France and Spain in the 1620s. He failed to learn from this and became involved in war with Scotland. Defeat for Charles in the Bishops' Wars of 1639–40 was followed by Scottish intervention against him from 1644 in the First English Civil War. This intervention greatly contributed to his defeat, notably at the battle of Marston Moor that year.

From a very different background, Oliver Cromwell, the leading Parliamentary general and eventually as Lord Protector from 1653 to 1658, dictator, played the key role in defeating Scottish intervention, now on behalf of Charles, in 1648, and then in conquering both Ireland (1649–52) and Scotland (1650–2). The remaining Royalist bases in the Channel Isles, the Isles of Scilly, the Isle of Man, and the English colonies were all also conquered.

Empire led to a government of the British Isles as a whole, and this new style was to be dynamic overseas, notably in war with the Dutch in 1652–4 and with Spain in 1654–60, a war that added Jamaica but not the hoped-for Hispaniola (now Haiti and the Dominican Republic) to the empire. This was on a scale and very different to English imperialism earlier in the century. At that time, settlements were established on islands that the Spaniards had not colonized; although this was not an easy process. Bermuda, an uninhabited island remote from all others, was discovered but not settled (probably in 1505) by Juan Bermúdez, a Spanish navigator returning from Hispaniola. An English shipwreck in 1609 was followed, from 1612, by the arrival of settlers. Tobacco cultivation was swiftly established and the export of ambergris, a product of sperm whales used for flavoring. The first enslaved people arrived in 1616, indicating the variety of the slave trade, for Bermudan privateers were a source as was the obtaining of pearl divers from Venezuela.[1] The island was rapidly fortified in order to provide protection against possible attack, whether by Spain, France or pirates, and John Smith's map of 1624 showed numerous forts. However, the small size of the island and the far more abundant possibilities in North America restricted the size of the population. In contrast, the inherent difficulties of the task—notably disease, but also Spanish opposition—bore the major responsibility for the failure of the schemes for a colony on the Amazon, as well as of Sir Walter Raleigh's better-known plans for Guiana.

English settlements, meanwhile, were founded on St. Lucia in 1605 and Grenada in 1609, but opposition from native Caribs helped lead to their failure. Lasting English colonies in the Caribbean came from the 1620s: St. Christopher (usually known as St. Kitts, 1624), Barbados (1627), Nevis (1628), and Antigua and Montserrat (1632). As England was at war with both Spain and France in the 1620s, English schemes for new colonies were closely linked to bellicosity or, at least, to the likelihood of defending successfully against Spanish attack. This was a reason for the settlement of St. Kitts, where the first crop was tobacco, albeit being hit hard by a hurricane. Initially friendly, the Caribs there turned against the colonists, while the English had to share their possession with the French under a treaty of 1627, only for fighting to break out in 1629. One colony proved the basis for another, Nevis being settled from St Kitts. Sir Thomas Warner, who was responsible for founding the first English colonies in the West Indies in the 1620s, was appointed King's Lieutenant for St. Kitts, Nevis, Barbados and Montserrat, and in 1629 Governor of St. Kitts.

Conflict did not always lead to success, as in 1626 when an attempt upon the Spaniards in Trinidad failed. So also with the Puritan-run colony on Providence Island, off the coast of Nicaragua, which the

Puritans saw in terms of their vision of a struggle between good and evil. Intended to enrich the godly at the expense of Spain, the colony, established in 1630, was presented as a means to support the struggle against popery in Britain. Ironically, trade proved more lucrative than privateering, and the island's economy came to be founded on tobacco grown by enslaved Africans. That vulnerable colony did not last, and Spanish control was re-established in 1641 (although an English role there was subsequently to recur). Moreover, that was not the sole colony to fail, as Carib attacks ended English attempts to settle on Tobago in 1639–40 and 1642–3.

Nevertheless, the colonies that succeeded were to be important bases for subsequent expansion, and, without these, it would have been far more difficult to make later gains at the expense of Spain and France. Colonies also helped in a transfer of English energy in the Caribbean from buccaneering to a more regulated process of activity and expansion; although buccaneering remained very important to the established authorities in the second half of the century, notably so on Jamaica but also in other West Indian colonies.

This was an aspect of the powerful role of private interests in imperial development, practice, profit creation, and fiscal-sharing. At the level of colonial establishment, aristocratic entrepreneurs and mercantile investors were important.[2] Yet, these were not discrete or isolated groups, for imperial enterprise extended across the social span and with far more having a degree of "agency" than might be appreciated. Some who seemed outside the structure, notably pirates and private traders breaching company monopolies, were, paradoxically, also within it due to the multiple arrangements and linkages of imperialism. Indeed, these arrangements that extended to non-White natives and to the subjects of other empires conditioned, even challenged, if not helped undercut, imperial rhetoric and policy; yet while also making them work.

Further north, it was not until a base was established by the Virginia Company at Jamestown in the Chesapeake in 1607 that a permanent English colony was founded on the eastern seaboard. Spain regarded this colony as an invasion of its rights and protested its foundation, but, although the defenses at Jamestown (the vulnerability of which is apparent to the modern visitor), were prepared to resist Spanish attack, it did not come: Virginia was too distant from the centers of Spanish power, and more effort was put into preventing Sir Walter Raleigh from establishing himself in Guiana.

Jamestown was thought to be a good location for inland exploration and for acquiring furs. The context was very different to the launching of English colonialization in Australia in 1788 as a government-run, militarized convict settlement. Despite heavy initial losses of settlers, largely due to the impact of disease in an unfamiliar environment, the Virginia colony expanded as a result of the continued arrival of new settlers and the willingness to put an emphasis on growing food. And, after much bloodshed, Native resistance was overcome in 1622–4 and 1644. Disappointingly, no gold or silver was ever found there. Nor was it possible to trade with the Spanish colonies in order to obtain sugar and tobacco that could be profitably sold in England, as Spain was determined to exclude foreign traders. The bankrupt Virginia Company failed in 1624, but not all of its investors wanted to surrender the charter which had to be taken away, the Native uprising providing the excuse. The colony was continued with a royal governor. A key opportunity for profit arose when tobacco became the major crop in both Virginia and Maryland. Tobacco's limited capital requirements and high profitability fostered investment and settlement, while, because tobacco was an export crop, the links with England were underlined.

In 1620, the Pilgrim Fathers, a group of Protestant nonconformist separatists or "saints" as well as "strangers" who had been recruited by Thomas Weston or his agents, sailed from England on the *Mayflower*, made a landing at Cape Cod, and established a settlement at New Plymouth. This was the beginning of the development of a colony in New England, a term first used in 1614 by Captain John Smith when he described the coastline north of the Hudson, and popularized by his *Description of New England* (1616), which matched English interest in Virginia.[3] The Pilgrim Fathers, who had leased a concession from the New England Company, sought to create a godly agrarian world, and believed their righteousness made them more entitled to the land than the Natives,[4] although it was not only Protestant nonconformist settlers who saw Natives as savages. In Philip Massinger's play *The City Madam* (c. 1632), the villain is ready to sell his sister-in-law and nieces to the heroes who are disguised as "Indians" seeking women for sacrifice.

In Shakespeare's *The Tempest* (1611), a forceful native response to settlement was offered by Caliban:

> "This island's mine…
> Which thou tak'st from me…." (I.ii)

This response was placed in the play by his diabolical origins, malign intentions and behavior. The modern approach of playing Caliban as the victim of Western colonialism, and of treating Prospero and Miranda as having selfish reasons to stigmatize him unfairly and thus as unreasonable in their criticism, represent a different power-relationship, one that captures the idea of a monstrous "other," but provides a sympathetic tone, with Caliban's otherness frequently represented by his color.[5]

The New England settlers were greatly helped by the impact on the latter of (probably) a plague in 1616–18 and of smallpox in 1634. The separatists were followed by other settlers who were not separatists but who were also zealous for a Godly commonwealth. These more mainstream Protestants, sponsored by the Massachusetts Bay Company established in 1629, founded Boston in 1630. This colony expanded rapidly, and the Natives were unable to confront the growth of the English presence. The settlers' brutal defeat of the Pequots in a brief war in 1637 confirmed the Puritans' position and their conviction of divine support. Settlement spread, for example in the Connecticut River Valley from 1634, and with it a new landscape was created. By 1642 there were over 15,000 English settlers in New England, and by 1650 nearly 23,000. An emphasis on spreading settlement can lead to an underrating of the role of ports, particularly Boston, and, more particularly, the importance of the beginning of the annual sailing season and the arrival of ships that brought immigrants, products, money and news: When they might be due to arrive was the focus of continual discussion and concern.

The English also colonized Newfoundland: Humphrey Gilbert, Raleigh's half-brother, had claimed it for Elizabeth I in 1583—being essentially laughed off by the English, French and Portuguese fishermen—and it proved difficult to develop the English presence from fishing stations to a settlement colony. In 1610, the newly-established Newfoundland

Company established a settlement at Cuper's Cove in Conception Bay, and, thereafter, the Company granted land to settlers on the Avalon peninsula, but it proved difficult to make a success of them. The hopes outlined in a pamphlet by John Mason, the Governor of the Conception Bay settlement, *Brief Discourse of the New-found-land with the Situation, Temperature, and Commodities thereof inciting our Nation to go forward in that hopeful plantation begun* (1620), proved deceptive as the climate was too harsh for farming. By 1630, the colony at Cuper's Cove contained only a few settlers, while George, 1st Lord Baltimore, who came to Newfoundland in 1627 to help the colony he had established at Ferryland in 1621, found the climate unpleasant, and became more interested in more clement climes further south (and ultimately obtaining a charter for Maryland). Nevertheless, the seaborne empire relied on flexibility and probing limits, and the Newfoundland settlements showed that it was possible to overwinter there, which provided the basis for a strengthening of the fisheries, as the fishing season was extended.

The bleaker environment of eastern Canada, however, proved unpropitious for Sir William Alexander, who in 1621 was granted a charter giving him and his heirs a claim to what are now the Maritime Provinces of Canada. The charter was renewed by Charles I in 1625, but it proved impossible to establish a successful settlement on the south shore of the Bay of Fundy. A ship sent in 1622 left the colonists in Newfoundland, and by 1623 only ten of them were willing to continue. Their experience of Nova Scotia did not persuade them to stay. Alexander's son established a colony at Port Royal in the Bay of Fundy in 1629 but, like Québec, which had been captured from France, it was handed over to France in 1632 as part of a peace agreement.

Nevertheless, the opportunities presented by colonies, and, more particularly, the profits derived from them, helped make their development, as well as the acquisition of new ones, normative. Disease hit hard, with yellow fever first definitively occurring in the New World in Barbados in 1647, and then spreading rapidly. However, the presence of settlers permitted a process of acclimatization and the development among survivors of a degree of immunity to tropical disease, an immunity that provided an important local resource for future aggression and development.

Given the military background and character of Cromwell's Protectorate government (1653–8), it is not surprising that its imperial emphasis should be martial, but that does not capture the range of factors involved in conflict with Spain, from supposed divine support to colonial ambition and commercial rivalry. That Jamaica became English was a result of the extent to which conflict between European powers increasingly dominated the history of the Caribbean, a process encouraged by the loot it offered, in both reality and imagination, and the value of its plantation exports, and one facilitated by the development of navies. The 1650s saw the Parliamentarians overcome the Royalists in the Caribbean, as well as Ireland and Scotland, taking Barbados in 1652 after a difficult struggle and holding off a Royalist squadron under Prince Rupert of the Rhine that year.

The pulse of empire under Cromwell was military and far more so than the militaristic trends under William, Duke of Cumberland in the 1740s and 1750s, and, even later, during the French Revolutionary and Napoleonic Wars, important as it then was. The military dimension was also demographic in that White settlement in the mid-seventeenth century English Caribbean was partly a matter of Royalist and Irish prisoners. The key episode was the Western Design launched by Cromwell in 1654, after he had made peace with the Dutch, and intended to bring the earlier plans focused on Providence Island to fruition: God's elect nation was to overthrow Spain's popish empire and seize its trade, beginning with the dispatch of the largest English fleet hitherto sent to the Caribbean and the seizure of Hispaniola. Cromwell brushed aside objections at a ministerial meeting that July:

> "We consider this attempt because we think God has not brought us hither where we are but to consider the work that we may do in the world as well as at home.... Now Providence seemed to lead us thither, having 160 ships swimming ... this design would cost little more than laying by the ships, and that with hope of greater profit."

10,000 troops were also sent, but the badly-led expedition was mismanaged—notably with logistics, never an easy task, poorly planned. About

1,000 troops died of hunger and thirst once landed, and about another 1,500 were killed by the defenders, who had their own strong motivation. With disease hitting home, the expedition, its failure blamed by Cromwell on a lack of divine favor arising from sin at home, had to be content with less well-defended Spanish colonies—namely, Jamaica, where the Spanish population was small, and Great Cayman which was largely populated by privateers.[6] Both were to be formally ceded to England under the Treaty of Madrid of 1670, which officially ended the war begun in 1654. The war had ended in Europe in 1659–60, with a formal treaty in 1667, but continued throughout the 1660s in the Caribbean as the issues there had not been settled.

The Caribbean islands were no mere adjunct to the English colonies in North America. Instead, they were more important, generated more wealth and, until the 1660s, attracted more settlers (readily-accessible Barbados proving the most popular destination). These islands were rapidly focused on commercial agriculture, and the labor-intensive nature of the resulting plantation economies led to a need for more settlers. At this stage, they were largely White workers provided by contracts of indenture, a practice of labor provision and control transplanted from England. In addition, Cromwell sent Irish prisoners to Barbados.

Some imported crops did not work, particularly grapes, olives, and wheat; but other transfers were successful, notably bananas, lemons, oranges and rice. Tobacco (also important on Cuba) and cotton were the major initial crops on the English colonies; then, from the 1640s, there was a shift to sugar, especially on Barbados. Sugar, which exhausts the soil less than tobacco, was to lead to the use of the enslaved, but this was not the inevitable socio-economic trajectory. Instead, a more mixed economic pattern that was less capital-intensive, and therefore possible for White settlers who did not possess much capital, was initially dominant; and this pattern continued to be important even after there was an emphasis on sugar. New settlers also provided the colonies with vital assistance against the serious inroads of war and, even more so, disease.

The ecological impact—in part deliberate, in part unintended—of the English was formidable. Their diseases ravaged Native societies, while hunting, a necessary search for food as well as a practice brought from home and greatly eased by the availability of guns, affected the local wildlife. The deliberate or accidental introduction of new species, including horses, pigs, cattle, rats, wheat, grapes, apples, peaches, and citrus fruit, harmed indigenous animals and plants, directly or indirectly. There was no sense of loss by the settlers, as these indigenous animals and plants did not play a role in Christianity as they did in Native religions. In a major change, the natural cover was cleared to make way for cultivation and water systems were altered, or at least disrupted, as new types of farming were introduced. Some animals proved easier to control than others: the feral hogs on Barbados and St. Kitts were hunted to extinction, but the arrival of rats did much harm to other species—especially birds, iguanas, and the indigenous tree rats.

The production of sugar was intensive and very hard—notably the act of hacking down the sugar cane—and required a large labor force. Slavery provided this more effectively than indentured White labor, which was not only less malleable, but also less attuned to the environment, particularly the climate. The impact in the late 1640s of yellow fever on the White settlers encouraged this process, and, as a result, there was much demand for enslaved people. Captain William Freeman (c.1610–82), who from 1670 in response to the French devastation of the family's St. Kitt's estate in 1666, developed a sugar plantation on the small island of Montserrat, and left nearly 700 letters written between 1678 and 1685, claimed that "land without slaves is a dead stock." By 1677, he had at least 51, and, from 1674, was one of the slave-trading Royal African Company's two agents in the Leeward Islands. As part of the range of activities typical of the settler class, including roles in both public service and private enterprise, Freeman also bought leases on Nevis plantations and acted as agent and banker for the Governor of the Leeward Islands, as well as advising the London-based Lords Commissioners for Trade and Plantations. In 1678, 40 percent of the 4,500 strong population of Montserrat was non-White, but by 1729 this was 80 percent of the 7,200 total.

A shift in cultivation was important, as, after the 1640s, tobacco (the price of which slumped in response to competition from Virginia and Maryland) was replaced by sugar as the main crop. Whereas tobacco, a less arduous crop to cultivate, was grown on smallholdings and its cultivation relied heavily on indentured labor; sugar meant plantations and the enslaved and therefore more investment. The enslaved suddenly appeared in Barbados' deeds in 1642 as a result of the first arrival of English slave ships there the previous year, and, by 1660, Barbados, which already in 1650 had exported 7,000 tons of sugar, had a majority of Black people. Although prices of the enslaved thereafter fluctuated annually, they fell over time, encouraging the demand and reflecting the increasingly sophisticated organization of the trade, which was, at once, responsive to both sources and markets. While important, price was not the sole factor favoring the use of the enslaved, as they also ensured owners a longer labor availability than that provided by the indentured servants (many of whom eventually died).

Land-hungry Barbadians, unable to afford the capital requirements of plantations on Barbados, also settled elsewhere, including in South Carolina, but notably on Jamaica where they sought to subjugate the African slaves of the previous Spanish settlers (slaves who had used the English conquest in 1655 as an opportunity to win freedom). The escaped slaves had joined the Natives who were willing to cooperate with the Spaniards against the English. Spanish resistance continued, but was overcome in 1660 as a result of the determined command of the talented Lieutenant-General Edward D'Oyley.

The spread of sugar production in Jamaica from the late 1660s was inextricably linked to the increase in slavery, both the hunting down of escaped slaves and the import of many new ones, including from Barbados. There were campaigns against escaped slaves in the 1670s and 1680s, and they withdrew further into the Blue Mountains. The population of Jamaica was transformed due to the import of many more slaves under English rule and, whereas in 1662 there were about 3,500 White people and 550 Black people, by 1673 they were each about 7,700, and by 1681 there were 24,000 Black people and 7,500 White people. Over 1,800 slaves were being brought to the island each year, in response to a clear demand, for, by 1675, there were 70 plantations able to produce 50 tons of sugar each year, and the Black population rose to 43,000 in 1700, when there were only 7,300 White people there.

With this rise in the population of the enslaved, Jamaica to a considerable degree switched from smallholdings to plantation monoculture; for, although slave buying there was widespread among the White community, large purchasers dominated the market, which both reflected their access to credit and also an accentuated social stratification. Furthermore, the market became more complex and was controlled by specialized traders. The value of Caribbean exports was enhanced as government loans could be raised on the basis of anticipated customs revenue on the goods imported into England and re-exported from there.

In contrast, the colony of the Bahamas relied on piracy. This reflected the local environment, but also the extent to which many Britons arriving in the Caribbean lacked the capital to plant and grow sugar and, instead, turned to cutting logwood (in what became Belize from 1638 and on the Mosquito Coast from 1655) or to piracy.

The growing resale of slaves within Jamaica further increased the already harsh instability of their lives, and their experience of it as arbitrary, cruel and impersonal, notably in the destruction of personal ties. In 1684, the Jamaica Assembly passed a new Slave Act that sought to codify slavery by regulating the control of runaways, the obligation to enforce slave law, and property rights over the enslaved, rights changed to increase those of creditors: If owners died in debt, the enslaved had to be sold in order to satisfy their creditors, which pushed the interests of capital to the fore. This provision helped to liquefy the enslaved as property assets; but moving enslaved from landed estates in this fashion added a further level of disruption to the fact that they were treated simply as property. Slavery was thus to be characterized by high labor mobility, rather than as part of a stable, albeit highly coercive, pattern of settled agriculture as it has sometimes been presented. In Jamaica, there was an unsuccessful slave uprising in 1694.

The harsh regime for the enslaved included the total absence of rights and the ever-present possibility of brutal control, which encouraged flight and (although less commonly) violent opposition, which, in turn, resulted in even stricter controls. Initially, the legislation largely treated servants and the enslaved in a similar fashion, but the enslaved were increasingly distinguished, being subject to a separate code from the Barbados Assembly in 1661, in contrast to the more piecemeal situation in 1652. The entire stance was far harsher: The preamble to the Barbados Slave Act described "Negroes" as a "heathenish, brutish and an uncertain dangerous pride of people" who required harsher punishment and laws accordingly. The word "Negro" was used interchangeably with slave, while description as "brutish," a word associated with beasts, further categorized and disparaged. "Pride," a word employed to describe a band of lions, further treated the enslaved as animals with the additional sense of being brutish or fierce. As such, the enslaved could not possess rights, in contrast to the position taken in Portuguese and Spanish laws, and one later taken in the French *Code Noir*. A clear legal difference was established in the Barbados Slave Act, as the enslaved were not to receive a jury trial of 12 peers, but rather to be tried in a slave court, in which two Justices of the Peace and three freeholders—all five inevitably White men—were to pass judgment. Severe punishment was to be inflicted on any "Negro" who struck a "Christian." The first offense was a severe whipping, while, for the second, the offender was to have their nose slit and face branded, a brutal disfigurement to demonstrate status and punishment. Even more ominously, the killing of a slave during punishment was not to be considered a crime. In contrast, the legislation of 1661 protected White indentured servants from such violence.

For the enslaved, life was totally disrupted, and more so than in the case of the widespread slavery within Africa. Alongside the extent to which European slave buyers in Africa tended to buy from particular areas, and thus from specific tribes, and plantation owners considered maintaining this in order to avoid conflict within their slave populations; there was also, in contrast, a widespread mixing of slaves from different backgrounds in a deliberate attempt to lessen their potential cohesiveness and rebelliousness, and this mixing helped ensure a lack of a common heritage, including language and religion. This was responsible for the development of creole languages and for the openness to Christian proselytism, and notably so for the children born into slavery, a group for which the term "enslaved" can be queried as they were slaves from birth.

The greater ability of Blacks to adapt to the Tropics was seen by Britons, on a longstanding pattern, as justifying their use for hard labor. Indeed, the harshness and brutality involved were not solely a reflection of serious racism, which in part indeed was the result rather than the foundation of slavery. Instead there was also an instrumentalism within the technology and opportunities of the age, although that instrumentalism was closely linked to racism. Slavery was justified by necessity and through reference back to the world of Classical Greece and Rome.

The growing imbalance of the numerical relationship between the enslaved and Whites led to the need for garrisons; and the removal of troops for whatever reason alarmed the Whites. The anxiety was communicated to British readers, creating an impression of the Caribbean, by publications such as *Great Newes from the Barbadoes, or, A True and Faithful Account of the Grand Conspiracy of the Negroes Against the English and the Happy Discovery of the Same* (1676). Government support, notably in the shape of troops, was therefore much in demand, a situation that looked toward the contrasting responses to the fiscal policies of the British government—namely, that of the Thirteen Colonies (the basis of the modern United States) that rebelled in 1775, and of the colonies in the Caribbean, none of which revolted despite their dislike of these policies.

Compared to the First Anglo-Dutch War, that of 1652–4, colonial ambition and commercial rivalry were far more to the fore in the next Anglo-Dutch conflict, that of 1665–7, a war that confirmed the English seizure of New Amsterdam in 1664. Its renaming as New York was an instructive aspect of the nature of empire as a process of defining identity. The strengthening of the English position in North America (as elsewhere) was a matter not only of relations, including conflict, with other European powers but also of the same with non-Europeans. Thus, in North America, there was conflict in New England in 1675–6, but in defeating the Native Americans then in King Philip's War, the English colonists also benefited from their Native allies. Colonists and Natives had created a transactional society based on a conscious interweaving of English and Native polities by individuals hoping to preserve their identities in a rapidly-changing world. The strong links established were ruptured, however, as well as transformed for those still allied, in 1675–6 in what in effect was a civil war as much as a conquest, and one based on racial conquest.[7] This was part of a pattern seen throughout imperial history, English/British and otherwise.

Not only conflict was involved. In accordance with a marriage contract of 1661, Catherine of Braganza, the Portuguese wife of Charles II, brought Tangier and Bombay (Mumbai) as a dowry when she married in 1662. At Tangier, an extensive defensive system was prepared, and a mole designed to protect the harbor (and in part built by slaves captured in the Mediterranean from North African ships). English place names were introduced. The cost of the defense of Tangier in the face of Moroccan pressure, however, led to its evacuation in 1684. English and Moroccan empire and state building had interacted in a process made more complex by domestic pressures and alternative international commitments. Tangier was evacuated when Charles II was trying to rule without Parliament, and therefore was not receiving parliamentary grants, and he could not afford the expense.

There was also the major strengthening of empire by means of trade and migration, notably with both seen in North America and the Caribbean. In contrast, there was no settlement history to English bases in India, Sumatra and West Africa, and empire there was commercial,[8] based on trading companies, buying, from fortified bases,[9] goods which in West Africa included local people enslaved and sold by other local people.

The emphasis for India was also transnational in the sense that there was not so much conflict, as the ability of the East India Company to grow within the framework of the Mughal empire. The seventeenth-century Company developed as a de-centered corporate structure in which Asian agency plays a major role, Asian understood both as the English in Asia, and as Asians themselves.[10] The Mughal Emperors were more able than the Company to bend transnational networks to serve their own interests. Force played only a small part in the relationship.

In the early eighteenth century, the British state became more intrusive and capable as a whole, and also, to a degree, as far as the Company was concerned, not least through the provision of military support. However, the settlement over Bengal, Bihar and Orissa under the Treaty of Allahabad of 1765 with the Mughal Emperor, Shah Alam II, following the Company's victory at Buxar in 1764 represented not some jarring transformation of a trading company into an imperial power, an approach considered in the following chapter, but, rather, the zenith of a long process in which the Company's presence was expanded from within existing Asian political and economic frameworks. Robert Clive, who signed the treaty as Governor of the Presidency of Fort William, and had as a servant of the Company, been an entrepreneur of military force, was also in part acting as a Mughal noble and a Bengali landowner. A major obstacle to understanding the Asian origins of the empire is the idea that Britain could succeed without operating within mutually beneficial frameworks of economic and political power.[11] This is clearly relevant for discussion of empire as a whole as well as the British empire, and, indeed, the slave trading networks of the period.

Meanwhile, in the uninhabited South Atlantic, the English settled the island of Saint Helena from 1659 and built a fort there. In 1673, the Dutch captured it but were driven out. Saint Helena became a key port of call, and there was no native resistance to overcome.

The context of empire changed in the second half of the seventeenth century. There had been much continuity from mid-century to the reigns of Charles II (1660–85) and James II (1685–8), notably in hostility to the Dutch[12] but also in the legacy of the mid-century civil wars for later imperial policy—for example, in Royalist hostility to New England as a Puritan stronghold.[13]

Yet, there was to be a major change as a consequence of William III's seizure of power in the "Glorious Revolution" of 1688–9. In 1672–4, in the Third Anglo-Dutch War, Charles II of England while allied to his cousin, Louis XIV of France, had fought the Dutch, although, crucially, with insufficient cooperation. However, from 1688 the two powers were opposed, notably in 1689–97 and 1702–13, and France, rather than Spain or the Dutch, was increasingly identified as the major opponent of England's imperial position in the British Isles and more widely. Indeed, from that perspective, imperial history very much does not match to century divides, as there was more continuity between the period over 1700 than between the 1690s and earlier decades. An empire linked to the political settlement after the "Glorious Revolution," notably parliamentary power, became etched more strongly in national consciousness and, increasingly, played more than a markedly subordinate role to trade. The two were not contrasted because empire, with the celebration of the patriot merchant, was seen as distinctly commercial[14] rather than territorial, let alone necessarily a matter of settlement. There was also a far greater definition of a trans-oceanic empire than hitherto, with the British Isles increasingly seen as a distinct sphere of imperial interest and identity. Yet, that was not necessarily the case as far as empire was experienced, for there was considerable overlap in this respect.

The vision and, increasingly, reality of a maritime commercial empire identified the opportunities and success of trade with trans-oceanic power as well as with the liberty of English (from 1707 British) politics, as established from 1688. This liberty and the rights entailed encouraged colonists to present themselves as English, later British, as indeed, differently, did the military protection offered by the state. There was a clear sense of superiority over other empires, which were presented as defined by territorial conquest and by a lack of freedom—notably as defined in 1685 by the revocation of the Edict of Nantes by Louis XIV of France (r. 1643–1715) and the consequent deligitimation of Huguenots (French Protestants). The corruptions and debilities discerned in other empires past and present were associated with a lack of liberty. This may seem bitterly ironic given the significance of slavery to the Atlantic imperial economy of Britain as of other Western European states, which is indeed the case but also a reflection of present-day values.

The passage to 1700 was far from inevitable. The successful Dutch invasion of 1688 could easily have been countered by the French strike planned for 1692 but wrecked by the English naval victory at Barfleur. The conquest of Ireland by William III's forces in 1689–91 might have failed. Louis XIV could have been more successful in the Nine Years' War of 1688–97. The fate of empire rested on developments and events in the British Isles and in Western Europe, but the consequences were apparent across the range of English imperial activity, most clearly in the British Isles but also more generally.

At the same time, much still rested in potential. Thus, by the late 1690s, the English state had already taken up anew the challenge of navigating in the Pacific, although it had no bases on the Pacific periphery. However, any voyage across the South Atlantic and round South America into the Pacific was long and risky, with problems of navigation, weather and seaworthiness. Future imperial horizons were being anticipated by exploration and publication, as with William Dampier, a former buccaneer who was given command of an expedition to acquire knowledge about Australia. His voyage led to the naming of islands, such as New Britain, New Ireland, New Hanover, and Rooke Island, the last after an admiral, and of features such as Capes St. George, King William, Anne, and Orford, St. George's Channel and Montagu harbor. With Cape Dampier, Dampier Strait and Dampier Island, the explorer was not forgotten, although he found nothing of apparent value in Australia.

He left a legacy of published works, including the very successful *A New Voyage Round the World* (1698), *A Discourse of Winds* (1699), and *Voyage to New Holland in the Year 1699* (two parts, 1703, 1709). Dampier's focus on observation was seen in his reporting on tides, which was highly significant for determining possibilities for landing. Discussion of tides brought together the perception of astronomical influences, the understanding of relations between forces and masses, and the application of knowledge. Similarly, Edmund Halley produced his chart of trade winds in 1689, the first scientific astronomical tables in 1693, and his "General Chart" of compass variations in 1701, all important tools for navigators. The last, a chart of terrestrial magnetism, was designed to enable navigators to chart the variation between true north and magnetic north (to which compass needles point), and thus to calculate longitude accurately.

Narratives such as that by Dampier, Lionel Wafer's *A New Voyage and Description of the Isthmus of Panama* (1699), William Funnell's *A Voyage Round the World* (1707), Edward Cooke's *A Voyage to the South Sea and Round the World* (1712), and Woodes Rogers's *A Cruising Voyage Round the World* (1712), helped create a sense of the Pacific as an accessible ocean open to profitable British penetration and one that could be seized from the real and imagined grasp of Spain. This possibility, which was also catered to in the cartographer Herman Moll's *A View of the Coasts, Countries and Islands within the Limits of the South-Sea-Company* (1711), created a context within which the British public was eager for new information. Moreover, the major financial speculation of the 1710s and early 1720s, the South Sea Company, drew on hope for profit from trade to the Pacific.

Contemporary interest in distant seas was seen in Jonathan Swift's novel *Gulliver's Travels* (1726), specifically the fictional Gulliver's voyage to Lilliput, which was located in the South Pacific, as well as Daniel Defoe's novel *Robinson Crusoe* (1726), which was based on the marooning of the Scottish buccaneer Alexander Selkirk on the uninhabited islands of Juan Férnandez in 1704–9. Once rescued, he took part in privateering on and off the coast of Ecuador and Mexico. Fiction played a role in many respects, helping indeed to locate advances in an "heroic" interpretation of exploration in terms of increased knowledge.

However, the hopes of trade associated with the South Sea Company and other schemes proved totally naïve. The distance to the Pacific helped ensure that, as yet, despite Spanish fears in the 1680s about Mocha Island, there were no significant concentrations of Western independents or marginals, "non-state actors," notably pirates, who, in pursuing their own interests, could establish a presence. This concentration had been the case in the Caribbean and Madagascar, with Mocha Island an equivalent to the latter as an outlier of the world of Atlantic piracy. Non-Western "non-state actors," such as the *wako*, were seen in East Asian waters. However, the extent to which Western trade was regulated, thanks to the role the British, Dutch and French East India Companies, and of the Portuguese and Spanish governments, affected the opportunities for Western equivalents and contributed to this sparsity of "independent" actors, and underlined the significance of government policy.

The Pacific was not yet of great importance to the British government and the extrapolation onto the Pacific of hopes, ideas, and models developed to deal with the Caribbean was at this point foolish, in terms not only of force-projection but also of the possibilities of the Pacific as opposed to the Atlantic. Yet, this extrapolation was symptomatic of the transfer onto the Pacific of ideas and hopes based on other regions.

The quite varied nature of empire had substantial impacts on those with which the British came into contact, indeed these impacts being part of the character of empire. There was also an impact on England, Britain and the British Isles, and across society, with individuals, families and communities all affected by the process—from military service to settlement, trade to the dispatch of convicts. The contexts, conjunctures and contingencies involved made empire a changing course of meanings, not least as imperial ideas, policies and practices adapted to the major political changes in Britain,[15] including with the changing fortune of commercial monopolies in the shape of trading companies.

At the same time, the networks and processes of empire saw much adaptation to cope with political and confessional divides.[16] Indeed, cross-confessional and trans-national links were central to the operation of empires, and, given their scale, this was even more the case than the situation with individual states that could be, or appear to be, more homogenous. Empire therefore was a challenge in governance, understanding and presentation. This was a challenge that developed as new circumstances provided a dynamic[17] to perpetuate and also change what was at once both an inherent conditioned stability and yet also a potential flux of instability.

5. THE EIGHTEENTH CENTURY

The key development in the British empire was not the establishment of significant power in India, nor the loss of control over the Thirteen Colonies that became the kernel of America, important as both were. Instead, the key development was the parliamentary union of 1707 between England (and Wales) and Scotland. Far from being inevitable, this union arose from another instance of the defensive character of imperial expansion. Centrally, there was English concern about the possible hazards posed by an autonomous, if not independent, Scotland in the situation of dynastic, political and international uncertainties created by the "Glorious Revolution" of 1688–9. The serious weakness of the Scottish economy in part arose from the failure in 1698–1700 to establish the colony of New Caledonia on the Gulf of Darién on the Isthmus of Panama, a failure that affected a very large number of Scottish investors. Nevertheless, there was only limited support for Union in Scotland, and its passage through the Scottish Parliament, depended in part on corruption, and was unpopular with many. The Union also reflected and anticipated the enormous variety in arrangements, norms and practices that was to characterize imperial society and governance.

As a result of the Union, Scotland retained a different national Church (the Church of Scotland was Presbyterian) and legal and educational system. It continued to be governed by Scots, but not through administrative and political institutions in Scotland. Instead, the Edinburgh Parliament was subsumed into its Westminster equivalent, with 45 MPs and 16 representative peers out of a total of 558 MPs and about 200 peers. These numbers represented a form of subordination, reflecting English concern about the possible hazards posed by an autonomous, if not independent, Scotland. Yet, it also became important to try and win these Scottish parliamentary votes; and, therefore, the political management of Scotland was important. This helped lead to some English anger at what was seen as the role of Scotland in Parliament and at the cost entailed.[1] There were also more realistic complaints in Scotland that its interests were ignored because of the cupidity of its representatives.[2]

The abolition of the Scottish Privy Council in 1708 also led to a significant change. Although the surviving Scottish officers of state sat in the British Privy Council, government policy was not formulated there, but in the Inner Cabinet. Moreover, the officers of the revenue and of the armed forces in Scotland answered to ministers in London.

For Scotland, there was therefore an explicit and an implicit bargain. These were to be present more generally in empire, and with the particular participation and to the benefit of specific groups that helped define the practice of empire. And this was the case not only in the British Isles but also further afield. Scots, in particular, came to play a major role in the expansion of empire, not least through disproportionate service in the army and the East India Company. Union also admitted Scots to a free trade area that comprised the British Isles and the colonies, and this led to Glasgow becoming a major trans-Atlantic port. Scottish-born, the journalist and novelist Tobias Smollett presented the ambiguities and contention underlining discussion of the value of imperial links. In his novel *The Expedition of Humphry Clinker* (1771), Matthew Bramwell, visiting Scotland, is perplexed:

> "I congratulated him [Lismahago] … on the present flourishing state of his country, observing, that the Scotch were now in a fair way to wipe off the national reproach of poverty, and expressing my satisfaction at the happy effects of the union, so conspicuous in the improvement of their agriculture, commerce, mnaufactures, and manners."

The cantankerous Lismahago, however, attributed this to "the natural progress of improvement," and presents the Scots as being losers from the Union:

> "Their trade has been saddled with grievous impositions, and every article of living severely taxed, to pay the interest of enormous debts, contracted by the English, in support of

> measures and connections in which the Scotch had no interest nor concern."

In further support of this argument, Lismahago presses on to talk of the great advantages England gained from the Union, namely:

> "...the settlement of the Protestant succession, a point which the English ministry drove with such eagerness, that no stone was left unturned to cajole and bribe a few leading men, to cram the union down the throats of the Scottish nation, who were surprisingly averse to the expedient. They gained by it a considerable addition of territory, extending their dominion to the sea on all sides of the island, thereby shutting up all back-doors against the enterprise of their enemies. They got an accession of above a million of useful subjects ... the Scots who settle in South Britain are remarkably sober, orderly, and industrious."

In turn, John, Lord Carteret, who was an English peer and then, as the Secretary of State closest to George II, the key figure in the government, had told the House of Lords in 1743: "[I]t is hardly possible to do justice to the Scottish or Irish, without raising a clamour among the English."[3]

It is instructive to think of James Boswell in London in 1762—a proud Scot, declaiming on his ancestry and enraged by English anti-Scottish prejudice, yet desperate to achieve professional and social acceptance in England. So also with Oliver Goldsmith, an Irishman who studied medicine in Edinburgh, settling in London in 1756. Goldsmith was to work for Smollett, and both at the *Critical Review* and the *British Magazine*. Far from being radicals keen to see the overthrow of the empire, the two men were conservative and supporters of the Church of England and of the social order.[4]

For Smollett, there were also particular crises of Scottish consciousness and concern, each linked to periods of especially harsh Scotophobia related to British politics. The most pressing crisis arose beginning in 1745, with Bonnie Prince Charlie's march at the head of a largely Scottish

Jacobite army toward London later that same year, but only, in the event, as far as Derby—nevertheless, the greatest crisis faced by the eighteenth-century British state. The atrocities in Scotland subsequently committed by the victorious British army after the battle of Culloden in 1746 fired Smollett's ire, and he reflected eloquently on them, both at the time and later. The opening lines of his *The Tears of Scotland,* written in 1746, declaimed:

> "Mourn, hapless Caledonia, mourn
> Thy banish'd peace, thy laurels torn."

The Tears of Scotland includes some grim language:

> "The ravish"d virgins shriek in vain,
> Thy infants perish on the plain."

Later, Smollett offered a bitterly ironic passage in the *Adventures of an Atom* about the atrocities, one similar in style to the biting work of Jonathan Swift when discussing Ireland. Separately, Smollett made it clear in *The Tears of Scotland* that divisions within Scotland explain conquest:

> "What foreign arms could never quell,
> By civil rage and rancour fell....
> The sons against their father stood."

A harsh governance of Highland Scotland was based on a lack of trust, with Captain James Molesworth, then serving in the garrison at Fort William, reporting in 1750:

> "[T]he thievish and the rebellious spirit are so intimately connected, that those measures which crush the thief, cannot fail to disconcert the rebel; let vigilance and force make the Highlanders honest, reason and interest will make them loyal ... that natural hatred of the English so industriously ... fomented among these people."[5]

More generally, Scotland was losing its capacity for important independent political initiatives, but doing so with prominent Scots cooperating with English ministers and, in practice, the latter role players in Scottish factional politics, a situation that had long been the case. Indeed, whereas Oliver Cromwell, having conquered Scotland, relied on Englishmen to govern it in the 1650s, now the reliance from London was on Scottish politicians,[6] notably Archibald, 3rd Duke of Argyll (earlier Earl of Ilay), Lord Keeper of the Great Seal of Scotland from 1733 until his death in 1761. Largely as a result, Scottish politics were less contentious in the 1750s than their London counterparts.

At the same time, a sense of opportunity in Scotland was discerned at the end of that decade by Charles Townshend, a visiting English politician whose stepson was Henry, 3rd Duke of Buccleuch and 5th Duke of Queensberry, a leading Scottish magnate. As part of a wider mingling of élites, Townshend—who was a member of the Board of Trade and in 1755, had married Caroline Campbell, daughter of John, 2nd Duke of Argyll and widow of the eldest son of Francis, 2nd Duke of Buccleuch––wrote:

> "[I]t is a very rising country: industry is general: the improvements are rapid: the lowest rank of subjects is emancipated from traditional slavery: commerce driven from England by high taxes, luxury and abuse, seeks the simplicity, frugality and exemptions of Scotland, and this part of Britain must in time, from these causes, succeed to the plenty, prosperity, cultivation, wealth, luxury, abuses and decline of England."[7]

Links between the two kingdoms deepened and improved, ranging from postal services to marriage, and from political management to medical care in the shape of the movement of doctors. Scottish-educated doctors were found across England, William Withering being physician to the Staffordshire County Infirmary from 1767 to 1775.

For Smollett, as for other Scots, such as the Edinburgh poet Robert Fergusson (1750–74), there was an attempt to reconcile the contrasting emotions bound up with sympathy for past practice, and the identity it provided, with, on the other hand, the commercial ethos of the "Improvers."[8]

Moreover, the foundation and running of a range of companies and institutions, such as the British Linen Company, the Commission of Annexed [Jacobite] Estates, and the Board of Trustees for the Improvement of Fisheries and Manufactures helped to create new semi-public spaces in which the new Scottish governing cadre, however self-interested, could develop practices of cooperation and improvement among themselves and with the government. They were also agencies for new ideas and, in particular, for an emphasis on commercialization, the latter helping to drive up rents and other charges, and thus to challenge established socio-economic patterns, the last generally a disruptive feature of empire.

The Annexing Act of 1752 sought to transform the Highlands by using the Jacobite estates to make them modern in socio-economic and political-cultural terms, the latter including the ending of Gaelic distinctiveness. In practice, as so often with empire, a lack of understanding, contradictory goals, and the strengths of existing patterns, combined to ensure a considerable degree of failure for the government strategies of change, as opposed to the more effective osmosis of new influences.[9]

The influence, alleged and real, under George III of his former mentor when Prince of Wales, John, 3rd Earl of Bute, who became a Secretary of State in 1761–62 and First Lord of the Treasury in 1762–63, in England led to a fresh crescendo of Scotophobia in 1762–63. It did not help that his surname was Stuart. This criticism directly involved Smollett, who, as part of a government press campaign, replied in the *Briton*. Under vicious attack, Bute resigned in 1763. Nevertheless, this anti-Scottish prejudice, now more strongly established, continued.[10] Thus, a London newspaper, the *St. James's Chronicle* of 17 December 1771, complained: "They send us whole cargoes of their staple commodity, half-bred doctors and surgeons to poison and destroy our health." That newspaper had long used the Jacobite and Scottish cards to attack government measures.[11] Given the relative skill and sophistication of Scottish medicine in this period, its readiness to adapt to new research, and, as a related point, its links with the United Provinces (Dutch Republic), a major center of such research, this was an especially foolish approach. The modernization of the medical curriculum in Scotland strengthened the role of hospital-based research, and led to a welcome willingness to try methods.[12]

Wales experienced similar cultural, economic, social and political pressures to Scotland, albeit from a different background. British cultural norms had a growing appeal there, but England preponderated, and to a degree not seen in Scotland. The Welsh gentry increasingly intermarried with their English counterparts, while a greater number of heirs were educated in England. Alongside new cultural organizations specifically for the Welsh, there was the increasing presence of English ideas and practices. The talented Welsh also flocked to London, Thomas Jones, a painter of Welsh scenery, studying at Oxford and, from 1762, living for many years in London.[13]

The situation clearly varied in Wales by geographical and social context. In 1776, an American traveler recorded of Shropshire: "Call the people in this country Welsh and you offend them: go into Wales and you can offer them no greater insult than to call them English. Is this Patriotism? It is a love of one's own country."[14] In *Humphry Clinker*, the fictional Matthew Bramble came from anglophone Monmouthshire, near England, and not from Welsh Wales; and, in contrast, the far greater sense of difference in the latter was captured in 1735 by John Campbell of Cawdor, MP for Pembrokeshire and possessor of estates there and in Scotland, when writing to his son:

> "On Sunday there came here ... two Highlanders in highland clothes without breeches, with long swords and each a pistol stuck in his girdle, they brought your uncle Philipps eight dogs.... The Highlanders came by Shrewsbury, through Montgomeryshire and Cardiganshire. The people in England were very civil to them and pleased with their dress, but when they came some miles into Wales the people were afraid of them and the folks of the inns would not have given them lodging. They were forced when they came into an inn to say that they would pay for what they had and to behave themselves civilly and so doing they would not be turned out of a public house, saying this with their pistols in their hands frightened the folks into compliance, or else they must have lain under the hedges, and maybe got no victuals, but this was among the Wild Welsh; in our part of the country [Pembrokeshire] they know a little better."[15]

The determination of the Scottish, Welsh and Irish Protestant élites and mercantile groups to link their fortune and fate with that of the British state was important to imperial identity and strength. The conceptual languages of Britishness and empire were used until the seventeenth century to describe the British Isles, but the linkage of the two concepts then came to encompass a wider political community, the full range of English-speaking territories in the Western Hemisphere thus being members of a single body. This, however, did not much alter the views of the English political élite, for whom Britain was essentially an extension of England, and that at a time when stereotypes of a distinctive Englishness hardened.[16]

There were many, however, who did not appreciate the confident association of Britishness with liberty. Today, this point would be made in particular about enslaved Africans, but it was not only relevant to them. In the British Isles, this was especially true of the Catholic Irish and also in Scotland. In Ireland, the nature of Britishness and of rule from both London and Dublin varied greatly by individual, community, religion, place and time. There were violent responses to state authority,[17] and, if but the same was true in England, it was not to the same extent.

In the Scottish Highlands, the suppression in 1746 of the Jacobite rising of 1745 was followed by a harsh pacification of what was seen as a barbarous threat that involved the breaking up of the clan system as part of an attempt to alter the politics and society of the region. This was the imperial episode to which the government devoted the most attention in the 1740s, with power affirmed by roadbuilding and fortification.

Moreover, although there was concern about transoceanic interests, these were less significant than those in Western Europe, a point demonstrated in 1747 when a planned expedition against the French colony in Canada was shelved in order to focus on the French naval and military threat in Western Europe. In addition, the British bases in Gibraltar and Minorca, captured in 1704 and 1708, respectively, reflected British concern about the strategic position in the Western Mediterranean. This was an imperialism focused on Europe. Furthermore, in 1748, as part of the peace with France, the 1745 gain of the major French naval position in Canada, Louisbourg on Cape Breton Island, was returned, despite opposition criticism.

Such points need to be borne in mind given the general tendency to write about transoceanic imperial ambitions without due qualification. It is easy for example, to note the enthusiasm surrounding the outbreak of war with Spain in 1739, the War of Jenkins' Ear, and Edward Vernon's capture later that year of Porto Bello, to comment on the singing of "Rule Britannia," and not to note that, although the war with Spain continued until 1748, it was largely abandoned in practice from 1742. More generally, despite the memoranda received from projectors, there was no master-plan for transoceanic expansion on the part of government. The peace settlement in 1748 encapsulated compromise with France and Spain, not only in its clauses but also in a more general acceptance that difficult issues should be postponed, in part by leaving them to commissioners.

This was an abrupt failure to the bold earlier hopes of major gains from the Spanish empire, the existing "known world" of the Americas and the "new world" of the Pacific. In 1713, the journalist George Ridpath noted "some people promise themselves mountains of gold from the South Sea," the term used for the Pacific.[18] In *A New Voyage Round the World by a Course Never Sailed Before* (1725), a work set in 1713–17, Daniel Defoe used a maritime account in the service of colonialization, pressing for the establishment of a colony on the tip at South America, which would have given an entry into the Pacific as well as a base in the South Atlantic south of St. Helena.[19] Projects and plans had been pushed to the fore when war broke out with Spain in 1718 and 1739 and when war appeared imminent, notably in 1726–7 and 1729. They indicated the combination of a rush to the head with pragmatism, and in both goals and means, a combination that repeatedly characterized imperialism.

These tendencies were linked to a systematization of the world in terms of the suitability for British expansion and (separately) settlement. Thus, Defoe's *New Voyage* included a section: "An Observation concerning the soil and climate of the Continent of America south of the River de la Plata, and how suitable to the genius, the constitution, and the manner of living of Englishmen, and consequently of an English colony." At the same time, a justification of slavery, directly or indirectly, played a major role in Defoe's writing.[20]

Britain's imperial position changed in the 1750s, which was the decade in which what is generally (but mistakenly) held to characterize "the British empire" came to the fore. In practice, attitudes and interests interacted, but did so in a particular context, and one that was unpredictable in its origins and development. Contingency and conjuncture were always significant to the history of British imperialisms. Governmental and public sensitivity to imperial issues rose in the 1750s, with a conscious echo being offered of the rivalry of Carthage and Rome, which was deployed as a parallel to that of Britain and France. Protestantism, rivalry with Spain and France, the many, varied and widespread benefits of empire, and the linked opposition (as contemporaries noted) to Jacobitism, France, Spain and Catholicism, helped together to create a practice and language not only of English nationalism, but also of British nationhood. Yet the latter developed alongside the still strong senses of English, Scottish, Irish, and Welsh identity, as well as the weaker ones of colonial identities.[21]

Enthusiasm for imperial expansion reflected both political positioning, and the strengthening of the public engagement with expansion as a way to ensure commercial strength and maritime destiny. However, in practice, the running together of an empire of the seas with territorial empire represented a conflation that posed serious problems in policy as well as conception.

The outbreak anew of hostilities with France in 1754 were important, not least because they centered on North America and there was not a European dimension to the war with France until 1756; which contrasted greatly with the situation with France in the early 1740s. The defense of the Low Countries (the Austrian Netherlands and the United Provinces, the modern Belgium and Holland/the Netherlands) from France had played a key role in British foreign policy and strategy from the fourteenth century and, more immediately 1689, but alliance between Austria and France from 1756 ended French expansion in that region until war between the two broke out in 1792. As a result, British attention could focus elsewhere, which was a prime instance of the dependence of imperialism, whether in attitude, ambition or policy, or other contexts.

War with France from 1754 helped foster interest and ambitions, not only at the governmental level, but also in terms of public discussion.

Moreover, rivalry with France helped provide a common issue, linking diplomatic mercantile, military, naval, European, transoceanic, and cultural anxieties and themes, and resonating them within a strong context of popular assumptions. The revival of France from the 1730s as a commercial, colonial, and naval power, and the failure of the Dutch and Spain to match this, ensured that empire for Britain came to focus on opposition to France, which, indeed, remained the dominant theme until the end of the nineteenth century. In part again this was a matter of British defensiveness: This was central until the defeat of Napoleon in 1815, and revived thereafter, notably at the close of the 1850s.

Conflict with France was very different to the situation in the medieval period. It no longer was a matter of control over parts of mainland France. Instead, the traditional theme of control over the British Isles, with Ireland a key issue in conflict until 1798, was supplemented across the oceans. Thus, in the 1750s the longstanding theme of conquering the Spanish Main declined and, instead, the focus was on North America, where the apparently imperilled fate of the British colonists ensured that themes of liberty, Protestantism and Britain all under challenge, could lend popular interest to the more abstruse issues of borders and Native American allegiances.

At the same time, looked at closely, North America posed the tensions integral to empire. Indeed, moves into the interior of North America, notably the Ohio Valley, challenged the ability of the British state to direct affairs; while the concern with land and territory in the interior did not match the standard focus on "blue water" issues.

This contrast was also linked to a tension over the direction of empire. With William, Duke of Cumberland, the authoritarian Captain-General of the Forces from 1745 to 1757, and an opponent of the "Patriot" politicians who had earlier pressed for "blue water" conflict with Spain, there was an emphasis on control over territory. Protégés of the Duke were given authority in Gibraltar, Minorca and Nova Scotia, and Cumberland's support for a forward policy in North America was very important in the escalation of tension with France in 1755. This prefigured the comparable emphasis for empire on the role of the military and associated landed values in the French Revolutionary and Napoleonic period. Cumberland's view of empire was also seen in 1748 in his interest in putting a British garrison into Ostend in modern Belgium as part of the peace settlement: He intended Ostend as a fortress against France and not as a trading center. Aside from Cumberland, there was to be a separate authoritarian strand to empire in the use of the navy to enforce imperial control and regulations.[22]

An either/or approach focused on populist or governmental trajectories for imperialism, or on rival tendencies within each or both is inappropriate. Imperialism does not match to such dichotomies and, instead, there were significant overlaps. Moreover, this was within a context of adversarial domestic politics and unpredictable international tensions. Thus, the major expansion of empire in mid-century appears more coherent and even inevitable in retrospect than was the case at the time. Indeed, the last was made readily apparent by the divisions in 1762 over whether to retain Canada or the Caribbean sugar islands Martinique and Guadeloupe when making peace with France.

Foreign policy in the early 1750s had related heavily to European power politics, and North America was secondary until 1755. Even then, in 1756, it was the collapse of Britain's alliance system in Europe that was of most concern to government. As so often, however, war radicalized policy, leading to a greater concern for security and gains, a process seen both in North America and in India. Public interest was far more focused on the former, which also affected governmental options. In comparison far less note was taken of developments in India. There, after Robert Clive's victory at Plassey in 1757, the East India Company with difficulty consolidated its position in Bengal, while the French were defeated in southern India. In December 1761, John Johnstone wrote from Calcutta: "The company are now in the highest pitch of glory, possessors of lords of almost Hindostum!"[23] In practice, the situation even in Bengal was unsettled until after victories in 1764 led to peace in 1765; while elsewhere the British position was more limited.

In contrast, repeated and serious French defeats in 1758–62 provided opportunities for British politicians and commentators to rethink the nature and range of maritime North American and Caribbean empire. There was a sequential character to imperial activity. Thus, the fall of Louisbourg in 1758 led to that of Quebec in 1759, and the latter was a prelude to the capture of Montreal in 1760. In 1761, freed by the fall of Canada with the surrender of Montreal to Britain the previous year, a large British force conquered Dominica and then, in 1762, Martinique. In 1761, bold commentators could respond to the issue of whether Britain should retain Canada or Caribbean gains by calling for the retention of both and, indeed, calling for additional conquests, including Louisiana.[24]

The prospect, and then in 1762 reality, of Spanish entry into the war on the side of France helped expand the range of British ambition, but also posed the questions of the purpose of gains and of priorities as a whole. In 1762, Arthur Dobbs, Governor of North Carolina from 1754 to 1764, an Irish MP and supporter of Scots-Irish (Protestant) migration to Ireland, offered a scheme for the improvement of the New World under the aegis of Britain and to her profit, a project he had backed for years and one that indicated the significance of ideological factors, both political and religious, to imperialism. He urged the need:

> "to publish manifestoes in the Spanish tongue on landing … declaring the Spanish colonies free states to be governed by laws framed by themselves after the model of British liberty under the protection of Britain as a perpetual ally with a free trade most favourable to Britain … and to retain, as cautionary pledges of the future friendship and fidelity of these colonies, Vera-Cruz, Havana, Portobello and the isthmus of Darien, Cartagena, Hispaniola and the other Spanish islands. Spanish Florida to be entirely ceded to Britain … to send missionaries to civilise and Christianise the natives where the Spaniards have no settlements and to form them into regular polities under the direction of governors truly Christian and educated for that purpose in Britain at the expense of the public."[25]

As a reminder of the problems seen with territorial conquest, Sir John Molesworth, a Tory MP, regarded conquests in Spanish America as a "wild" project, as "we could neither hold nor cultivate them without exhausting and depopulating the Mother Country." One of a number of claims about the risks about imperial expansion, this was an argument that had much weight prior to the sustained rise in population that began in the late eighteenth century and made it possible to support emigration and consider a different demographic to empire. Molesworth, instead, pressed for the capture of leading positions in Spanish America as a means to force Spain to abandon France.[26]

In the event, imperial success led to the capture of Havana and Manila from Spain and Martinique from France, all in 1762, and to a moment of exuberance. The news of the fall of Havana was received in Salisbury during a choral concert in the annual music festival—to shouts of applause, the choir at once burst into the song "Britons, Strike Home." In his *Travels through France and Italy* (1766), published after his tour in 1763–5, Smollett wrote of Monaco that it "might be laid in ashes by a bomb-ketch [firing mortar shells] in four hours by sea"; while the Gulf of La Spezia was described in terms of "an admirable station for a British squadron." For Rome, Smollett, with total implausibility, wrote:

> "[T]he popes will do well to avoid misunderstandings with the maritime protestant states, especially the English, who being masters of the Mediterranean, and in possession of Minorca, have it in their power at all times, to land a body of troops within four leagues of Rome, and to take the city, without opposition … altogether incapable of defense."[27]

Yet, as a reminder of the ambivalence of attitudes, these captures also reflected a formidable effort and led to a sense of imperial overstretch that were to lead directly to the post-war crises in public finances and colonial governance.

By 1763, when the Seven Years' War ended, Britain was the most powerful European empire in the world, with "blue water" transformed into Britain's destiny and Britain's empire the leading European one in North America and South Asia. In exchange for returning Cuba in the Peace of Paris of 1763, the British received unconquered Florida that was extended, at the expense of French-ruled Louisiana (now transferred to Spain), as far as the Mississippi, creating for the British the separate colonies of East Florida and West Florida. The right to cut wood in Belize was also gained from Spain, while Minorca was returned to Britain.

Returning Guadeloupe, Martinique and St. Lucia to France, the British kept Dominca, Grenada, St. Vincent and Tobago.

However, this situation prefigured that at other victorious closes to war in 1815, 1856, 1918 and 1945, for these achievements had to be protected, and there was now more to defend. Empire therefore became a defensive project anew, albeit in each case, in a different context to the pre-war one. This was even more the case when the close to war registered failure, as in 1783, although not to the same extent, 1748 and 1802.

Imperial rivalry with France came more to the fore from the 1750s, in part because French alliance with Austria from 1756 meant that France no longer had to fear her Continental neighbors. Instead, it was possible for France to focus more of an effort on exploiting British imperial problems, notably in 1778–83. This again pushed the onus of empire into a defensive context. Whereas repeated imperial failure in North America and Minorca in 1754–7 had been rapidly remedied, this was not to be the case with the War of American Independence. As a result, the empire thereafter appeared more precarious, a situation particularly felt in postwar 1783–7 and again in 1798–1803, years of wartime crisis followed by precarious peace.

While competition with France and its allies was a symbol of national vitality and an issue of governmental credibility, the context had shifted from the 1760s because of a far stronger engagement than in previous inter-war periods with the governance and internal issues of Britain's imperial possessions. These were seen as a potential cause of strength or weakness, and that was a theme that was to remain strong until the close of empire in the twentieth century. From the 1760s, the nature of authority and financing of power in the North American and West Indian colonies and the territories of the East India Company came to the fore. Far from the focus being one on territorial expansion, much of the struggle to maintain Britain's imperial position involved the attempt to consolidate and enhance Britain's overseas presence by means of a beneficial direction of the trade of colonies. This was most obviously seen with the attempt to sell Indian tea in order to improve the finances of the East India Company.

Fear of French *revanche* underlay the government's contentious desire to build up the defensive strength of the North American colonies, and there was also a fear of French *revanche* in India in alliance with hostile local powers, particularly the Marathas and Mysore. International rivalry and, even more, a perception of such rivalry, was the basic condition of thought regarding the empire, as it led to urgent concern about how best to strengthen it. Yet, these issues were increasingly set alongside serious divisions within the British political world over how best to organize the empire. This political world extended to include the North American and West Indian colonists, as well as officials in India, but the terms of the resulting relationships were unclear. For example, the policy of the government in limiting the westward expansion of the North American colonies at the expense of the Native Americans became a matter of resented authority. Moreover, the grant of civil recognition to Quebec's Catholics by the Quebec Act of 1774, intended to strengthen imperial stability there, also accentuated New England concerns about the intentions of the British government. That legislation and the treatment of the Native Americans were reflections of the more general degree to which empire was a matter of diversity and compromise, is a situation exemplified by the weakness of frontier garrisons and their dependence on transactional acceptance and agreement by both Native Americans and settlers.[28]

The ways in which policy, and regulation as an aspect of it, were to be framed, formulated and enforced, were themselves matters of contention to a far greater degree than before, or during, the mid-century wars. In consequence, the role of foreign policy in framing discussion about empire, or in expressing views about it, declined in importance.

The politics of imperial consolidation and expansion were quite varied in character, both in the metropole and on the periphery; and this related to controversy over the nature of this consolidation and expansion. Again, underlining a long-term theme but one that was not consistent in its sensitivity, British ministers might see the strengthening of Westminster's imperial authority as a means to share burdens and strengthen the colonies, but it is not surprising that critical commentators discerned an authoritarian prospectus.

Modern discussion also takes differing views on this issue as it does on the extent to which imperialism, British and otherwise, was a syncretic system, dependent on the cooperation of local élites, most notably in India where British rule relied heavily on existing ideas and practices of governance that were developing prior to British conquest. Yet these practices were now applied in a way that took note of British wishes and power.[29]

In contrast to an emphasis on hybrid forms albeit adapted ones, there has also been an emphasis on the coercive character of empire. The former approach stresses consensus and continuity, the latter force and discontinuity, which were particularly apparent in the harshness of slavery.

This range is appropriate not only for relations with native peoples, but also for discussion over the character and process of economic and fiscal links. Bengal, the major area of increased British power in India, provides an instructive instance of the way in which profit was not simply a matter of seizing and using power. Victory in war enabled the British to take a major role in regional trade, a role that meant imposing particular habits, terms and meanings for goods, markets and people. Once East India Company power was forcibly established in Bengal in mid-century, a process that began in 1757 and was complete by 1765, there was an alteration in the political economy of trade as control over customs was monopolized. The authority of local landed chiefs was banished from rivers, ferries and tollways, and intermediate units over markets were ended. As a consequence, in an anticipation of what would later be called globalization, the colonial marketplace was opened up to the freer flow of imperial commodities and investment. The gathering of information was central to this policy. Long-distance trade rose and prices became more uniform. Published lists of prices challenged the immense variety of wholesale and retail rates that had once characterized markets where trade was subject to different political authorities.[30] The role of the Company also facilitated British commodity exports to India, particularly woollen textiles, and these exports rose in the 1760s and, even more, from the late 1780s.[31]

Yet, far from proving a cash cow, the viability of the conquests in India, and indeed of the entire position of the Company, were challenged by the combination of dividend demands by the shareholders, the heavy costs of defense, the difficulties of revenue collection in India, and weakness in the market for tea, a major source of Company finances. This hit governmental fiscal expectations, particularly when, in 1772, the Company sought both the rescheduling of customs payments and a loan. Tea imports into North America apparently offered a way to tackle Company finances.[32] Tea therefore was both reality and symbol of the process by which India became an integral part of the empire in tandem with attempts to integrate America more firmly into it.[33] In 1778, Spiridion Roma was commissioned by the Company's directors to paint the ceiling of their Leadenhall Street headquarters. His *East Offering its Riches to Britannia* showed India and China, both as women, presenting their riches, a standard gender depiction in Classical imperial ensembles in stone and one that Britain sustained.

The capture of Manila in 1762 increased British interest in the Pacific, even though Manila was returned to Spain in 1764. Exploration in the Pacific and elsewhere owed something to scientific interest, but was also driven by the widespread sense that the British maritime dominance recognized by the Peace of Paris of 1763 would be challenged in the future, and that any such war would focus even more on colonial and maritime rivalry than the Seven Years' War had done. At the popular level, there was also widespread interest in Pacific exploration, and this encouraged, and was sustained by, publications such as Alexander Dalrymple's *Historical Collection of the Several Voyages and Discoveries in the South Pacific Ocean* (1770–1). A copy of the first was taken on James Cook's first voyage to the Pacific, on which in 1770 a landing in Botany Bay led to the claiming of Australia for George III.[34]

As with the manufacturing exports to Africa linked to the British role in the slave trade, there was also an important local dimension to the East India Company in particular British towns. The Company notably brought wealth and activity into Portsmouth with new employment and investment possibilities. There was also local investment in the Company. The range of relationship included growing numbers of Company officers gravitating toward Hampshire's coastal communities for rest and recuperation, while retired officers followed suit and took up permanent residence. The Company helped to make Portsmouth more aware of the outer world, an instance of a process taking place more generally in British society but one that was most marked in ports. Food, clothing and furnishings were all affected, and the religious character of Portsmouth became more varied. There were naturally tensions, not only between town and Company, but also, at times, difficult relations with the navy that owed much to clashes over the use of naval facilities. Furthermore, the navy could be difficult over its convoying responsibilities, a more general problem in the relationship of trade and state, but the relationship with the Company was essentially cooperative. The Company had its own military forces and this could cause tension in Portsmouth, with issues of recruiting, housing and logistics, but it is important to note the degree to which disputes were essentially contained.[35]

The gain of an Indian-based Oriental empire, however, encouraged comparison with imperial Rome. This comparison was particularly made because, unlike Britain's North American empire, but like that of imperial Rome, the new empire in India had no ethnic underpinning and was clearly imperial. Power in the Orient produced a number of disturbing cultural and political resonances. It seemed to position Britain as the descendant not of republican Rome, with what was seen as its virtues and vital energies, and an empire ruled by a dedicated leadership in combination with representative assemblies that could be compared with Parliament—but, instead, of Imperial Rome, the Rome of the Emperors (not just the empire) with its self-indulgent decadence. Anxieties about the effects of empire upon metropolitan culture were frequently expressed. The figure of the nabob, as in the extortionist Sir Matthew Mite in Samuel Foote's play *The Nabob* (1772), was particularly troubling because of the potential impact of their great wealth, not least in purchasing parliamentary influence. The nabob also encapsulated longstanding anxieties about new money.[36]

The situation in the Caribbean differently involved oppression and brutality in the treatment of slaves. This was the century in which the largest number of slaves crossed the Atlantic, with the British the major shippers. In part, this involved the brutal movement of the enslaved to British colonies. There was also the sale to the colonies of others. Thus, the Asiento contract to transport slaves to Spanish America given to France in 1701 was gained by Britain in 1713 and seen as of value to its economy as a whole, an anonymous memorandum in the papers of Sir Robert Walpole, first minister from 1720 to 1742, commenting:

> "This trade is truly national being carried on entirely in British shipping, and managed by British merchants both in

> Africa and America, and the goods sent out are principally the product and manufactures of Great Britain, or such goods as have been purchased with the product and manufactures of Great Britain, the returns are made either in gold or silver, or in commodities necessary for the carrying on our own manufactures, or in other useful and valuable commodities."[37]

A similar theme about the fiscal benefit of a slave-plantation economy in which Britain played a central role in the West was offered in 1798 by Charles, 1st Earl of Liverpool, the longstanding President of the Board of Trade:

> "[T]he great importation of sugar and coffee from the West Indies by the last fleets, amounting in value, as I am informed, to £4,000,000 was sold instantly at a very high price in a very few days, to be carried to Hamburg and other foreign markets, and very little was left for the consumption of this kingdom, which makes the present price of these articles at present so high. The return for this vast exportation will be principally in gold and silver bullion. The London market is said to be full of money, which sufficiently manifests itself by the rise of the stocks."[38]

This benefit also helped finance the war with France and its allies.

The triangular trade of British exports to West Africa, the enslaved thence to Britain's colonies, and plantation goods thence to Britain, depended on credit and the ability to wait for payment. Britain's financial strength provided both. The crucial role of finance, particularly of the sugar commission business, ensured that London, where the business centered, was as heavily involved in the slave trade as Liverpool from which there were more sailings.[39] Financial buoyancy was particularly important in long-distance trade in which new ships lasted only two or three voyages, financial returns were seriously delayed, and merchants, therefore, needed to obtain long-term credit on favorable terms.

The trade brought opportunities and prosperity to British manufacturers. The export of goods to Africa as part of the triangular trade helped broaden the range of groups in British society who were interested in the slave trade and who, directly or indirectly, profited from its expansion. This increased the penetration of the slave trade in the British economy and in British society. Britain's largest industry, the woollen textile industry, benefited greatly from the development of the slave trade. The share of these textiles in the export of British-made goods to Africa, essentially West Africa, rose from 6.5% in 1660 to 64.9% in 1693, a year in which European markets were greatly affected by war; and from then until 1728 never dropped below 47.1%. Moreover, the percentage of British exports to Africa produced in Britain rose from less than 30% in the 1650s and 1660s to about two-thirds by 1713–15.[40] This opportunity helped manufacturers to cope with periods of difficulty in their usual markets, and led to innovations, notably in the production of lighter cloth, as the African market was pursued.[41]

In 1731, underlining the abiding issue with statistics, John Crookshanks, Secretary to the Commissioners discussing commercial differences with Spain, drew attention to the significance of the movement of New World plantation products to Britain, but also to the problems of fixing exact figures:

> "[T]he balance of trade with a particular kingdom or upon a single branch cannot be ascertained, unless we trade in cattle as the patriarchs did. The consideration of the Guinea [West Africa] trade makes this plain. £500 from England to Africa produces £5,000 in Jamaica, which last sum merges in the return from the English colonies, without any possibility of distinction."[42]

At the same time, there was a high rate of migration as well from the British Isles—notably of indentured servants. For example, benefiting from more predictable and rapid trans-Atlantic crossings, with a significant change in both occurring in the period from 1675 to 1740, between 30,000 and 50,000 White migrants arrived in Jamaica in the first half of the eighteenth century, and the cultivated area there increased greatly; although, tellingly again, this information refers to the land under imperial control, not that tilled by escaped slaves. But for disease, such migration would have led to a British New World dominated by the West Indies, with nearly three million people in 1760, compared to only 1.7 million in British North America; but disease prevented that outcome. Similarly, with disease again a key feature, the African-descended population of the United States equals that of the Caribbean, although nearly ten times as many African migrants went to the Caribbean.

The willingness to accept non-British European migrants was seen with the Plantation Act of 1740, under which it was possible for all bar Catholics to become eligible for naturalization after seven years in a British colony, a measure that threw them open to all European Protestants (and thus to those for whom the monarch was not the head of the Church); and that was only fully ended in 1773. The French and Spanish empires conspicuously lacked such tolerance, although that did not prevent people evading regulations.

Alongside the racial oppression of Blacks that understandably attracts so much modern attention, there were serious social tensions within the settler community, much of which was poor, and many of whom indentured servants or wage laborers. Racial issues were frequently affected by these social tensions, with poorer White people often resentful of free Black people and harsh to Black slaves.

Meanwhile, opportunities within the White community varied greatly, for, in contrast to the poor White people, élite families were able to seek not only to exploit the local resources, but also to control the institutions of local government and to become representatives of their state; an always shifting, but generally prosperous, combination. At the same time, there was a strong sense of local rights and privileges, leading to frequent disputes over the power and pretensions of governors. Thus, having earlier survived two assassination attempts, Daniel Parke, the Virginian-born Governor of the Leeward Islands from 1706, was lynched in 1710 by colonists in Antigua when he ignored pressure to let the legislature control its defenses. More significantly, no one was punished.

The surveying of the British colonies, which was very much to the benefit of the élite, readily displayed economic, social and racial landscapes. The utilitarian origins of the plans that were produced ensured that a premium was placed on accuracy of measurement and representation;

and successfully so as recent tests for Jamaica suggest error of less than two percent for the gross dimensions of plantations. Planters there wanted precise information for land use management and fields planted with major export crops were plotted more carefully than areas of woodland or than land planted with provision crops in what were known as "Negro grounds."

The crisis of 1745–6 caused by the Jacobite rebellion had been rapidly overcome, and had led to the further integration of Scotland into the empire. The rebellion in Ireland of 1798 was to be followed, in 1800–1, by Union with Ireland. In contrast, the crisis with the Thirteen Colonies that turned continually violent in 1775 spread and was sustained, thanks to successful foreign intervention, to encompass pressure on the entire empire. This crisis also accentuated a wider anxiety about the nature of British society and, in particular, the extent to which it had been corrupted by success and luxury.

The origins of the American War of Independence owed much to the terms of benefit within the imperial political economy as mediated through a series of disputes, particularly those over taxation. Trade proved one of the ways in which first confrontation and then conflict were waged, with peacetime colonial boycotts of British trade followed by wartime privateering. Yet, underlining the variegated nature of the empire, whereas in America, Nova Scotia and the Leeward Islands, there was marked opposition to the Stamp Act of 1765 and, specifically, the sense that the levying of taxation for revenue purposes by a Parliament that included no colonial representatives was a dangerous degree of political innovation, this was not true of the major West Indian colonies.[43] The latter, particularly Jamaica, were the wealthiest British colonies in the New World.[44] Repealed in 1766, the Stamp Act was followed in 1767 by a Revenue Act that imposed customs duties in the colonies on a variety of goods, most valuably tea. This taxation was designed to pay the costs of civil government and thus end dependence on colonial assemblies, a longstanding complaint on the part of governors. The American colonies responded with fury, but the West Indian colonies accepted the legislation.[45] The tea duty was retained in 1769 when the other duties introduced in 1767 were repealed. The duty symbolized Parliament's right to tax, and public finances benefited.

Smuggled Dutch tea, however, challenged East India Company sales and, in 1773, the government passed a Tea Act that abolished British duties on the tea re-exported to America and allowed the Company to sell its tea directly to consignees to the American colonies, a measure designed to cut the cost of tea there and thus boost sales. The Americans were still to pay the duty on the imported tea. This was condemned by Patriot activists, unwilling to accept Parliament's right to impose direct taxes on the colonies. Whereas in Ireland, the West Indies and the Floridas there was a need, despite grievances, for the settler groups to stick with Britain, the "political space" of Whites in the American colonies that rebelled provided an opportunity to consider different outcomes and methods, and to establish new practices and structures accordingly.

Thus, the Boston Tea Party on 16 December 1773, in which tea was seized and thrown into the harbor became a stage to a more serious prospectus. This action, and the government response, including the Boston Port Act of 1774, which closed the port and moved the customs house until the Company was reimbursed for the tea, dramatized the breakdown of imperial authority.

The crisis also indicated divisions within the empire/trade nexus, in particular merchants' longstanding reluctance to accept the disruption and other costs of war.[46] Merchants hit by American boycotts of British imports, including those in 1768–70 and from 1774, tended to prefer commercial continuity to the defense of imperial authority. Moreover, in the Thirteen rebellious colonies, there was no economic or military dependence on British naval bases as there was in Antigua, Bermuda, Jamaica and Nova Scotia.

If wars in 1739 and from 1754 had stemmed from imperial disputes, the terms of the British response had then been set by political divisions in the metropole, conflict had rapidly extended to European waters, and the implications for Britain's alliances became a key issue in foreign policy. From 1775, in contrast, the empire was the source and site of war as the conflict focused on imperial authority, and not on protection from external challenges. Hopes from many of the colonists, and on the part of Britain, particularly with the Howes' instructions in 1776 and the Carlisle Commission in 1778, that it might be possible to settle the crisis by adjusting governance proved misplaced. Instead, the conflict in North

America became from 1776 one both for independence and for the allocation of imperial dominions, notably Canada. French entry in 1778 made the entire situation seem more desperate, Spain followed in 1779 and the Dutch in 1780. The war did not lead to military success, and, indeed, in 1777 and 1781 there were serous failures in North America, at Saratoga and Yorktown, with British forces driven to surrender. Yet the latter simply meant a new stalemate, and there was little assumption in North America that Yorktown meant the close of the conflict, not least because Britain held apparently impregnable New York. Instead, it was in Parliament that the battle had a decisive impact in the spring of 1782 in undermining political backing for the North ministry and leading to a new government pledged to negotiations.[47]

The British had lost the Thirteen Colonies in North America, West Florida, several Caribbean islands, and Minorca during the war. Under the Treaty of Versailles of 1783, Tobago was ceded to France, and West and East Florida to Spain, which restored Minorca. Spanish hopes of gaining Gibraltar and Jamaica in war and peace proved fruitless.

The breakdown of the imperial link in 1775–6 had indicated that the British government and political system, with its overlapping and interacting systems of policy-discussion, formulation and execution, was unable to deal with the serious issues of management posed by the nature of the empire and the politics of the period. Although the failure in North America did not produce the wider crisis that was feared and indeed might have been anticipated,[48] it was unclear in 1783 whether the system would be more successful in confronting pressing issues of management in Britain and Ireland, issues that included the governance of British India.

Both before and after 1793, there was interest in territorial expansion but, prior to the outbreak of war with France that year, expansion was largely at the expense of non-European powers, and there was caution about pushing colonial claims against European states.[49] From 1793, in contrast, there were also the tempting prizes of the colonies of France and her allies, which from 1796 included both Spain and the Netherlands. Furthermore, policy toward non-European states from 1793 was affected by the likely interaction with the war.

In the late 1780s, William Pitt the Younger, Prime Minister from 1783 to 1801 and from 1804 to his death in 1806, was not keen at all on war with France, but was also anxious to strengthen the British role in the Indian Ocean, which helped lead him to contest French influence in the United Provinces as the Dutch were a regional power there. Pitt expressed interest in 1788 in a settlement with France by which Britain gained Mauritius, Réunion and France's positions in India in return for support for French gains from the Turkish empire.[50] Yet nothing came of this idea.

Relations with America after 1783 indicated that trade did not necessarily depend on empire because this trade revived after American independence. However, trade was still widely expected to flow from empire: There was apparently a one-way relationship alongside the more difficult one with independent states. This assumption encouraged interest in South and East Asia and the Pacific, for they seemed to offer new opportunities for both types of trade. The focus generally is on spreading territorial empire—in India, Australia and to a lesser extent elsewhere, for example Malaya—but a desire for trade was as crucial. There was very much seen in an increased engagement with China, as well as the foundation of a trading base at Penang in Malaya in 1786, and growing speculation about prospects in the Pacific.

The establishment in 1788 of a British settlement in Australia owed much to the loss of America, where many criminals had been sent. In 1786, the British government decided to found New South Wales in order to provide a penal colony, a course recommended by Sir Joseph Banks, an advocate for value from a new Pacific presence. Geopolitical advantage was also pursued, both pre-empting the French and providing a base that would project British power into the Southern Hemisphere (which caused concern in Spain) and provide naval supplies. In turn, British activity in the Pacific reflected maritime predominance and the relative situation of the leading naval powers. In the waters of the southwest Pacific, the British added to their empire Lord Howe Island (1788), the Chatham Islands (1791), and Pitt Island (1791), the names all commemorating ministers of the time. Captain William Bligh made intelligible charts of Fiji, the Banks group and Aitutaki in the Cooks, Captain Severs "discovered" the Kermadecs and Penrhyn Island, and Captains Gilbert and Marshall the islands that bear their names. In 1789, Lieutenant John Shortland coasted the shores of Guadalcanal and San Cristobal.

Commander George Vancouver, who had been on James Cook's second and third voyages, was sent to the Pacific in 1791 in order to carry out survey work and to secure Britain's possession of the Nootka Sound coastline on what is now Vancouver Island. Competition over this coast had nearly led to a major war: In 1789, the commander of a Spanish warship seized the British ships and depot recently established at Nootka Sound and, when the news reached London in 1790, there was a major naval armament.

Ultimately, Spain backed down, in part because it was clear that France could not provide support, and accepted a settlement that established the rights of the British to settle to the north of the areas occupied by Spain prior to the 1789 seizure. British whalers and traders were also to be able to operate "in the Pacific Ocean or in the South Seas, or in landing on the coasts of those seas in places not already occupied, or for the purpose of carrying on their commerce with the indigenous people of the country or of making establishments there."

Meanwhile, in addition to the firepower offered by muskets, the British were helped in Australia by numerical superiority. This was accentuated by the impact of Western diseases on the indigenous Australians, in contrast to the disease balance in Africa. Tactical developments were also important—notably the use of light infantry, especially in night-time encirclements of indigenous Australian camps. The net effect was a total change in control over a large area. A pattern of dominance was developed that was to be applied elsewhere in the Pacific.

Australia became the key base for this activity. The first British sealing operation off New Zealand was established in 1792, and the first sealing station began operating on the east coast of New Zealand a decade later. The search for seals led to the "discovery" of sealing islands, such as Antipodes Island in 1800, Auckland Island in 1806, and both Campbell and Macquarie Islands in 1810. Other voyages sought to supply the new colony in Australia until it could feed itself, and traders imported pork from Pacific islands, especially Tahiti.

Much of Latin America, meanwhile, became part of the world of British informal empire, with important trading and financial interests bringing Britain profit and influence. This was not, however, the situation Arthur Dobbs had envisaged in 1762. There were no British military bases, and, indeed, although Montevideo was briefly seized, the British attempt to capture Buenos Aires in 1807 was humiliatingly defeated and Montevideo soon after abandoned. Nor was there a direct relationship between the British and the Native (Indian) population, other than on the Caribbean coasts of Honduras and Nicaragua. Yet, the important role Britain played in Latin America during the nineteenth century, with exports there matching those to America by the late 1810s, was a testimony to the longstanding relationship of trade and policy, and its implications for empire, whether it be formal or, as in this case, informal.

Naval power, amphibious capability, and transoceanic power projection ensured that the British could be in a dominant position. In 1793–1802, it proved possible to conquer islands in the West Indies and the Dutch base at Cape Town while slave risings were crushed—notably on Grenada and St. Lucia. On St. Vincent, the native Caribs attacked in 1795 (in response to French encouragement) only to be defeated in 1796 after the destruction of their homes and provision grounds, and then forcibly expelled from the island, being sent first to the Grenadines and then to Roatán. The British position in the Mediterranean was also developed, most lastingly with Malta, but with shorter term bases, including on Corsica, Elba and Sicily. In 1793, the Corsicans requested British protection and the following year the French forces there were defeated. A democratic constitution was established with an elected Parliament and a British viceroy and there was talk of the island passing under the British Crown, only for the French to reconquer the island in 1796.

Once war resumed with Napoleon in 1803, the British seized St. Lucia, Tobago, Demerara, Essequibo (now both in Guyana), and Surinam in 1803–4, following with the Danish West Islands—namely, St. Croix, St. Thomas and St. Johns, in 1807, Martinique and Cayenne in 1809, and Guadeloupe, St. Eustatius and St. Martin in 1810. Fort Louis, the last French base in Africa, fell in 1809.

The war destroyed or greatly weakened the imperial systems of the other European states and provided military and diplomatic incentives for Britain to seize their territories, so that the period 1793–1815 marked the apogee of one method of territorial gain—the acquisition of the colonies of other European powers—even though the other method, the gain of non-European-ruled territories, continued thereafter, especially in India and Australasia.

The seizure of the extra-European territories of other European powers in 1793–1815 was bound up with foreign policy, understood as the formal diplomacy of the state. This was less the case with the acquisition of non-European-ruled lands, as initiatives were taken by local officials and by non-governmental bodies, most importantly the East India Company. However, British military strength and reputation were very important to this expansion during the French Revolutionary and Napoleonic period. Strategic considerations, particularly vulnerability and opportunity, were key to this expansion, and were more urgent than the earlier tendency (seen during the inter-war period of 1783–93) to regard territorial expansion as necessary to consolidate commercial positions.

There were many reasons behind colonial activity, not least settling convicts as with Australia. In West Africa, due to the actions and pressure from Abolitionists in the 1780s, freed slaves were settled from 1787 in coastal Sierra Leone, although such a formulation underplays the extent and role of Black presence and agency, which, more generally, has attracted attention in recent years.[51] The St. George Bay Company established in 1790 was brought under the Sierra Leone Company in 1792, the year in which the town of Freetown was established. In turn, in 1808, Sierra Leone became a Crown Colony.

Not all ideas and initiatives bore fruit. In 1793, Sir Erasmus Gower, the captain of HMS *Lion*, which had conveyed the first British envoy to Beijing, reported that, *en route*, he had stopped in Cochin China, in what is now Vietnam, adding: "I think we shall establish an advantageous trade with these people … and there is a very proper place for a settlement which we have called New Gibraltar."[52] This, however, remained only an aspiration, evidence indeed of the extent to which trade and empire were constrained by practicality, even as they were exalted by hope and power.

War, nevertheless, transformed this relationship, not least by enhancing military strength and exigencies and reducing concerns about cost. In 1786, Charles James Fox had been worried about "sacrificing political importance to gain and peace," as, he claimed, the Dutch had long tended to do,[53] but the last combination was no longer an option for Britain from 1793.

A structural or systemic account of British empire-building can make war, naval power, imperial expansion and maritime hegemony appear not only as obviously linked, but also as inevitably leading to a synergy of success. This is misleading and, in particular, underrates the multiple difficulties posed to Britain's domestic and international situation. Even if the synergy appeared clearcut overseas after the major defeat of the French and Spanish fleet at Trafalgar in 1805, there was still the danger that defeat on the European Continent or simply the collapse of Britain's alliance system would lead to an unwelcome return of colonial gains in order to obtain peace, as occurred in 1748 and 1802. The possibility that Austria might settle with Napoleon as late as the beginning of 1814 made this a continuing danger. Trade and empire had to be fought for, by Britain, both on its own and as part of an often complex and difficult foreign policy involving compromises with allies.

The audiences at Birmingham's New Street theater were left in little doubt about Britain's spreading power. The "pantomimical interlude" on 17 August 1791 was "a grand serious pantomime in one act called Soldiers' Festival, or The Night before the Battle … with an exact representation of the siege of Quebec, an engagement between the English and French armies, and the death of General Wolfe." The events of 1759 thus depicted clearly still resonated, but, five days later, something more recent was promised:

> "A pantomime exhibition called Botany Bay; or, A Trip to Port Jackson, with entire new scenery, painted for the occasion … in which will be introduced a picturesque view of the coast of New South Wales … arrival of the Grand Fleet [in 1788], landing, reception, and employment of the convicts. To conclude with the ceremony of planting the British flag, on taking possession of a new discovered island, with a dance by the convicts, and the grand chorus of 'God Save the King.'"

Distant events were thus staged far from the sea in a major manufacturing center whose prosperity in part rested on manufactured exports.

Economic growth, mercantile expansion, frequent wars and imperial apotheosis. All seemed, and seem, connected, as indeed they were, but the nature of this connection, and the extent to which there was a series of synergetical relationships, are questions open to debate, as they also were to contemporaries. The political opposition of the 1790s, naval mutinies of 1797 and even more the Irish Rising of 1798 also clearly showed that Britain was not a unity, whether in imperial matters or anything else; and this was more generally true. There is no smooth pattern in the growth of empire.

6. THE NINETEENTH CENTURY

The dominant image for empire is of a line or square of redcoats confronting charging natives. The geographical focus is on India and, toward the close of the century, Africa. Ideas associated with David Livingstone and Rudyard Kipling resonant—the dark forests of Africa for the former, distant hill-stations and mountain valleys for the latter.

In practice, expansion on land relied on *Pax Britannica* at sea, naval hegemony providing the secure background to force projection. This hegemony combined with industrial growth and a liberal entrepreneurial ethos to encourage and sustain the commitment to free trade and a liberal international order that was to be a defining feature of nineteenth-century British imperialism.

This commitment to free trade was also to be of great importance for economic growth across the world, although the globalization, or at least openness to markets it fostered, caused major problems of adjustment, and the benefits it brought were spread very unequally. Trade, rather than costly expansion on land, was the source of Britain's status as the world's wealthiest nation—and thus of her power—more particularly, the resources that were to underwrite government revenues.

Yet, this was not the case in 1793–1815 for conflict on land as well as at sea had then been very important, as France and its allies were defeated. This hard-won success involved wideranging operations that were part of a global strategy drawing on imperial resources. This was seen clearly with the concentration of strength in 1801 to support an attack on the French forces in Egypt to resolve a crisis begun by the French conquest three years earlier. The British, in response, operated in both the Mediterranean and the Red Sea, and combined planning with Indian Ocean resources to a hitherto unprecedented extent. The successful attack on Tipu Sultan of Mysore in India in 1799 was designed to shut off the prospect of French exploitation of success in Egypt, a geopolitical relationship that anticipated imperial moves a century later. Britain then moved forces into the Red Sea to support the main attack from the Mediterranean. A base was established in 1799 on the island of Perim in the Straits of Bab-el-Mandab at the mouth of the Red Sea. However, this could not prefigure Aden, which was seized in 1839 and held until 1969, because the island was waterless and therefore evacuated. Plans included an expedient use of informal empire, in the shape of an extension of influence into the Hijaz in order to thwart any French use of the Red Sea. In the event, British troops, some from India and some from Cape Town, marched from the Red Sea to the Nile.[1]

War with France and its allies helped lead to far-flung ambitions for empire, with the British established strongly in the approaches to the Pacific. The French possessions in India and the Indian Ocean were captured, the last in 1810, while first Cape Town (1806) and then Batavia (now Jakarta 1811) were taken from the Dutch. Not all the hopes of Pacific power were realized. The brief capture of Buenos Aires in 1806 led to speculation about freeing South America for British trade and spreading power by means of expeditions to Chile and Mexico, but these ideas proved abortive. Moreover, Spain became an ally of Britain in 1808, thus closing down further opportunities.

The international peace Congress of Vienna (1814–15) set the seal on Britain's wartime triumph over France and marked the beginning of a period in which the empire was faced with no effective threats. British control of a host of wartime gains, including Cape Colony, the Seychelles, Mauritius, Trinidad, Tobago, St. Lucia, Malta, the Ionian Islands, Sri Lanka, Essequibo and Demerara (the last two the basis of British Guiana, now Guyana), were all recognized. Britain ruled a far more widely flung congeries of possessions than any other empire in the world then or previously. This was also very much an empire that had been tested in war and that, if necessary, was ready for further conflict. The governmental dimension of imperial rule was to the fore, rather than that of commerce, military figures played a major role in this governance, and there was a strong emphasis on control over imperial subjects.[2]

Imprisonment was not only part of the nature and tone of empire in Australia. Instead, this was also important to the development of empire in the South Atlantic. There, Napoleon was imprisoned on St. Helena from 1815 when the British also annexed Ascension Island. In 1816, Tristan da Cunha and Gough Island followed, in order to prevent them being used by France or America. There was particular concern that these islands might serve as a base for a rescue attempt for Napoleon, although none was made. There was also anxiety, in the aftermath of the War of 1812, about the Americans establishing bases, this anxiety looking toward Britain's acquisition of the Falkland Islands in 1833.

The British thwarted both Argentina and America in doing so, the government being concerned about the potential threat that the islands in other hands might pose to British seaborne and political interests in South America and the southern oceans. Viscount Palmerston, the Foreign Secretary, was influenced by the views of William Gore Ouseley, envoy in Rio, then capital of Brazil, who argued that, if the Falklands were developed as a center for trade, ship repair and shipbuilding, they would assist British maritime activity. Britain had been concerned about American views after the Monroe Doctrine about Continental integrity from European power-projection was declared in 1823, but America proved reluctant to cooperate with Argentina against Britain. Meanwhile, in West Africa, Bathurst in Gambia was gained in 1816.

Aside from defeating France, the British were also successful in South Asia in defeating local powers, a process that culminated in a rapid defeat of the Marathas in 1817–18, with far more success than the previous Anglo-Maratha war of 1803–6. The subsequent treaties led to major gains of territory, and the remaining Maratha leaders had to accept terms that brought them under British protection.

Yet, as a reminder of the abiding need to consider changing contexts and conjunctures in clarifying imperial history, key elements of Britain's advantage arose from policies, priorities and rebellions within the imperial systems of real and potential rivals, from the Saint-Domingue rebellion in 1791–1804 and the sale of Louisiana to America in 1803, both lessening the French Atlantic,[3] to the end of the Latin American mainland rule by Portugal and Spain in 1809–25. Britain played a major role in fostering these changes, but scarcely acted alone.

So also, in terms of contexts and conjunctures, with the end of the sustained burst of French Revolution and Napoleonic warfare. Instead, although great care is necessary in suggesting coherence, let alone central direction—especially effective central direction—in imperial policy, both ministers and public opinion were cautious about fresh territorial expansion. There were two major reasons. First, the fiscal situation was very difficult: the cost of the long period of war from 1793 had led to a massive and unprecedented rise in the national debt. The consequences were exacerbated by post-war depression and by a reluctance to raise taxation. Secondly, there was not the immediate problem of competition from France. Indeed, Britain was not directly involved in war on the continent until 1854, and the Crimean War with Russia (1854–6) was both short and waged in alliance with France.

Earlier than 1854, turning away from Europe's conflicts gave Britain the opportunity to expand elsewhere, as did British naval dominance; although there was no overall plan for colonial conquest or indeed the expansion of influence and control. This can be seen by considering some of the bolder ideas. Some of these took note of new technology. For example, as advanced from the late 1820s, the British idea of a steam route to India via the Euphrates River first involved a railway across Turkey to the river, then continuing with a steamship service on the Euphrates to the port of Basra, and then another by sea down the Persian Gulf and across the Arabian Sea to Bombay (Mumbai). A key British protagonist, Francis Rawdon Chesney (1789–1872), explored the route in the 1830s and subsequently supported the Euphrates Valley Railway Company set up in 1857. However, the problems faced by the project ensured that the focus in the 1840s and 1850s, instead, was on the steamships on the Euphrates, which took the British maritime presence in the Persian Gulf into the interior, and not on the railway. In contrast, the emphasis on the route to India avoiding the long haul round southern Africa came to focus on a Suez Canal.

There was also interest in a Euphrates railway from Indian rail circles––notably, William Patrick Andrew (1807–87), a Director of the East Indian Railway, and the founder of the Scinde Railway Company established in 1855 to build a line from Karachi to Kotri linked to a steamship service on the River Indus. He wrote a series of geopolitical rail works, notably, *Indian Railways. As Connected with the Power and Stability of the British Empire in the East, the Development of its Resources, and the Civilisation of its People; with an analysis of the projects now claiming public confidence*

(1846), *The Scinde Railway and its relations to the Euphrates Valley, and other routes to India* (1856), *European interests in the Euphrates Valley Route* (1861), and *The Euphrates Valley Route to India in connection with the Central Asian Question* (1873). Andrew became President of the Euphrates Valley Railway Company, which sought to gain a concession to construct a first section from Izmir on the Aegean to Aydin, and presented itself as a British alternative to the French-dominated Suez scheme.

British governmental financial backing for the Euphrates Valley Railway Company was sought in 1857, but, without firm financial support from the Turkish and British governments, the idea of a rail or rail-river route to India across South-West Asia lacked viability, not least with British merchants preferring the Red Sea route. Indeed, a railway from Alexandria on the Mediterranean to Suez was floated by these merchants in the 1840s and built in 1852–8 by Robert Stephenson, an engineer of empire who was also an opponent of the idea of a Suez Canal. Publications in favor of the Euphrates route—for example, by William Beaumont Selby in 1864 and Thomas Chenery, later editor of the *Times*, in 1869—lacked credibility. That the idea for a Euphrates route, however, had been advanced so speedily showed how rapidly an empire of rail had gripped the imagination, and, less positively, without much attention to economic or political practicality.

Meanwhile, crucially, there was no foreign power able, if it wished, to provide large-scale support to non-Western opponents of Britain, a situation very different to the Cold War of the twentieth century. Thus, Burma fought Britain in 1824–6 without foreign assistance, either European or Asian, and notably not even Chinese. Burmese expansion, especially the annexation of Maripur in 1819 and of Assam in 1821, was seen as a challenge to both the East India Company's position in Bengal and its determination to support nearby protectorates, and differing notions of sovereignty and borders created serious problems that led to a war won by Britain. In the subsequent peace, Arakan and Tenasserim were ceded to Britain, which helped ensure that the subsequent development of an independent Burma was limited, while these gains also eased the path for later British expansion in Burma and Malaya. At the same time, the war was costly in casualties (15,000 British and Indian soldiers died, mostly of disease) and expenditure (£5 million).

In contrast, the island of Fernando Póo, off West Africa, transferred from Spain in 1827 and used as a base for anti-slaving patrols and Protestant prosleytism, was returned in 1855 and Port Clarence was renamed Santa Isabel (it is now Malabo).

Divine sanction was sought and seen in successive British victories, and cast a retrospective glow over past triumphs. William Wordsworth, later Poet Laureat, in his "Ode for the Day of General Thanksgiving" for victory, held on 18 January 1816, urged "this favoured Nation … be conscious of thy moving spirit … thy protecting care."[4] In a potent psychological brew, a sense of mission was important alongside triumphalism, racialism and cultural arrogance, contributing to a view that Britain was bringing civilization to a benighted world and therefore fulfilling providential purposes, an approach that can be seen in the writings of many generally known for other themes, for example Wordsworth's predecessor as Poet Laureat, Robert Southey.[5] The result was a commitment, varied but insistent, to the imperial mission that encouraged persistence in the face of adversity.

The cultural manifestations and images of empire usually associated with the later "Age of Imperialism" in the late Victorian and Edwardian period did not begin there. The abolition of slavery in the colonies as a result of the Emancipation Act of 1833 (which came into force in 1834, freeing 311,000 slaves in Jamaica alone) contributed powerfully to this sense of superiority and came to encourage moral activism toward Africa, especially hostility to the slave trade in West, East and Central Africa. There was also a liberalism seen with the support for independence movements in the wider European world, notably the Latin American Wars of Independence against Spain and Portugal and the Greek War of Independence against Turkish rule.

Meanwhile, settlement colonies were expanded. In Australia, once a way had been found across the Blue Mountains in 1813, Lachlan Macquarie, the reforming governor from 1810 to 1821, commissioned the surveying and building of a road to the Bathurst Plains, where he established a government settlement in 1815. An active process of land grants helped encourage expansion, and the government sought to control this by organizing surveys, under John Oxley and Thomas Mitchell, which served as the basis for an expansion of government structures. Nineteen counties were declared in New South Wales in 1826.

The same process was seen in Tasmania, where the decision to establish a settlement should be placed in the context of bitter competition with France. In 1802, the French explorer Nicolas Baudin had appeared in Tasmanian waters which excited British concern. Moreover, there was a quest for new sources of timber for British warships. So also with the range of reasons behind British expansion into West and South Australia, and in New Zealand. In the case of Tasmania, the warship *Calcutta* was sent to establish a base in the Bass Strait to pre-empt the French. Convict settlers played a key role. The forest came right down to the water's edge, so that the convicts had to fell big trees to make room for their tents and huts. Then the expected store ship from Sydney was wrecked, and in the "starvation years" the settlers subsisted on kangaroo meat (the convicts entrusted with muskets to hunt kangaroo), wiping out the local population of kangaroo. Aside from the environmental damage of imperialism, this episode shows that coerced labor was not simply a matter of the enslaved and, as a related point, that the modern concept of "White Privilege" should be used with care.

William Pitt the Younger, Prime Minister from 1783 to 1801 and 1804 to 1806, and his mentor on the Board of Trade, Henry Dundas, also saw a much bigger picture than both competition with France, with which war resumed in 1803, and the quest for timber. They grasped the potential of a genuinely global empire linked by trade across the oceans as well as the means for holding strategic harbor locations that could contain the ambitions of all Britain's imperial rivals. The vision also provided a trade outlet for the new British manufactured products from the emerging industrial revolution, and would potentially be based on free trade. Having read the economist Adam Smith, whose work also influenced Pitt, Dundas saw free trade as benefiting Britain and as creating a global realm of co-operation. This was a very early version of the Pax Britannica that emerged after 1815. Amid all this, the indigenous population of the colonies could, it was believed, be uplifted by gaining the benefits of civilization.

In Australia, in practice, the indigenous population was hit hard from the outset by Western diseases, especially smallpox and influenza. These not only killed many, but also hit social patterns and morale. Resistance was also affected by the very fragmented nature of the indigenous "nation," which greatly lessened the prospect of cooperation. The extent to which a failure to adopt firearms on any scale lessened the chances for resistance is controversial. It can be seen as a sign of inflexibility, but also as a response to the limitations of early nineteenth-century firearms and to the difficulty of obtaining supplies. By the second half of the century, the settlers enjoyed an important technological advantage thanks to the spread of breech-loading rifles and were able to make rapid advances, especially in Queensland.

At the same time, the government by Britain of eastern Australia changed. With the exception of Van Diemen's Land, renamed Tasmania in 1853, all the Pacific coast was under New South Wales, but its Southern District became Victoria in 1851 and its Northern District Queensland in 1859, leaving the Middle District as New South Wales. Tasmania, Victoria and New South Wales were granted self-government in 1855 and Queensland in 1859.

In the Northland of New Zealand, meanwhile, there was a major influenza outbreak in 1808 that may have killed up to half of the population. The infection probably arrived with early traders from Australia. Measles was the other great killer in New Zealand and missionary diaries noted outbreaks in the 1820s and 1830s. More generally, the British settlement of New Zealand was made much easier by the disruptions and displacements of Māori tribes, and the drastic reduction of population by disease and internecine wars before 1840.

The Māori were enthusiastic early adopters of capitalism, trading potatoes and flax to Sydney, often in their own vessels, and feeding the first British arrivals in New Zealand. They grew large quantities of wheat, tobacco, potatoes and vegetables, and often had their own mills. However, as they lost land, the Māori economy shrank, and much of it had virtually disappeared by 1900. In contrast, the gold rush, which began from 1861, and the export to Britain of frozen meat from 1882, were both dominated by British settlers.

A French colonization expedition had arrived in New Zealand just after the signing of the Treaty of Waitangi in 1840 and the declaration of British sovereignty. The French established a settlement at Akaroa, and the town still has French street names, but a British warship swiftly proclaimed and demonstrated the sovereignty of the British Crown.

The failure of the British to honor the Treaty of Waitangi with the Māori led to the Northern War of 1845–6, in which Hone Keke chopped down the flagpole at Waitangi three times. The course of conflict in New Zealand indicated the extent to which Western power projection spanned the globe, but also that its progress was far from easy. The Māori used well-sited trench and *pā* (fort) systems that were difficult to bombard or storm, and inflicted serious defeats on the British, for example in 1846 at Ruapekapeka *pā* with its underground pits and tunnel. In 1860, in the First Taranaki War, the Te Āti Awa Māori were able to inflict heavy casualties on British troops at the *pā* at Puketakauere and Onukwkaitara. Elsewhere the British were more successful in using artillery bombardment to get the Māori to abandon *pā* at Te Kohia and Ōrongomāihangi, but the Māori were able to do so without heavy losses, a corrective to assumptions about Western firepower superiority. Without either side winning a decisive victory, a cease-fire was negotiated in 1861.

Farther north, conflict broke out in 1863 as the British sought to expand their control over land to the south of Auckland, control that involved road and fort construction. The major clash at Rangiriri (1863) saw the outnumbered Māori defend a position in which they were battered by artillery fire, but inflicted heavy losses on attacking infantry staging frontal attacks, before leaving their fortifications at night. The following year, at Pukehinahina, the Māori lured British forces into a *pā* before inflicting heavy losses on them and then retreating. In 1868, Māori forces under Titokowaru defeated colonial forces twice at Te Ngutu-o-te-Manu and once at Moturoa. Also on North Island in 1868, another Māori leader, Te Kooti, launched a vigorous attack on colonial settlements. The response was mostly by colonial and pro-British Māori forces as most regular units had now left, and Te Kooti found less Māori support than he had anticipated. By 1872, he had clearly lost. Militarily, the mobility of the colonial forces, was combined with the construction of roads, telegraph lines and Armed Constabulary stations while local Māori cooperation was crucial to success.

Meanwhile, there was a rapid process of British expansion in New Zealand. The settlements founded in the early 1840s, notably Wellington (1840), Auckland (1841), Nelson (1841) and New Plymouth (1841), were followed by expansion on the east coast of the South Island, notably with Dunedin (1848) and Christchurch (1850), and then with significant expansion in the 1850s, especially with Gisborne (1852), Invercargill (1855) and Napier (1855). Separated from New South Wales in 1841, New Zealand was granted self-government in 1852. In 1842, the Chatham, Bounty and Antipodes Islands were transferred by Britain. Further north, in the South-West Pacific, in the Solomon Islands, Britain declared a protectorate in 1893, in large part in order to thwart possible French expansion from the New Hebrides, an argument advanced by the expansionist Sir John Thurston, the High Commissioner for the Western Pacific.

In 1881, the Australian colonies pressed for a stronger British naval presence, but were unwilling to pay for it. However, the Colonial Conference held in London in 1887 accepted the idea of cooperative imperial defense and agreed, not only support for a trans-Pacific cable, but also that more British warships should be employed to defend Australasian maritime trade, while Australia and New Zealand, in return, were to provide annual payment. These projects in part reflected the development of Queensland and the sense that the Pacific was no barrier to further growth. Thus, the Torres Strait Islands were placed in 1879 under Queensland which also developed a strong interest in New Guinea. The construction of ports was a key element, as with Townsville, founded in 1864 to make it easier to export cattle, and soon offering opportunities for other products—notably, gold and sugar.

On the pattern of Virginian expansion and the outbreak of hostilities with France in the Ohio Valley, Australian, notably Queensland, attempts to seize New Guinea and the New Hebrides reflected interests that threatened international relations and led Britain in 1883 to divide them respectively with Germany and France in order to prevent disputes. British New Guinea was transferred in 1902–6 to Australia which had become a federated Commonwealth in 1901. Similarly, Britain and Spain defined the situation for the Philippines and North Borneo by the Madrid Protocol of 1885, which accepted the former as Spanish and the latter as British.

The naming of empire reflected the pantheon of imperial greatness. Thus, New Zealand added the towns of Nelson and Wellington to Hawke's Bay, while in Britain and elsewhere the empire was commemorated in the names of the streets of new residential areas and of public houses—the naming of the latter after imperial triumphs and heroes is an indicator of the social range of the celebration of war and empire. Heroism operated as an antidote to a boredom that could be a condition of imperial and home life.[6] Warfare and exploration provided new heroes such as Frederick, 1st Earl Roberts, for the pantheon.

The liberalism Britain proclaimed for its imperial role did not mean a cultural relativism, for the values dominant in Britain, including racism, affected the views of other peoples, a process discussed more recently in terms of Occidentalism.[7] This racism drew on the notion of sharply distinguished races, and supposed differences between them, that could be classified in a hierarchy whose genesis was traced back to the sons of Adam. Race was seen in physical attributes, especially skin color, but was linked also to alleged moral and intellectual characteristics, and to stages in sociological development. This approach encouraged a sense of fixed identity as part of a compartmentalized view of mankind, rather than an acceptance of an inherent unity and of shared characteristics. Religious and biological explanations of apparent differences between races were presented as important. Aside from the assessment of the inherent characteristics of other people, a belief in progress, and in the association of reason with European (more particularly British) culture necessarily encouraged a hierarchy dominated by the British, and thus a treatment of others as inferior and in need of enlightenment. This was a process greatly encouraged by Britain's leading role in technological advance and scientific understanding. The characteristics and development of other people were understood in terms of the suppositions of British culture, and led to, and supported the process of hierarchization.

This was linked to the idea that the British empire (and not other empires) was both apogee and conclusion of the historical process, and the product of both Classical and Christian civilization. There was a fascination with Classical Rome, seen, for example, in paintings and in the success of novels such as Bulwer Lytton's highly successful *Last Days of Pompeii* (1834). Classical Rome and modern Britain were often compared directly as in the preface to Charles Pearson's *Historical Maps of England* (1869) when, in a discussion of the size of the indigenous population, he wrote: "[O]ur troops have repeatedly fought in India against greater odds than the Romans ever encountered in the conquest of Britain."

Exploration, also celebrated in a heroic light, was a powerful contribution to the sense of the British as the purposeful bringers of knowledge and the standard-bearers of a single world order of beneficial purpose and consequences. Britain's colonial presence was closely linked to exploration, as in Australia.

Another form of exploration was offered by missionary work, which was important to the sense of British superiority and that of a providential role for Britain. Missionary work seemed necessary to fulfil this world, while, at the same time, the reputation in Britain of missionary work helped to disseminate ideas of empire. The mission societies provided the opportunity for individual missionaries to expand the reach of British society. John Beecham, a Methodist missionary, told a committee of the House of Commons in 1835:

> "No sooner does the gospel begin to operate in the mind of the heathen than it leads to the first step in civilisation, which was for the people to feel, under the teaching of the missionaries, that a more decent exterior is necessary; and thus the first step is taken in civilization, and clothing is introduced."

Missionaries were very much involved in establishing a British presence in the Pacific and particular missionary societies focused on specific places and groups—for example, the London Missionary Society in the Cook Islands and Samoa, and the Wesleyan Methodist Society in Fiji and Tonga. John Williams of the London Missionary Society set out to the Tahitian archipelago in 1817 and moved on to Samoa in 1830, returning to Britain in 1834 where he oversaw the printing of his translation of the New Testament into Rarotongan, only in 1839, with another missionary, James Harris, to be killed and eaten by cannibals on the island of Erromango in the New Hebrides (now Vanuatu). George Pritchard, a missionary for the London Missionary Society in Tahiti from 1824, became consul there in 1837 and then, after being expelled by the French in 1844, became consul at Samoa from 1845 to 1856.

Missionary activity spread British influence, not least as it frequently competed with indigenous or rival Western activity, notably in the shape of French Catholicism. The creation of mission schools was especially important, as English was taught side by side with Protestantism. These schools were heavily dependent on funds from Britain. Missionaries could support the extension of British authority, as with the protectorate over Bechuanaland proclaimed in 1884.[8] However, missionaries were also often ambivalent about, if not opposed to, British settlement—for example, in New Zealand—as they saw it as likely to harm native interests and hinder conversion. The relationship between missionaries and officials, as also between Abolitionists and officials,[9] could be ambivalent, and there was a fair amount of mutual mistrust. Governmental tolerance of other religions, which contributed to this ambivalence, was seen in Queen Victoria's proclamation to the People of India in 1858 which repudiated any right or desire to impose on the faith of her subjects and promised all, irrespective of religion, the rights of law.

Although not without many hesitations, not least with reference to the sensibilities of colonial populations, Christianity was important to the purpose of empire as understood by contemporaries. The Colonial Bishoprics Fund greatly expanded the institutional structure of the Anglican Church from the 1840s. There was also a presentation of the past in terms of religious mission, as with the interest in Crusading and later the Reformation struggle against Spain.[10]

The forcible abolition of *Suttee*, suicide by burning of Hindu widows, in Bengal in 1829 and the spread of British law and legal practice, were other aspects of a diverse process of moral utilitarianism that was important to the sense of mission and superiority; although those who suffered from government neglect during natural calamities, notably famine, as in India and Ireland, would have had a very different experience.[11] The British empire, not imperial rule by others, was held to equate with civilization. This displayed a confidence reflected in the Great Exhibition of 1851 and elsewhere. In the notes to accompany the globe he exhibited in a large circular building in Leicester Square in 1851–62, James Wyld, the leading British mapmaker and Liberal MP for Bodmin from 1847 to 1852 and 1857 to 1859, reflected a widespread British confidence in their superiority and rule:

> "What comparisons suggest themselves between the condition of the Pacific region in the time of Cook and now? What was then held by illiterate savages now constitutes the rising communities of New South Wales … the civilizing sway of the English crown…."

The sense of national distinctiveness and mission was also expressed in the export of the British constitution, an export symbolized by the building and layout of Parliament buildings, such as that for Canada in Ottawa that drew on the neo-Gothic example of the new Houses of Parliament in Westminster. The internal self-government of long-established colonies of White settlement was expanded from the mid-nineteenth century with the development of an external form of self-government known as "responsible government," which meant that colonial governors were henceforth to become politically "responsible" to locally-elected legislatures, rather than to London. This reflected both the extent of White settlement and the institutionalizing of a comparable parliamentary arrangement in Victorian Britain. The old composite monarchy of empire continued in new constitutional and government forms and alongside the new theme of an imperial nation.[12] Although the Colonial Laws Validity Act of 1865 declared colonial legislation that clashed with that from Westminster to be invalid, the Act was only rarely invoked. It needs hardly be said that the Native population was not consulted.

"Responsible government" was first applied when Lower (Quebec) and Upper (Ontario) Canada were joined together in the Province of Canada in 1841. Dominion status took this forward when the Dominion of Canada was established in 1867. This was closely linked to rail and the idea of a transcontinental railway, one that would secure British Columbia for Canada. Sir Frederick Bruce, the British envoy in Washington, saw the railway as crucial to the future of Canada, writing in 1867 to the Foreign Secretary:

> "As population and industrial development increase in Minnesota, Montana, and other North Western states [of America] which adjoin the British frontier, it is not difficult to foresee that the demand will arise for communication by the line of

> the Saskatchewan River which is said to offer the greatest facilities for reaching the Pacific. And if the Provinces aided by Great Britain are unable to meet it when it becomes necessary and show themselves incapable of providing greater facilities for the transit of produce from the Lake region through the St Lawrence to the Atlantic, the desire of the United States to drive their British rivals off the continent will be powerfully reinforced by the material interests of the North West which will be enlisted in favour of conquest or annexation. Whether the policy adopted by Great Britain in the Northern part of this continent contemplates provincial connection with the mother country as a permanent relation, or looks to it merely as a step toward provincial independence in the future, its success will materially depend upon our ability to deal in a sufficiently liberal and comprehensive manner with the transit question."[13]

Thus, the economic imperative was to the fore, but also as part of geostrategy.

The British North America Act of 1867, a key element of the Canadian Constitution, included a provision for an intercolonial railway. In turn, in 1871, it proved necessary for the Canadian government to pressure its British counterpart to guarantee a loan for the transcontinental railway that was pledged when British Columbia entered the Confederation that year. That America had such a railway was regarded as a comparative disadvantage for Canada, and therefore the British empire, as well as as a model that required emulation. There was a concern that, without such a rail link, British Columbia would go into the ambit of America's Pacific coast, not least after the American purchase of Alaska from Russia in 1867 put America both north and south of British Columbia.

The ethnic politics of imperial expansion were clear. Much of the labor was provided by 17,000 Chinese workers, although they did not feature in the Last Spike photograph, that commemorated the achievement. At least 600 of these workers died, many as a result of landslides or of the unsafe use of explosives. As in other countries, the Chinese were paid less than the other workers.

Land grants were an aspect of the financing of the railway. The Confederation project, a means to form a national identity within the empire, was linked to the British financing model of Canadian railways, which ensured that private corporations played the key role in developing the country. Thus, the construction of the Manitoba and North Western Railway began in 1881 after it had received a land grant of 1.4 million acres. Land grants paid little reference to the Native population which was confined to "Indian Reserves."

The development of "responsible government" was an important aspect of the extent to which imperial expansion and governance tested assumptions about how best to devise and sustain political arrangements, a process also seen in Britain. Flux was repeatedly to the fore, with new governmental systems needed as the authority of both the East India Company and the Hudson's Bay Company was ended. Ironically, the situation was very different in Sarawak with the Brooke family becoming a dynasty ruling from 1841 to 1946 when Sarawak was ceded to the Colonial Office thus becoming part of the Crown Colony of North Borneo. The family's position reflected the extent to which empire reflected a range of compromises with local circumstances and a variety of governing systems. Brooke had also served as Governor of Labuan, an island crown colony acquired from Brunei in 1846.

Later, other colonizing companies lost their charter rights, the Imperial British East Africa Company losing its charter in 1895, and the Royal Niger Company in 1899, and the British South Africa Company in 1924. Instead, the companies that came to the fore were economic interests without territorial control, such as Cable and Wireless, and the British Overseas Airways Corporation. Yet, underlining variety, Sabah in northern Borneo was run from 1881 by the British North Borneo Company, which was not dissolved until 1946 when the territory was transferred to the Colonial Office, although Sabah had become a British protectorate in 1888.

The changing position of individual colonies owed much to the extent and consequences of migration, although this was not simply a matter of the empire. In particular, between 1815 and 1901, America took over eight million immigrants from the British Isles, more than the entire movement to the empire. This was and a reflection of the way in which the British government, which discouraged this migration to America, played only a partial role in shaping migration patterns, although state financial support for colonialization and regulation of shipping by Passenger Acts were of some, albeit limited, importance.

Migration was affected by push, pull and means factors, from post-Napoleonic Wars' demobilization[14] to gold rushes, from steamship services to population growth in Britain, and from the Irish Famine of 1845–52, which created a new set of Irish frontiers within the empire,[15] to the provision of land. There was particularly large-scale emigration to America from Ireland, while Cornwall saw large-scale emigration in response to the pressure on copper and tin mining from the late 1860s due to world competition. There were many reasons for migration, permanent or short-term, family or individual, other than work, including military service, education, politics and marriage.

For many migrants, the intention from the outset had been to return to Britain having made money, but most migrants did not return. This contributed to the emotional wrench of emigration and thus to the psychological character of the empire (and the English-speaking world also) as a separated family. Actively propagated, both in the British Isles and in the colonies, this idea looked toward the notion of a Commonwealth. This idea of a separated family was enhanced by some specific aspects of emigration that diminished its wrench, including the degree to which it took place within, or with regard to, friendship, family, locality or occupational networks. Moreover, alongside young single migrants, many migrated as family groups.

Migration and, more generally, the empire, provided an opportunity for individuals and groups to try to pursue hopes and implement ideas, a situation that provided much of the dynamism of empire. This was seen for example with the sponsoring and organization by the Salvation Army of the emigration to Canada of 200,000 people between 1890 and 1930 in pursuit of the view of its founder, William Booth, that Canada offered the prospect of a virtuous regeneration.

Migration more generally illustrated the polycentric character of the empire, for it became the largest territorial space for population movements. Some involved British emigrants moving on, for example between Australia and New Zealand, but there was also much movement not involving Britons, and notably so for work. India was an important source of migrants to British Guiana, the West Indies (especially Trinidad), East and South Africa, Ceylon, Burma, Malaya and Fiji. In Natal in southern Africa, where railway construction started in 1876, the railway department became the biggest single employer of Indian labor in the 1880s and 1890s. The contract of 1875 for the first section of the line had stipulated that two-thirds of the laborers needed for building the line were to be recruited from outside the colony, a measure stipulated to prevent local labor rates from rising and thus an attempt to prevent rail from disrupting the local situation, and notably the relationships between employers and workers. Many of the Indians for the Natal railway were recruited in Mauritius. There were also African laborers recruited from Mozambique. George Nathaniel, Lord Curzon, Viceroy of India, observed in 1904 in a speech at the Guildhall in London: "[I]f you want to build a railway to Uganda [from Kenya] or in the Soudan [Sudan], you employ Indian labor."

At present, there is frequently a stress on the disruption and hardship involved in such work and migration. Long-term contracts of indentures are misleadingly treated as if akin to slavery. Nevertheless, it is important to note that the opportunities for employment provided by migration were also welcomed, or at least accepted, by many. Much of this migration was initially designed to replace or supplement the earlier movement of slaves to colonies where there was reliance on them for plantation labor, as in Mauritius. However, migration also provided labor across the empire including in Queensland where there had not been slavery. These labor flows complemented those of White migrants from the British Isles, although the conditions of work could become far worse. The end of slavery was not a description of a free or easy labor world, as the harsh conditions of the tea plantations of India and Ceylon readily showed. The ending of the slave trade itself produced the largest number of imperial settlers in West Africa, an area to which very few Britons went to stay. Instead, close to 100,000 enslaved people were freed by the navy from slave ships between 1808 and 1863 and largely settled in Sierra Leone, especially in Freetown where they greatly changed the ethnic composition of the colony.

Although China was an important source of migrants, especially for the Transvaal gold mines after the Boer War of 1899–1902, most migration within the wider Indian Ocean economy was within the empire. These labor flows helped make the empire more effective as a series of regional economies and, to a lesser extent, as an economic unit. Labor, entrepreneurial initiative and energy, and capital were all provided.

Migration within, into and outside the empire, however, created many unfamiliar ethnic interactions (for example, Irish and Chinese in competition in Australia[16]) as well as greatly expanded the scale in existing interactions, leading, for example, to the development of an Indian community in London.[17] Interactions produced issues, if not tensions, that were problematic for governance, not least for concepts of legal, political and social status. The projection of ethnic hierarchies and notions of cultural superiority with relation to the changing patterns and anxieties of imperial advance and rule involved both specific contingencies but also practices and ideas of cultural relativism.[18] Fashionable intellectual ideas played a role, not least in legal re-drawings of the ethnic complexity, but most of the situation was addressed through practices of social inclusion and exclusion, not least through endogamy.

Alongside imperial links in a system of influence and governance from the center moderated by local issues, initiatives, and responses, there were also shifts in imperial focus. For example, with the end of slavery and the rise of competition—notably, in sugar from other Caribbean countries, especially Spanish-ruled Cuba, and from European sugar beet—the relative significance of the West Indies within the empire declined greatly and notably so in London. Under the Sugar Duties Act of 1846, all duties on imported sugar were equalized in 1851, hitting the British colonies. Meanwhile, a crisis in the British plantation societies was especially marked in Jamaica. Labor availability and discipline were crucial to the ability of estates to hold down costs, but the end of the apprenticeship system in 1838 was followed by large numbers of former slaves leaving the plantations, notably in Jamaica and Trinidad, in order to seek unsettled land for their own where they followed subsistence agriculture. Former slaves thus became independent farmers to the degree they were able to get land.

This option was not so available in smaller colonies, such as Antigua and Barbados, which lacked free land, and the estate system therefore remained more effective. In the larger colonies, emancipation led to a fall in estate productivity and profitability, as, despite the possibilities offered by the adoption of steam power in the shape of steam milling in place of windmills, sugar production continued to be labor-intensive. Free labor proved more expensive and less reliable (generally meaning cowed) than slaves, greatly increasing the operating costs. Many estates were also affected by debt and a lack of liquidity, which meant that there was insufficient investment in new technology. In Jamaica, significant areas went out of cultivation. Individual colonies, moreover, were hit by particular events, a bad hurricane in 1847 precipitating the end of sugar exports from Tobago. There was some substitution, notably by cocoa on Grenada, but none of great scale; and the Royal Commission appointed in 1896 reported that, excluding Jamaica, sugar products were responsible for 75 percent of the exports of the British Caribbean. The price for unrefined sugar had fallen by nearly 50 percent from 1881 to 1896.

As the exports of the former British plantation economies declined, so they were less able to attract investment, afford imports from Britain and elsewhere, and develop social capital, which hit living standards and has affected the legacy of empire there. In 1815, the West Indies had been the leading market for British exports, but by 1840 they had been passed as a market by India, Australia and Canada in that order; and, linked to this, the role of the Caribbean in British shipping needs also diminished. The severance of commercial links with America as a result of post-1783 protectionist legislation was also a major problem.

Moreover, the Caribbean receded from attention—with the exception of the Morant Bay Rebellion in 1865, a protest initially against the harsh treatment of Blacks that turned violent in part due to militia opening fire. In response, Edward Eyre, Governor of Jamaica, declared martial law and deployed troops who behaved with much slaughter. In addition, martial law was used to try and execute many while many homes were burned down by troops. This repression led to much criticism in Britain, as well as support. In practice, both the troops and Eyre broke the law. Eyre was recalled and criticized in Parliament by the Secretary of State for the Colonies for a lack of sound judgment and impartiality, but legal action against him failed and the government eventually covered his legal expenses.[19] Understandably, the rebellion, its intentions, course, repression and aftermath has become a major episode in imperial memorialization, notably in Jamaica where was published Don Robotham's *"The Notorious Riot": The Socio-Economic and Political Bases of Paul Bogle's Revolt* (1981) and where Bogle, charged with incitement to riot and hand, is commemorated both by being named a National Hero of Jamaica in 1969 and depicted on coins and currency, mentioned in many songs, and depicted in a statue in which he holds a Bible and a machete.[20]

Britain, meanwhile, became less active in the Caribbean as a territorial power. British claims on the Mosquito Coast of modern Nicaragua became more modest in the 1850s. Suzerainty had been claimed there until 1850, but the British protectorate came to an end with the recognition of Nicaraguan sovereignty in 1860, although the interests of the Miskitos, long allies of the British, were protected and there was no full incorporation of the area into Nicaragua until 1894 (and that after a confused conflict that also involved Honduras and British Marines).[21] The northward extension of the protectorate in Honduras was recognized as coming under Honduran sovereignty in 1859, as were the Bay Islands, Lord John Russell, the Foreign Secretary, expressing his concern that year about the health of island bases in the Tropics. These British withdrawals reflected a lack of political and public commitment to a long-standing part of Britain's informal empire, and certainly no wish to extend British influence or possession.

Instead, the Indian Ocean was an increasingly significant part of the empire. To a certain extent, the nature of this dynamic has been lost, or at least minimized, as a result of referring to it as India. This underrates the place of India, its troops, emigrants, economy and port cities within a dynamic oceanic system. While centered on nearby waters, notably the Arabian Sea, the Persian Gulf, and the Bay of Bengal, this system stretched out to the Red Sea, where Aden, seized in 1839, was placed under the government of Bombay. It also stretched out to East Africa, South-East Asia, and China, and farther, to Australasia, into the Pacific and, less prominently, into the Atlantic. This system represented the refraction of earlier links—for example, between India and both Burma and the Persian Gulf—and the development of new links, such as between India and South Africa, that reflected the significance of British imperial expansion and enterprise.

This expansion involved competition with other Western powers, for example France over Tahiti in 1842–4, a competition in which France was successful, but also conflict with non-Western powers. That contrast was important to the character of empire but also helps explain why an account of empire based on 1816–1913, the usual approach, is unrepresentative for empire as a whole because for much of its history, and notably in 1689–1815 and 1914 on, this was very much in the context of competition with other European powers. In South Asia, in contrast, there was major conflict in 1839–49, in Afghanistan, Sind and the Punjab. These led to a focus on the North-West Frontier of India that remained pertinent until the late 1930s.

British India, meanwhile, was linked by rail, the shareholders of which were guaranteed in 1849 an annual return of five per cent by the East India Company. James, 1st Marquess of Dalhousie, the Governor-General from 1848 to 1856, was a keen supporter of rail, as, in Britain, he had been as President of the Board of Trade in 1845–6. Dalhousie emphasized in 1853 that railways would enable Britain "to bring the main bulk of its military strength to bear upon any given point in as many days as it would not require months, and to an extent which at present is physically impossible." He also stressed the economic and social advantages from the expansion of railways. Dalhousie, who had unsuccessfully supported a degree of government direction in the development of a system of British rail routes, pressed in India for a network of major trunk lines, notably to provide lines between Bombay, Calcutta, Lahore, Delhi and Madras. The plans were ambitious and Dalhousie also saw the potential of future developments: thus, even when single track was installed, the bridges were to be strong and wide enough for eventual double-tracking. Dalhousie's plan was followed, with the lines built from the major administrative centers—Bombay, Calcutta and Madras, each of which were ports. A utilitarian modernizer, Dalhousie also backed uniform postage and the telegraph for India, where he greatly extended British territorial power.

Large amounts of capital and labor were deployed, and many Indians died in the construction of railways. The last point may be seen as an instance of nineteenth-century imperial racism, and that could then be amplified by reference to the deaths of Chinese rail workers in construction elsewhere. At the same time, death rates in rail construction were generally high—indeed very high, by modern standards—and that included workers in Britain as well as British labor elsewhere. The damage and disruption caused by railways was very varied, including to wildlife and local drainage and routes. The Indian Forest Service was set up in part due to concern about deforestation for railways, both in construction and for powering the locomotives.

The railway route mileage of British India (which included what is now Pakistan and Myanmar) rose, thanks to private railway contractors, from 5,400 in 1872 to 25,511 in 1901 and 42,528 in 1931, the comparable figures for British-ruled Ceylon (Sri Lanka) being 70 in 1872, 297 in 1901 and 951 in 1931. The track mileage was second only to America. Economic advantage was a key element, as in the concentration of railways on the Bengal coalfield, a pattern seen across the world. Usage developed rapidly, both for freight and for passengers, but the carriage arrangements and fare structure in terms of classes very much benefited wealthier travelers, who tended to be British. The grandeur of imperial railway stations was particularly present in the Victoria Railway Terminus in Bombay completed in 1929. With a massive dome, this multi-towered building borrowed from many styles including Classical, Gothic, Byzantine, Moorish, and what was seen as Indian.

In Burma (Myanmar), the first line opened in 1877, from the port of Rangoon to Prome, and was seen as important to the export of rice from the Irrawaddy valley to India. A second line, from Rangoon to Toungoo, followed in 1884—this one instead following the valley of the Sittang. The British annexation of Upper Burma after the Third Anglo-Burmese War of 1885–6 led to the extension of the latter line to Mandalay in 1889, in turn being that extended to Mytikyina in 1898. Two years earlier, the rail companies in Burma were combined into the Burma Railway Company. In Ceylon (Sri Lanka), coffee, a major export crop produced in the interior near Kandy, took 10–12 days to be moved to the port of Colombo, a distance of 73 miles, by bullock carts. Begun in 1858 and taken over by the government in 1861, the line to Kandy, the historic capital in the interior, was completed in 1867.

The railways the British built in India helped ensure that troops and their supplies could be moved to areas of imperial tension, as in 1897 when they were sent to the North-West Frontier (of modern Pakistan) to assist in overcoming resistance among the Waziris. With railway expansion significant in the 1880s and 1890s, railheads—notably Peshawar, Quetta and Chaman—played a key part in British planning, both on that frontier and with regard to power-projection into neighbouring Afghanistan where there were no railways. In turn, these railheads and the routes from them had to be protected; while an anxious eye was kept on the development of the rival Russian rail network into Central Asia.

Many imperial careers came to involve railways, as with Percy Girouard (1867–1932). Born in Montreal, he graduated from the Royal Military College of Canada, worked for two years on the Canadian Pacific Railway in London (1886–8), was commissioned in the Royal Engineers (1888), in charge of the Woolwich Arsenal Railway (1890–5), built the railway across the Sudan desert from Wadi Halfa (1896–7) that was important to the logistics of British conquest, was President of the Egyptian Railways (1898–9), became Director of Imperial Military Railways in South Africa (1899–1904), High Commissioner of Northern Nigeria (1908–11), and Commissioner of Kenya (1909–12).

With a very different trajectory to India, there was also a new, albeit different, agenda of concern about China, the Opium War of 1839–42 being essentially about trade not territorial security. Yet, British troops in China and the cession in 1842 of Hong Kong represented a new commitment. Lower tariffs on British goods were enforced at the expense of China's right to regulate its economy and society. Combined with the successful British intervention against Egyptian forces in modern Lebanon and Israel in 1840, an impressive demonstration of power against a modernizing and empire-building non-Western power, this suggested a "tipping point" toward British imperial primacy. These years saw a major contrast to 1807–9 when British forces had failed in Egypt and in the intimidation of the Turkish empire, and failed to persuade China to accept a British garrison in Macao. Moreover, after 1815, the European situation provided opportunity for British expansion abroad.

The focus tends to be on India, but there was also a dominance of the Mediterranean, both directly—in Gibraltar, Malta, the Ionian Islands (conquered in 1809–14) and (later) Cyprus (1878), Egypt (1882), and Israel (1917)—and indirectly, for example in Greece. Minorca, however, was returned for good to Spain in 1802, although imperial echoes remain with sash windows and gin. The gain and loss of possessions reflected geopolitics, politics and the possibility of defining acceptable constitutional settlements. Thus, in the face of Russian expansion and in response to British support, Cyprus became a British protectorate in 1878, but it was not annexed until 1914. In contrast, in the aftermath of a rebellion in 1848, and in light of pressure for union with Greece, the less strategically significant Ionian Islands had been ceded to Greece in 1864 as a way to help the new pro-British king. Cyprus was better placed than the Ionian Islands to support British interests in the Suez Canal, which had been opened in 1869, and in any action in Egypt. Britain intervened there in 1882, in part in response to a developing crisis that forced the pace of Cabinet politics and also due to a wish to match French and Russian advances.[22] Although the Khedivate of Egypt remained an autonomous province of the Turkish empire until 1914, a British quasi-protectorate over Egypt was established, and Evelyn Baring, Lord Cromer, who had held office in India in 1872–6 as Private Secretary to the Viceroy, ran the Egyptian government until 1907 as Consul General and Adviser to the Khedive. British racial stereotypes about Arabs affected their stance in Egypt, which was seen as akin to India in some respects, but without the "martial races" of the latter. Cromer himself regarded Islam as a medieval religion that held Egypt back but his paternalism, Protestantism and racism helped make British rule unpopular.[23] Egypt was seen as securing the Suez Canal and as a base for intervention in Sudan, which was eventually successful in 1896–9. The latter intervention owed much to Britain's Mediterranean position and control of Egypt, with Britain taking on longstanding Egyptian interests in southward expansion.

Meanwhile, thanks to suppressing rebellion in India in 1857–9, a rebellion since variously described including as the Indian Mutiny and the First War of Independence,[24] the last the term popularized by Jawaharlal Nehru, Prime Minister from 1947 to 1964, the British had greatly strengthened their position there. Moreover, governance was transformed when power was transferred from the East India Company to the Crown in 1858. Alongside extensive power projection against Persia and China, as well as in South-East Asia, Britain became a major Asian power, one in no way limited to India. At the same time, the nature of the British presence, both in terms of sovereign claims and with reference to colonialization, varied greatly. There was no comparison to the overcoming of indigenous resistance in Australia. And New Zealand showed a fresh example of variety. The British negotiated with the Māoris, but also pursued a colonization that helped lead to conflict.

Very differently, the British role in supporting independence for Latin America helped delimit the empire. South America was the only one of the three inhabited continents entirely or partly in the Southern Hemisphere in which Britain did not become a major colonial power—the variety of Australasia, Africa and South America both today and in the past leading to the questionable use of the concept of "The Global South," a term used in 1969 by Carl Oglesby, an American activist and academic. British Guiana became an important plantation colony, especially for the production of sugar, and expanded into the interior, but this expansion was challenged by Venezuela and the colony remained relatively small. In 1898, Cuba and Puerto Rico were conquered from Spain by America, not Britain. Yet much of Latin America was part of the British "informal empire" in large part due to the scale of British investment. Thus, in Uruguay by 1900 there was £36 million of British investment, £11 million of which was in railways, much to support the beef exported to Britain. So also in Argentina.

Such investment was an aspect of the shared interests that were crucial to empire, interests often very much linked to Britons "who went native," which often included local marriages. Thus, in Argentina, a railway was built from Buenos Aires to the major river port of Rosario, beginning service in 1886. Mariano Billinghurst (1810–92), the son of a British immigrant and an Argentinean mother, was the concessionary and a railway pioneer typical of the Anglo-Argentinians central to the British presence. Separately, British railway builders helped introduce football to South America—notably, to Argentina and Uruguay. In 1913, when Argentina took 41 percent of British investment in Latin America, 34 percent of British investment in Latin America was in railways and 38 percent in government bonds.

This was a contrast with the conquering and violent nature of British "Forward Policy" in Africa at this point and shows the extent to which there was variety in goals and practice, both between ministries and across the world. For example, a forward policy in Egypt was pursued in 1882, but had been rejected in 1859. Again, the combination of the replacement of Benjamin Disraeli's Conservative government in 1880 by a Liberal ministry that was opposed to bold expansionism, and also the political and logistical problems of operating in Afghanistan, challenged the efficacy of the "Forward Policy" that the government of India had been pursuing and encouraged the British to draw back, evacuating Kandahar in Afghanistan, and, instead, to seek to stabilize their position to the east on the "North-West Frontier." William Gladstone's Liberal government was initially reluctant to intervene in Egypt but circumstances, including the murder of Europeans in Alexandria, helped reframe the context.

The 1880s and 1890s brought a major burst of territorial expansion, such that by 1900 Britain had an empire covering a fifth of the world's land surface with a population of about 400 million people, whereas that of France included only 52 million. It is easy to underrate Britain's colonial wars as none was a war for survival or transformed British society, but their cumulative impact for Britain was important, not least psychologically, and their individual impact on other societies was often highly destructive as well as formative of a new politics defined by British rule or, at least, control or influence. Britain's role was part of the wider story of Europe's imperialism, but it was larger than that of any other state, and the greater British ability and willingness to support territorial expansion affected not only Britain and the areas she seized, but also other powers, both imperial and non-imperial.

The British benefited from large numbers of local soldiers, particularly Indians, whereas in Africa there was also an important use of indigenous troops. In Nigeria, where the Oil Rivers Protectorate was established in 1885, the West African Frontier Force, at the decisive battle of Omdurman in 1898 the Sudanese brigades in General Kitchener's force, and in Somaliland, native levies. The ability to win local support was in part a product of local rivalries, which greatly helped the British in many cases, although it also ensured a degree of instability in imperial control.

The British benefited in their imperial conquest and rule, across its span, from their ability to elicit—by coercion or willingly—local support, which in large part arose from divisions within polities, reflecting the fact that many were composite states. Thus, a Zulu civil war that followed conflict with Britain in 1879 provided the British with cooperative chiefs. The British also benefited from the multipolar character of power in many areas, such as West Africa and Malaya, and their consequent ability to tackle problems in a sequential or separate fashion, rather than to have to face a powerful regional opposition. At the same time, imperial experience was more effective for Britain because cumulative.

Attitudes within Britain shifted. There was a greater emphasis than hitherto on territorial control, and sovereignty became more crucial than the informal influence symbolized by Charles Gordon and David Livingstone, in part because the profit motive was subordinated to geopolitics and notably the response to the real or apparent plans of other imperial powers. At the same time, geopolitics was seen as linked to commercial advantage, as with the bold schemes of Cecil Rhodes in Southern Africa. The doctrine of "effective occupation" developed at the Congress of Berlin in 1884–5 encouraged a speeding up of annexation. The British moved into Uganda in part to pre-empt Germany, and into Sudan likewise with France. In Southern Africa, Portugal was bullied in order to help ensure that British power could move northward and not be thwarted by the Portuguese attempt to link their colonies of Angola and Mozambique.[25] In West Africa, there was greater interest in expanding a presence in response to rapid and ambitious French expansionism. In 1895, a boundary agreement for Sierra Leone was concluded with France. The establishment there of a protectorate over native chiefs led to considerable resistance until 1899, notably by the Mende, Temne and Loko tribes, including opposition to a hut tax to raise colonial revenue. This resistance was an aspect of the degree to which local groups shaped the practice and thus policies of British imperialism.[26]

Attitudes to empire in the high-Victorian period are a matter of contention, not least over the extent of support in Britain for imperial expansion and, as a related but different question, the impact of this expansion on developments in Britain. Literary works provide an indication of the cultural impact, although there were variations by genre and author. It is frequently most instructive to consider authors not generally noted for imperial engagement, such as Arthur Conan Doyle, the inventor of Sherlock Holmes. This was not least because such an assessment offers a qualification of the suggestion that the presence of empire in the British consciousness was somewhat limited,[27] a suggestion that has been criticized on empirical grounds.[28]

Empire is always present in the Holmes' world. Without its people, wealth, impact and mysteries, the Holmes stories would have been far less interesting. His essential loyalty was displayed in his lodgings rented from Mrs. Hudson, where, as recorded in "The Adventure of the Musgrave Ritual" (1893), he would "proceed to adorn the opposite wall with a patriotic V.R. [Victoria Regina] done in bullet-pocks." London is the center of imperial networks and empire a source of renewal and material wealth for Britain. This is very much seen in *The Hound of the Baskervilles* (1902) in which Sir Charles' wealth comes from the South African goldfields. Before he returns to Britain, his successor, the young baronet, Sir Henry, has spent his entire adult life in Canada on the prairies, and he represents youth, virility and a confidence in the future also seen in the Australian-born characters in the stories.

Empire indeed helped bring Britain wealth. It dominated the production of many important goods. Gold and diamonds came from South Africa, wheat, copper, timber and fish from Canada, tin from Malaya, cocoa from Ghana, palm oil from Nigeria, cotton from Egypt, tea from India, and sugar from the West Indies. Britain was also the largest overseas investor and the greatest merchant shipper in the world, as well as the center of the world's financial system: Commodity prices, shipping routes and insurance premiums were all set in London, as was the Greenwich meridian on which time zones were based from 1884. The expansion of the service sector, focused on the City of London, was fundamental to Britain's economic strength and influence. Thanks to her prominence in submarine telegraphy, Britain was also at the center of the world's communications.

Empire was very important to Britain, both in Doyle's life, and for the Holmes stories. In Britain, empire was staged actively in music-hall, melodrama, and blackface minstrelsy, and across all of society. Exhibitions, such as *The Empire of India* held in London in 1895, or the *Stanley and Africa* one five years earlier, were much-visited.[29]

So also with new technology. Jack Hunt, a private in the Scots Guards, described in a letter to his brother the entry into Pretoria, the capital of Transvaal, in 1900 during the Boer War: "When we marched into the market square headed by Lord Roberts to raise the flag, they took our photo by the cinematograph so I expect you will see it in some of the music-halls in London."[30]

Earlier that year, large London crowds, many of them clerks and medical students, applauded the relief of Mafeking from a long Boer siege. The garrison commander, Robert Baden-Powell (1857–1941), became an iconic figure. Joining the army in 1876, he had already served extensively before the siege of Mafeking—namely, in Southern Africa, West Africa, and India. Baden-Powell very much presented the Fourth Anglo-Ashanti war of 1895–96 in West Africa (in which he served) as a moral cause intended to pacify and develop the area, and to stop slave-trading and raiding.

Empire was not simply a matter of power politics, military interests, élite careers, and an ideology of mission and purpose that appealed to the propertied and the proselytizing. It also had relevance and meaning throughout a society affected by the growth of popular imperialist sentiment. This influence was reflected in the jingoistic strains of popular culture—for example, the ballads of music hall and the images depicted on advertisements for mass-produced goods. In Doyle's *The Sign of the Four* (1890), Jonathan Small "earned a living at this time by my exhibiting poor Tonga at fairs and other such places as the black cannibal. He would eat raw meat and dance his war-dance: so we always had a hatful of pennies after a day's work," the pennies referring to coins thrown in by ordinary citizens. On the other hand, some of the workers appear to have been pretty apathetic about imperialism.

Empire reflected and sustained widespread racist assertions and assumptions, both of which were amply demonstrated in the literature and press of the period. Empire also provided the occasion and stimulus for a new concept of exemplary masculinity focusing on soldier heroes, such as Wolseley, Gordon, Roberts, Kitchener and Baden-Powell, who, in a fusion of martial prowess, Protestant zeal and moral manhood, were all seen as national icons. Their victories were gained at the expense of numerous non-Europeans, often slaughtered by the technology of modern weaponry, as in Kitchener's victory at Omdurman (Sudan) in 1898. The zealous Charles Gordon, who died unsuccessfully defending Khartoum against the Mahdists in 1885, was presented as a quasi-saint resisting a vast force of Muslims, and sacrificing himself to that end. The impact of such controversial imperial events was enough to threaten prominent politicians such as Gladstone, who was held responsible for the failure to send a relief force until too late. In Doyle's "The Adventure of the Resident Patient" (1893), Dr Watson looks at his newly-framed picture of Gordon. Kitchener's success was regarded in Britain as the appropriate response and as a purging of guilt.

Alongside the occasional flaw, the idea of imperial masculinity as noble was frequently presented in Holmes stories, as with the Australian sea captain in "The Abbey Grange" (1904):

> "[O]ur door was opened to admit a fine a specimen of manhood as ever passed through it. He was a very tall young man, golden-moustached, blue-eyed, with a skin which had been burned by tropical suns, and a springy step which showed that the huge frame was as active as it was strong."

Captain Croker himself uses the commonplace language of empire, addressing Holmes' requirement that he comes clean about events: "I believe you are a man of your word, and a white man," the latter a racist commonplace for being honest.[31] To complete the account, Watson becomes "a British jury … and I never met a man who was more eminently fitted to represent one," and Holmes the judge, and Croker are swiftly cleared. In *The Hound of the Baskervilles*, Sir Henry Baskerville is a positive force, his vigor indicated by his not smartly dressing "the part" that Sir Henry, when returning from Canada, has to remedy in purchasing new clothes and boots. Manliness was a matter not only of supporting the cause of imperial federalism, but also of meeting the pressure for conscription, or, at least, volunteers.

The adventures of Holmes' longer foreign stories were located in India and the United States. Imperial struggle, notably the sieges of the Indian Mutiny (1857–9) and the Boer War (1899–1902), offered drama for the entire empire, although these struggles also had the capacity to focus dissatisfaction with imperial rule or ambition.[32] Imperial clashes were re-enacted in open-air spectacles in Britain: The tableau and pageant became art forms. Newspapers spent substantial sums on the telegraphy that brought news of imperial conflict. Moreover, army service was a glorious route out of the slums for many working-class men.

Empire was a crucial component of British nationalism, especially toward the end of the century. The imagery of government fuelled this: Victoria was made Empress of India in 1876, thus making empire serve the monarchy and vice versa[33]; the journal *Punch*, an influential creator of images, popularized empire in its cartoons; and public buildings were decorated with symbols of empire. The expansion of empire was seen as furthering moral, as well as national, goals by spreading what was seen as liberal government and the rule of law, and by providing opportunities for Christian proselytism.

Whereas Agatha Christie had her protagonists follow empire (formal or informal) abroad, as in T*he Man in the Brown Suit* (1924), *Murder in Mesopotamia* (1936), *Death on the Nile* (1937), and *They Came to Baghdad* (1951), that was not the practice for Holmes. He could readily have taken a steamer to Cape Town, Kingston or Halifax, but did not do so, and indeed was less traveled than Doyle. Yet Empire was very much present in the Holmes stories because of its presence in Britain. This was a very varied phenomenon. It included Britons who had lived there before coming home, as with the Honourable Philip Green in "The Disappearance of Lady Frances Carfax" (1911), who, having been "a wild youngster," makes his money in South Africa. In "The Adventure of the Solitary Cyclist" (1903), Violet Smith's uncle, "Ralph Smith … went to Africa twenty-five years ago, and we have never had a word from him since." In response to an advertisement in the *Times*, she "met two gentlemen, Mr. Carruthers and Mr. Woodley, who were home on a visit from South Africa. They said that my uncle was a friend of theirs, that he died some months before in poverty in Johannesburg, and that he had asked them with his last breath to hunt up his relations."

There were many born in empire who came to Britain, as with Jinny O'James, "the mature woman of the world" with a past, and Professor James McMurdo O'Brien, the two Australians in the non-Holmes "A

Physiologist's Wife" (1890). Australia is again at the fore in "Lady Frances Carfax," with Holmes telling Watson:

> "that we are dealing with an exceptionally astute and dangerous man. The Rev. Dr Schlessinger, missionary from South America, is none other than Holy Peters, one of the most unscrupulous rascals that Australia has ever evolved—and for a young country it has turned out some very finished types. His particular speciality is the beguiling of lonely ladies by playing upon their religious feelings, and his so-called wife, an Englishwoman named Fraser, is a worthy helpmate … he was badly bitten in a saloon-fight at Adelaide in '89."

Empire was more widely a background for detective stories set in Britain, as in Godfrey Benson's *Tracks in the Snow* (1906).[34]

There was also empire as a source of wealth and a focus for investment. Thus, in "The Adventure of the Dancing Men" (1903), set in 1898, Holmes reveals to Watson his knowledge that the latter had chosen not to invest in South African securities, which are subsequently clarified to mean the goldfields. In "The Adventure of the Stockbroker's Clerk" (1893), Hall Pycraft is quizzed on the stock price of New Zealand Consolidated and British Broken Hills, the latter a reference to the Broken Hill Proprietary Company, which was founded in 1885 to work the silver-rich Broken Hill ore body found in Australia in 1883. Readers would have been expected to understand the reference. Canadian Pacific Railway shares are part of the loot in "The Adventure of Black Peter" (1904). There were also in this story South American securities, from Argentina, Costa Rica and Brazil. The varied products from empire mentioned in the stories include the "Penang lawyer" type of walking stick referred to in "The Adventure of Silver Blaze" (1892).

The Britons going abroad can be sometimes unworthy, such as James Armitage, who is transported in 1855 for fraud in the "The Adventure of the *Gloria Scott*" (1893). The ships falls victim to a very violent convicts' rising. Like his compatriot Evans, Armitage then makes his money in the Australasian diggings where he is able to lose his former identity, and the two men return to England as "rich colonials" and buy into rural status, only to be exploited as a result of the *Gloria Scott*. At the close, Armitage's heartbroken son, Trevor, like Gilchrist in "The Adventure of the Three Students" (1904), in an act of imperial cleansing, leaves England. Trevor goes "out to the Terai tea planting, where I hear that he is doing well." The Terai is an area of northern India and southern Nepal some of which Britain had annexed from Nepal in 1816. Tea cultivation was successfully introduced in the Darjeeling Terai in 1862 and helped supply Britain's apparently insatiable demand for this product of Empire.

The villain in "The Adventure of the Priory School" (1904), James Wilder, the Duke of Holdernesse's secretary and his unacknowledged illegitimate son, who has "always a taste for low company," is sent "to seek his fortune in Australia." The assumption is that he would fit in there, and, at least, find opportunities. In Oscar Wilde's play *The Importance of Being Earnest* (1895), Jack Worthing proposes to send the spendthrift Algernon to Australia, although the latter responds that he would "sooner die…" and, told the choice is "this world, the next world, and Australia," replies, "The account I have received of Australia and the next world, are not particularly encouraging."

In "The Adventure of the Veiled Lodger," to India, but for different reasons, goes "a young Edmunds, of the Berkshire Constabulary. A smart lad that! He was sent later to Allahabad." Set in 1890, though published in 1927, his career reflects the extent to which the British presence in India increasingly moved from the military to the police.

The most contentious presentation of the empire to modern eyes would be *The Sign of the Four* (1890) with Jonathan Small's description of the Mutiny and the subsequent account of Tonga, the Andaman Islander. Small's account of his earlier life is the deep-history of the story, but does not come until the close of it, thus providing both a lengthy denouement and a second narrative for the novel, one shot through with a degree of drama and violence even greater than the chase on the River Thames involving Holmes and Watson. Going out to India as a soldier, Small loses a leg to a Ganges crocodile, thus providing an additional exoticism, and a reminder of the hazards of India, military service, and life. Small then becomes an estate overseer, finding both a role and stability, only to encounter the horror of the Mutiny:

> "One month India lay as still and peaceful, to all appearance, as Surrey or Kent; the next there were two hundred thousand black devils let loose, and the country was a perfect hell … the whole sky was alight with the burning bungalows.… Dawson's wife, all cut into ribbons … hundreds of the black fiends … a fight of the millions against the hundreds … nothing but torture and murder and outrage … fanatics and fierce devil-worshippers."

Small was then recruited under threat of death by three Sikhs into a conspiracy to kill a Hindu pretend-merchant transporting a duplicitous rajah's jewels. In an instructive note about tensions between the non-British inhabitants of India, Abdullah Khan, one of the Sikhs, tells Small that he, Khan, cannot trust Hindus, "But the Sikh knows the Englishman, and the Englishman knows the Sikh."

The murder is discovered. Sent to the prison settlement at Blair Island on the Andamans, where he was "bullied by every cursed black-faced policeman who loved to take it out of a white man," including a "vile Pathan." Small cures and befriends Tonga, a young islander, and the two men escape to hunt down the officer who had tricked Small on the prison colony. Tonga is identified by Holmes with reference to a gazetteer that describes the islanders as fierce, intractable, hideous and cannibals, providing a disturbing background. In the chase on the Thames, the language becomes far more derogatory: Tonga "this savage, distorted creature … never have I seen features so deeply marked with all bestiality and cruelty … half-animal fury … unhallowed dwarf … venomous, menacing eyes." Subsequently, Tonga is described by Small as "that hell-hound … the little devil." Fired at by Tonga with a poisoned dart, Holmes and Watson shoot together and hit Tonga who falls into the river.

This novel has an ironic counterpart in modern cultural politics. Visiting Port Blair on South Andaman Island, I noted the memorialization at the Cellular Jail of the "firebrand revolutionaries against the brutalities of the British barbarisms," in the words of the plaque erected in 1979 by Morarji Desai, Indian Prime Minister from 1977 to 1979. There is no mention, despite the islands being part of the wide-ranging southern

Indian Chola Empire in the eleventh century, of the islands only being Indian because India succeeded to the British imperial position in 1950: Benefiting from their firepower and amphibious capability, the British had overcome opposition by the local indigenous population in 1859. When Doyle wrote his account, the prisoners there were kept in miserable circumstances. Small himself gets a little hut and takes part in digging ditches, yam-planting, and, far more easily, drug-dispensing. The Cellular Jail for political detainees, a different form of regimentation, was not built until 1896–1906, and its single cells were designed to help limit the spread of disease.

Changing memorialization was, and is, also the case with the Mutiny. The emphasis in Doyle's day was on the brutal treatment of British women and children, especially the massacre at Kanpur (Small's Cawnpore) of over two hundred people in 1857, the details of which still have the capacity to shock.[35] The fate of the women and children were also at issue in the Holmes' short story "The Adventure of the Crooked Man" (1893). Now the emphasis has moved, instead, to British atrocities. These were indeed harsh, plentiful, and not restricted to punishing the rebel soldiers. Indeed, alongside hostility to the massacres by the rebels, there was criticism in Britain about the harsh and often arbitrary nature of the reprisals.

Doyle's treatment of the Andaman Islanders reflects the sense of civilizational conflict and progress, and the defense of British imperialism, seen also in his non-Holmes *The Tragedy of the Korosko*. This appeared as a serial in *The Strand Magazine* in 1897, as a book in 1898, and, in an adaptation by Doyle, as the play *Fires of Fate* (1909), which, in 1923, became a film. The story is very much set in the here-and-now of the British conflict with the Mahdists of Sudan. In the Doyle novel, Cecil Brown presents the Dervishes (Mahdists) as uncompromising believers in destiny, the proof of how bigotry leads toward barbarism, and a dire threat to the civilization of Egypt, which is protected by Britain. Brown feels that Britain has taken on the excessive burdens of being the global policeman, only for Colonel Cochrane to argue that he has:

> "a very limited view of our national duties … behind national interests and diplomacy and all that there lies a great guiding

> force—a Providence in fact—which is for ever getting the best out of each nation and using it for the good of the whole. When a nation ceases to respond, it is time that she went into hospital for a few centuries, like Spain or Greece—the virtue has gone out of her. A man or a nation is not placed upon the earth to do merely what is pleasant and what is profitable.... That is how we rule India. We came there by a kind of natural law, like air rushing into a vacuum."

There is also an opportunity for Doyle to advance his view of Anglo-American Manifest Destiny:

> "...[T]he English-speakers are all in the same boat ... we and you have among our best men a higher conception of moral sense and public duty than is to be found in any other people ... these are the two qualities which are needed for directing a weaker race.... The pressure of destiny will force you to administer the Whole of America from Mexico to the Horn."

The *Korosko,* a boat on the Nile, has a fate very different to that in Agatha Christie's *Death on the Nile* (1937), but, by then, Egypt, and indeed the entire course of the White Nile, are under British control.

A hero of empire featured in "The Adventure of the Devil's Foot," an effective Holmes story that was published in 1910, but set in 1897. The tall, craggy, fierce-eyed Leon Sterndale, "the great lion-hunter and explorer" with a "tremendous personality," kills the villainous Mortimer Tregennis with a rare West African ordeal poison he "obtained under very extraordinary circumstances in the Ubanghi country." Having in effect been his judge, Holmes, impressed by the "lawless lion-hunter," lets him go to Central Africa to complete his work.

Explorers were famous in Britain and the West. Henry Morton Stanley (1841–1904), who had made his fame as an explorer of Central Africa, was the Liberal Unionist MP for Lambeth North in 1895–1900, having been defeated for the seat by a Liberal by a narrow margin in 1892. Stanley did not stand in 1900 when Doyle unsuccessfully stood as a Liberal Unionist in 1900 as he was to do again in 1906. Ernest

Shackleton, the Polar explorer, and an Anglo-Irishman opposed to Irish Home Rule, was a Liberal Unionist candidate for Dundee in 1906, but did badly in that Liberal stronghold where Churchill was to be easily elected as a Liberal in a 1908 by-election.

Reference to lions in "The Devil's Foot" underlined the extent to which the Tropics were associated with danger, not least dangerous animals, which was an aspect of their alien quality. This was seen, for example, "with the giant rat of Sumatra, a story for which the world is not yet prepared," as mentioned by Holmes in "The Adventure of the Sussex Vampire" (1924). So also in the index of his notes and items he retains, with "Venomous lizard or gila. Remarkable case, that!"

A somewhat different hero of empire is Holmes himself in his years of post-Reichenbach Falls deception, as described in "The Adventure of the Empty House" (1903). He traveled for two years in Lhasa, into which a British expedition in fact fought its way in 1904, passed through Persia and Mecca, and visited the Sudanese capital Khartoum, which would have been a very brave mission, before giving the Foreign Office a report. There is not, however, in this travel account, the suppressed violence of Colonel Sebastian Moran, a hunter "in the dark jungle of criminal London." The jungle is an image that Doyle frequently uses, including for the upper atmosphere in the non-Holmes "The Horror of the Heights" (1913). Once Moran, an excellent "heavy game shot"—in many respects like a tiger himself—is captured, Holmes scorns him by describing his capture in terms of standard tiger-hunting technique in India. Hunting is frequently used also as a descriptor for Holmes, but his ethos and methods are different to Moran. The use of such language identifies Holmes in terms of manliness, and both rural and imperial values and practices. Thus, in "The Adventure of the Abbey Grange" (1904) while tracking down a visitor from Australia, he remarks of the steamer lines "we will draw the larger cover first." In contrast to Holmes, the fictional Moran is very much a child of empire. While born in London, in 1840, and educated at Eton and Oxford, he was the son of the one-time British envoy to Persia, and had served with the Bangalore Pioneers in India, including in the Second Anglo-Afghan War (1878–80) in which Watson had been wounded. The author of two books on his hunting exploits in India, he was obliged to leave it and the army due to his unacceptable behavior there.

In "The Adventure of Speckled Band" (1892), set in 1883, and Doyle's favorite Holmes short story, Dr. Grimesby Roylott has to go to Calcutta to try to rescue himself from being an "aristocrat pauper." A successful doctor but lacking in self-control, he was convicted and imprisoned for beating his native butler to death: Roylott was angered by robberies in the house. He brings back to Surrey his love of strong Indian cigars and his passion for Indian animals. One plays a crucial role in the plot, although the account of the animal is flawed.

Africa, as a land of extremes, emerged in another context in "The Adventure of the Blanched Soldier" (1926), a story set in 1903 in which James Dodd, a veteran of the Middlesex Corps of the Imperial Yeomanry as Holmes ascertains, seeks the detective's help to find his wartime friend, Godfrey Emsworth, only to discover that the latter, when wounded in the Boer War, had staggered into a leper colony and become ill. In Doyle and most popular fiction, Africa is very much the testing ground of imperial manliness, and not for example to the same extent the Asian adventures of the day—whether successfully relieving the Legations of Beijing from Boxer besiegers in 1900, or accompanying Colonel Francis Younghusband and his expedition to Lhasa in 1904, an invasion driven by those on the spot, that exceeded the British government's wishes.

Manliness is shown in both exploration and hunting, and there are elements of both in Holmes' adventures in Britain. Thus, in "Black Peter," Holmes, Watson and Inspector Hopkins wait among the bushes at night in order to find Peter Carey's killer. Watson treats humans and animals as interchangeable in character:

> "[I]t brought with it something of the thrill which the hunter feels when he lies beside the water-pool and waits for the coming of the thirsty beast of prey. What savage creature was it which might steal upon us out of the darkness? Was it a fierce tiger of crime, which could only be taken fighting hard with flashing fang and claw, or would it prove to be some skulking jackel, dangerous only to the weak and unguarded? In absolute silence we crouched among the bushes, waiting for whatever might come … an absolute stillness … it was the darkest hour which precedes the dawn."

A different form of identification of humans and animals was provided by Holmes' description of Charles Augustus Milverton, in the impressive story of that name published in 1904:

> "Do you feel a creeping, shrinking sensation, Watson, when you stand before the serpents in the Zoo and see the slithery, gliding, venomous creatures, with their deadly eyes and wicked flattened faces? Well, that's how Milverton impresses me."

London Zoo had been opened in 1828, with a reptile house following in 1849. Milverton was based on the half-Portuguese blackmailer Charles Augustus Howell (1840–90), who was found in Chelsea with his throat slit and a coin in his mouth.

There is also an element of necessary hunting in the "campaign" against Milverton, whom Holmes has compared to "the Evil One," the Devil. This campaign is described by Watson with a Gothic flourish: "As a flash of lightning in the night shows up in an instant every detail of a wide landscape." Holmes himself uses the image of "a sporting duel between this fellow Milverton and me." In breaking into Milverton's house, there is an air of the Tropics: Having used his burgling kit, which, Holmes remarks, contains "every modern improvement which the march of civilisation demands," he and Watson confront "the thick warm air of the conservatory and the rich, choking fragrance of exotic plants [which] took us by the throat."

The impact of empire on Britain is found throughout the stories, including those set far from the ports. Thus, in "Silver Blaze," the trainer on guard, Ned Hunter, has "curried mutton" for dinner, the strong, spicy taste of which provides an opportunity to drug him. In addition, Mrs. Hudson offers curried chicken for breakfast in "The Adventure of the Naval Treaty" (1893). In *A Study in Scarlet* (1887), the suspect smokes a Trinchopoly cigar, one made of Indian tobacco that was popular in Britain this period.

The heyday of the Holmes stories marked a highpoint in London's grand imperial history. London provided the setting for Victoria's Golden and Diamond Jubilees in 1887 and 1897. Prominent visitors, such as the Khedive of Egypt in 1900, were entertained by the Mayor and Corporation of the city. Whitehall had grand new ministerial buildings, notably the New War Office (1899–1906) and the New Public Offices (1899–1915). The Mall was conceived as a great ceremonial route with, at one end, Buckingham Palace's new façade as well as the enormous Victoria memorial in the *rond-point* in front of the palace, and, at the other, Admiralty Arch (1912), which provided an opening onto Trafalgar Square and the north end of Whitehall.

The empire was expanded greatly in the late nineteenth century. There were serious defeats along the way to imperial expansion, especially at Isandlwana (1879) and Maiwand (1880) at the hands of the Zulus and Afghans, respectively. The latter saw Watson, a fictional army doctor, wounded, while 962 of the outnumbered 2,500-strong British force was killed and the colors of a regiment were lost. The flavor of this very difficult imperial conflict can be readily captured, the Reverend Alfred Cane writing of a sortie against the village of Deh Khoja:

> "[W]e began by shelling the place. There was no reply so 800 of our infantry advanced to the attack when at once a galling fire was opened on them from loop holes round the village. Our men rushed on and entered the village on the south side but only to find it filled with armed men firing from the windows, doors and roofs. It was a hopeless task … had to return in hot haste under the same heavy fire."[36]

Nevertheless, the British were usually successful in battle, notably over the Zulus in 1879, in particular at Ulundi, and the Second Anglo-Afghan War ultimately led to British victory: Ayub Khan, who had been victorious over the British at Maiwand, was decisively defeated at Kandahar after an epic relief march by General Roberts from Kabul to Kandahar in August. Victory at Tel el Kebir (1882) left Britain dominant in Egypt, while the fate of Sudan was settled at Omdurman in 1898, when artillery, machine guns and rifle fire devastated the attacking Mahdists, with 31,000 casualties for the latter and only 430 for the Anglo-Egyptian force. The writer Hilaire Belloc observed in *The Modern Traveler* (1898):

"Whatever happens we have got
the Maxim Gun; and they have not."

Technology and resources were not only at stake on the battlefield. In 1896, the British invading force built a railway straight across the desert, from Wadi Halfa to Abu Hamed. Extended to Atbara in 1898, it played a major role in the supply of the British forces. A succinct Doyle Sudan contribution was "The Début of Bimbashi Joyce," published in *Punch* on 3 January 1900 and not a Holmes story. Barbaric Sudan is described in the opening paragraph as: "That country of darkness. Sometimes the sunset would turn those distant mists into a bank of crimson, and the dark mountains would rise from that sinister reek like islands in a sea of blood." British force was presented as benign: "...[I]t was time for civilisation to take a trip south once more, traveling, as her wont is, in an armoured train." British command emerges in a positive light.

In his "The Green Flag," published in the *Pall Mall Magazine* in June 1893, imperial service redeemed Irishness and in particular those involved in the anti-landlord Irish National Land League of 1879–82. Set in Sudan, this story told of an attack by a far larger number of Mahdists or "fanatics." Each side benefits from artillery, which obliges the British to rely on bravery. The "fighting blood" of the Irish was crucial, but that was a clash of identities: "You are not fighting for England. You are fighting for Ireland, and for the Empire of which it as [sic] part,"' remarks Captain Foley. The Mahdists are described as looking "like a blast of fiends from the pit.[37] And were these the Allies of Ireland? ...[T]he murder of the wounded, the hacking of the unarmed...." In the end, the Irish rally for the army, but under the Green Flag, reform the square, and die bravely.

The Sudan theme continued with "The Three Correspondents," published in *The Windsor Magazine* in October 1896, in which three journalists defend themselves from Mahdist attack, Doyle commenting "The law-abiding Briton is so imbued with the idea of the sanctity of human life that it was hard for the young pressman to realize that these men had every intention of killing him, and that he was at perfect liberty to do as much for them." Doyle's portrayal of the Irish in "The Green Flag" corresponded to that of his letter in *The Irish Times* on 3 October 1900, which had closed with an attack on intolerance in Irish politics, adding that he, like many, was "whole-souled in one desire that Ireland should become prosperous, happy, and reconciled to that great empire which has been so largely built up by Irish valour and Irish intellect," a stance very different to the development of anti-imperialism in Irish republicanism.[38] Britain's opponents in two wars that engaged Doyle had earlier been successful, the Boers in 1881 in the First Boer War, and the Mahdists in 1885, and were not overcome until 1900–2 and 1898–9, respectively.

Doyle was far from alone. Sudan was to the fore for many writers. A.E.W. Mason's *The Four Feathers*, a successful novel of 1902, was a presentation of British operations in Sudan as a definition of manliness and heroism. Sudan also appeared in the popular adventure stories for boys by the war correspondent George Alfred Henty. These included *The Dash for Khartoum: A Tale of the Nile Expedition* (1891), two on the Boer War—*With Buller in Natal* (1900) and *With Roberts to Pretoria* (1901)—and *With Kitchener in the Soudan* (1902). In the last, Henty presented the conquest of Sudan as a "stupendous achievement," the Preface declaring: "Thus a land that had been turned into a desert by the terrible tyranny of the Mahdi and his successor, was wrested from barbarism and restored to civilization; and the stain upon British honour, caused by the desertion of Gordon by the British ministry of the day, was wiped out." (The last a reference to the events of 1885.)

A different form of heroism was offered by Churchill in *The River War. An Historical Account of the Reconquest of the Soudan* (1899). He wrote of the Mahdists: "They lived by the sword. Why should they not perish by the magazine rifle? A state of society which, even if it were tolerable to those whom it comprised, was an annoyance to civilised nations has been swept aside.... The Government was a cruel despotism"[39] —which, indeed, was the case.

The very positive image of the army seen in these works by Doyle and others, was linked to a more general feeling that manliness was best developed and shown through military training and action, with appropriate ethos shown accordingly. British character and values were to be molded by fighting for Britain, and manliness thereby protected. In addition to the depiction of war in newspapers as well as Baden-Powell's

Boy Scouts, this feeling was reflected in the reorganization and modernization of the militia and volunteers into a Special Reserve and the Territorial Force, later the Territorial Army.[40]

While some acquisitions such as Uganda were made with reluctance on the part of government, much British imperial expansion, especially in 1880–1914, arose directly from the response to the real or apparent plans of other powers, particularly France and Russia. However, the search for markets for British industry was also important. Thus, both economic and political security were at stake and, as a result, the imperialist surge of activity at the close of the century has been seen as marking the beginning of a long decline from the zenith of British power, and of imperial position starting to fray under pressure at the same time that it continued to expand and, thereby, encounter additional problems.

The nature of the empire also changed as sovereignty and territorial control became crucial goals and replaced the pursuit of influence and of island and port possessions that had been the characteristic features of much, although by no means all, British expansion earlier in the nineteenth century. Suspicion of Russian designs on the Turkish empire, and of French schemes in North Africa, led the British to move into Cyprus (1878) and Egypt (1882); concern about French ambitions in South-East Asia resulted in the conquest of Mandalay (1885) and the annexation of Upper Burma (1886); while Russia's advance across Central Asia led to war panics, notably in 1885, and attempts to strengthen and move forward the "North-West Frontier" of British India and also to the development of British influence in southern Iran and the Persian Gulf, through which the British routed the telegraph to India. French and German expansion in Africa led Britain to take counter measures in Gambia, Sierra Leone, the Gold Coast (Ghana), Nigeria and Uganda—all moves in the "Scramble for Africa" by the European powers.

Specific clashes over colonial influence with other European powers increasingly interacted from the late 1870s with a more general sense of imperial insecurity as confidence was put under pressure by the growing strength of other states. More clearly, in the 1880s, there was public and governmental concern about naval vulnerability. In 1883, William Henry Smith, a Conservative politician, who had been First Lord of the Admiralty in 1877–80, told the House of Commons of:

> "...the duties to be discharged by the Navy, and which are of a very varying nature throughout the world, because heavier duties fall upon the Navy of this country than fall upon the Navies of all other countries taken together. We have a large commerce, and practically we have to perform what are called the police duties of the seas, and we have, in consequence, to maintain an iron-clad Fleet equal to any emergency."[41]

This he explained later that year was difficult:

> "[A]t this moment, ironclads have to be employed in the China and Australian Seas, in the Pacific, on the Coast of North America, and in the West Indies. Our Fleet is scattered in a manner in which the Fleet of no other power can be scattered; and while it is discharging duties in three or four different seas, if, unfortunately, we should be engaged in a war, Foreign Powers might be able to concentrate their forces against our Navy."[42]

In 1889, this concern led to the Naval Defense Act, which sought a two-power standard: superiority over the next two largest naval powers combined. The importance of naval dominance was taken for granted but also encouraged by a careful dissemination of navalist ideas.[43] It was a pre-requisite of an ideal of imperial, and therefore national, self-sufficiency that peaked in the late nineteenth century.

The response to the Russian advance could be the advance of territorial control notably on the "North-West Frontier," and, for the Balkans, in Cyprus. Yet, there was also a need in some areas to rely on less direct influence, notably in East Asia. There was a concern that the expansion of Russian control in China, more particularly Manchuria, would limit British trade and influence, and the fear that Russia would develop a stronger maritime presence in the Pacific where Britain had existing interests to protect. These concerns affected British policy in China and, more especially, the attempt to develop a strategic relationship with Japan, with which an alliance was signed in 1902 and renewed in 1905 and 1911.

Empire Day was launched in 1896 on May 24, Victoria's birthday. While in 1871, having defeated France, Wilhelm I (King of Prussia) became Emperor of Germany, Victoria, five years later as a result of the Royal Titles Act, became Empress of India—an empire that was to last until the sub-continent was granted independence in 1947, with the title being inherited by her four successors. Streets, towns, geographical features and whole tracts of land were named or renamed in her honor, including the Australian state of Victoria, the city of Victoria on Vancouver Island in Canada, Victoria Falls on the Zambezi, and Lake Victoria in East Africa. So also with the naming of places after other members of the royal family and after British politicians—for example Salisbury (after the Marquess of Salisbury) in Southern Rhodesia, now Harare in Zimbabwe.

The naming of Rhodesia reflected the ambition and activity of Cecil Rhodes who favored the idea of a railway from Cape Town to Cairo, a means to help anchor the developing British presence in Sudan, Uganda and Kenya. This key developer of the British imperial presence in southern Africa is now more generally discussed in terms of racist politics, notably the pursuit of advantage alongside and by means of White dominance.[44] Rail was also seen as a way to develop links to the Indian Ocean, while British colonies were also designed to help British settlers and to protect Protestant natives. The East Africa Protectorate established in 1895 was the basis for Kenya.

Imperial status was also part of the recreation of Victoria in the late 1870s. She was coaxed from reclusive widowhood to a new public role by Disraeli, who, as Prime Minister in 1868 and 1874–80, combined imperial policies with social reform and who sought, in doing so, to foster a sense of national unity and continuity. He realized that monarchy was a potent way to lead the public and control the consequences of the spread of the franchise, a view gently mocked in Gilbert and Sullivan's comic operetta, *The Pirates of Penzance* (1879), in which the pirates, victorious over the maladroit police, rapidly surrender at the close when summoned to do so in the name of the Queen.

At once an opportunistic and skilful political tactician, who was also an acute and imaginative thinker, Disraeli was able to create a political culture around the themes of imperial ambition, national identity, and social cohesion, and to focus popular support for the Conservatives on these themes as an alternative to the arrogant Liberal moral certainty in which Gladstone flourished. Disraeli carefully manipulated Victoria into accepting his view and playing the role he had allocated her.

The government of Victoria's empire was very varied. In some colonies, notably in much of Africa, there was straightforward imperial rule by representatives of the British state, whereas in India there was a careful attempt to incorporate existing hierarchies, interests and rituals. There, the princely dynasties were wooed, from the 1870s, by the creation of an anglicized princely hierarchy that gave them roles and honors, such as the Orders of the Star of India (established 1861) and the Indian Empire (established 1878), in accordance with British models and interests—a process that was also to be followed in Malaya and in parts of Africa. This process led to a stress on status and not race, which is easy to criticize, not least because the resulting emphasis on inherited privilege served as a brake on inculcating values of economic, social and political development. This policy was also a response to the large amount of India that had been left under princely rule.

Nevertheless, in practice, the search for support in India and elsewhere was not restricted to the social élite. Instead, the search was a multi-layered one, extending to the co-option or creation of professional and administrative groups, able to meet local as well as imperial needs. Moreover, princes were downgraded to knights in these orders, a subtle demotion that suited British interests.

Dominion status, self-government under the Crown, took the process of "Responsible Government" further, offering a peaceful, evolutionary route to independence.[45] Canada became a Dominion in 1867, Australia in 1901, and New Zealand in 1907. Although the Colonial Laws Validity Act of 1865 had declared invalid any colonial legislation that clashed with that from Westminster, the Act was only rarely invoked. This was a federalism that worked. Meetings of prime ministers from 1887 helped give the Dominions a voice in imperial policy and also offered a means of coherence. During the Boer War, the empire—especially Australia, Canada, Cape Colony and New Zealand—in response to a strong commitment,[46] sent troops to help the British forces, actions which helped foster Dominion nationalism within the empire, rather than having this nationalism act as a separatist element.

Imperial subjects in Britain in the Doyle stories were generally White. Daulat Ras, the Indian at St. Luke's, an imaginary Oxford college, in "The Adventure of the Three Students" (1904), is defended by Holmes from Watson's unfounded suspicions and the misdirection they represent. The guilty party in the theft of the question paper in fact is Gilchrist, a prominent athlete and "fine, manly fellow," in other words the standard hero, who then decides, in a *Four Feathers* fashion, to seek redemption in empire: "I have determined not to go in for the examination. I have been offered a commission in the Rhodesian Police, and I am going out to South Africa at once." With the story set in 1895, this is the frontier of empire, and Holmes concludes the story by telling him: "I trust that a bright future awaits you in Rhodesia. For once you have fallen low. Let us see in the future how high you can rise." Formed in 1889 as mounted infantrymen, the British South Africa Police operated in Rhodesia and took a major role in the Matabele wars of 1893–7, which led to the extension of control by the British South Africa Company under Cecil Rhodes. In 1909, this force merged with the Southern Rhodesia Constabulary, which was the police force for the cities of Salisbury and Bulawayo.

Aside from the fictional Daulat Ras, Doyle himself was concerned about the miscarriage of justice suffered by George Edalji (1876–1953), the son of a vicar of Parsee descent from India married to an Englishwoman. George became a lawyer and was unjustly convicted in 1903 of animal maiming. Racial prejudice played a role in the conviction, which was a serious miscarriage of justice. Doyle's involvement in the case helped make it more prominent. He played a major role in seeking to have the conviction overturned and in 1907 Edalji was granted a pardon. Doyle was a great supporter of the British empire and a very fair man,[47] and not invariably harsh to others at a time when empire was very frequently seen at least in part in racial terms.[48]

In contrast to Daulat Ras, in *The Sign of the Four*, Lal Rao, the butler at Pondicherry Lodge, a British house named after an Indian city, is a confederate of Jonathan Small. Mrs. Bernstone gives Lal Rao "far from a good character." In "The Adventure of thc Three Gables" (1926), however, there is a hostile and derogatory account of Steve Dixie that is unremitting in its nastiness. It is unclear whether Dixie is an American or a West Indian:

> "If I had said that a mad bull had arrived, it would give a clearer impression of what occurred. The door had flown open and a huge negro had burst into the room. He would have been a comic figure if he had not been terrific, for he was dressed in a very loud gray check suit with a flowing salmon-coloured tie … broad face and flattened nose … sullen dark eyes, with a smouldering gleam of malice in them … the savage … hideous mouth."

Holmes adds to Watson's account: "…[T]he smell of you … his woolly head … he is really rather a harmless fellow, a great muscular, foolish blistering baby, and easily cowed."

Outside the Holmes corpus of mysteries, and while Holmes had apparently been disposed of in the Reichenbach Falls, Doyle added the mystery "The Black Doctor" (1898), which presented Aloysius Lana, an effective doctor trained in Glasgow and working in a village ten miles south-west from Liverpool:

> "[H]e came undoubtedly of a tropical race, and was so dark that he might almost have had a strain of the Indian in his composition. His predominant features were, however, European, and he possessed a stately courtesy and carriage which suggested a Spanish extraction. A swarthy skin, raven-black hair, and dark, sparkling eyes under a pair of heavily-tufted brows made a strange contrast to the flaxen or chestnut rustics of England, and the newcomer was soon known as 'The Black Doctor of Bishop's Crossing.' At first it was a term of ridicule and reproach; as the years went on it became a title of honour which was familiar to the whole countryside, and extended far beyond the narrow confines of the village."

Lana is not in fact Black, but the key element is not his color. It is his British-trained medical skill and personal behavior that leads to his integration into rural society:

> "A remarkable surgical cure in the case of the Hon. James Lowry, the second son of Lord Belton, was the means of introducing him to county society, where he became a favourite through the charm of his conversation and the elegance of his manners. An absence of antecedents and of relatives is sometimes an aid rather than an impediment to social advancement, and the distinguished individuality of the handsome doctor was its own recommendation."

At a garden party, Lana meets Frances Morton of Leigh Hall, the daughter of a local squire, and the story ends with the news of their marriage, which is even more one of integration as Aloysius, a Catholic, has married in the local Anglican Church. This story captured the possible porosity of the élite to those who could fit into its parameters. As the case of Benjamin Disraeli, who had been born Jewish, amply showed, this integration was not only a matter of fiction.

Yet, alongside expansion as well as changes designed both to mold and to benefit from the situation of flux in the empire, cracks were appearing in the imperial edifice. Due, in part, to the diffusion within it of British notions of community, identity and political action, there was a measure of opposition to imperial control, with the Indian National Congress formed in 1885 and the Egyptian National Party in 1897. There were links between anti-imperial movements, at least in so far as ideology and rhetoric were concerned, with Irish Home Rule rhetoric being used by Indian nationalists.

The most immediate challenge to empire during Doyle's adult life prior to the outbreak of World War One in 1914 was the Boer War of 1899–1902, in practice the Second Boer War. It was waged with the Afrikaner (Boers Whites of Dutch descent) republics of the Orange Free State and the Transvaal in Southern Africa. Regional hegemony was a key issue. British leaders found it difficult to accept Boer views and were willing to risk war in order to achieve a transfer of some power in southern Africa. The Boer War is often seen as a classic instance of "capitalist-driven" empire-building. However, Alfred Milner, the aggressive Governor of the Cape Colony and High Commissioner for Southern Africa in 1897 to 1901, was essentially driven by political considerations, his own ambition, and his strong sense of imperial mission on behalf of a British race.[49] The British ministers were greatly influenced by the fear that if, given the gold and diamond discoveries, the Boers became the most powerful force in Southern Africa, it might not be long before they were working with Britain's imperial rivals, especially the Germans in South-West Africa, and threatening her strategic interests at the Cape. The Prime Minister, Salisbury, remarked that Britain had to be supreme. Ministers in London thought (wrongly) that the Boers were bluffing and would not put up much of a fight if war followed; while the failure of the British to send sufficient reinforcements persuaded the Boers to think it was the British who were bluffing. The Boer republics declared war , but only after Britain had isolated them internationally and had done everything possible to provoke them.[50]

Initially, the outnumbered and poorly-led British were outfought by the Boers' effective combination of the strategic offensive and a successful use of defensive positions. In "Black Week," in December 1899, British forces suffered heavy casualties in a series of battles, including Magersfontein and Colenso in which frontal attacks were foolishly pursued. Thomas Hardy's poem "The Dead Drummer" (1899), better known from 1901 as "Drummer Hodge", is a powerful elegy for a young drummer.

More effective generalship by Roberts and Kitchener transformed the situation in 1900. Moreover, far from empire proving a reactionary monolith, the army proved adaptable, both tactically and organizationally as when, responding to Boer tactics, there was use of mounted infantry to a great extent. Britain's larger force was applied methodically with the overrunning of the Boer heartland in the Transvaal. The British then turned to the more difficult task of countering Boer raiders. Boer guerrilla operations proved a formidable, but ultimately unsuccessful, challenge, not least because of the British combination of methodical force with flexible mobility.

The ability of Britain to allocate about £200 million and to deploy 400,000 troops was a testimony to the strength of her economic and imperial systems. Yet, income tax had to be doubled to pay for the war, which also greatly pushed up government borrowing. The Conservative policy of low taxation with financial retrenchment had to be abandoned under the pressure of imperial expansion. Doyle's role as both doctor and writer in defense of British interests during the war led to his being awarded a knighthood, one that was bestowed by Edward VII in person in October 1902. Arthur Raffles, a successful short story creation in 1898 of Doyle's brother-in-law, Ernest Hornung, is killed in 1900 in the Boer War at the very close of the short story "The Knees of the Gods." His companion, Bunny Manders, has already been wounded in that story.

In the end, as with other British imperial conflicts of the nineteenth century, the Boer War was a cause of the more general background of an apparently continuously expanding empire. In 1901, Asante in West Africa was annexed, while an expeditionary force was sent to the interior of British Somaliland, in order to confront the rising by Sayyid Muhammad 'Abdille Hassan who in 1899, had declared holy war on Christians. By 1905, the British had forced a peace on their opponents. In 1903, the army of the Emirate of Sokoto was smashed at Burmi in northern Nigeria. The following year, Younghusband advanced to Lhasa, the capital of Tibet, in order to thwart alleged Russian influence and dictate terms. In Kenya in 1905, tribal opposition was overcome. And so on. There was a strong degree of force underlying imperial expansion and consolidation.

Moreover, opposition to British control or influence in the colonies and in the informal empire was still limited in scope, certainly in comparison to the situation after World War One; and there was also a considerable measure of compliance with British rule. In Ireland, the preferred option was Home Rule under the Crown, not republican independence, which at the time was the preference of only a minority. Large numbers of Irish continued to serve in the empire, notably in the army; and the earlier concern about a "Fenian threat" to empire was lessened.[51] There had been rural violence, notably in the 1830s and 1830s, and some urban terrorism, but it was small-scale.

Many Scots benefited greatly from the empire, with about 16 percent of the capital paid out as compensation when slavery was abolished and repatriated to Britain being sent to Scotland. The degree to which the Scots retained considerable independence within the United Kingdom––including their own established Church and legal and educational systems—also militated against political nationalism. The National Association for the Vindication of Scottish Rights, sought recognition of equal partnership in the Union and the empire, but it was short-term (1853–6) and had scant immediate impact. In 1886, in part in response to developments in Ireland, a Scottish Home Rule Association was founded. The Liberals supported this policy, but it got nowhere in Parliament. However, the Conservatives, as part of the modernisation of government, established a separate Scottish Office in 1885.

The process of political reform that saw the expansion of the male franchise and the election of county councils ensured that, although there was no Home Rule, the grounding of empire in democratic practice and accountability increased. This made it easier to be a Scottish Conservative, a Liberal or Liberal Unionist like Doyle. Democratization did not mean that empire was inherently stronger, or indeed weaker; simply that the links of identity and means of power were changing.

7. THE TWENTIETH CENTURY

The promise of a steadily "wider" empire was held out in 1902 when Arthur Benson's words for "Land of Hope and Glory," the first of Edward Elgar's *Pomp and Circumstance* marches, were first heard as part of the Coronation Ode for Edward VII (1901–10). The empire was indeed not only the most extensive and populous in the world, but was still expanding rapidly. It was also developing. For example, the Viceroyalty of Lord Curzon from 1899 to 1905 saw reform in the government of India, not least the establishment of a Railway Board in 1901, a process formalized in 1905. Curzon was committed to the seriousness of a Russian challenge and had been Under-Secretary of State for Foreign Affairs in 1895–8.

Britain continued to be the greatest naval power, merchant shipper and shipbuilder and the largest overseas investor in the world. Much of Britain's commerce and finance were not linked to formal empire, the Chilean nitrate industry for example being developed by over £12 million of British capital between 1882 and 1896. Yet empire was still key to the economy, the source of many important goods, and the market for many British exports.

The empire was seen as both product and part of the nation. The British nation was not regarded as limited to Britain, and the values that accrued to empire offered an extensive fluidity that encompassed Britons abroad. Voluntarist bodies were at once imperial and national—for example, the Tariff Reform League, the Navy League and the Emigration Committee of the Royal Colonial Institute. There was a female dimension, the Victoria League, established in 1901, supporting female emigration and serving to underline the role of empire as a place of domesticity, family and the virtues of home.

Yet, despite the strength of the empire, there was a mounting sense of challenge, and for other imperial powers as well—for example a

France faced by German strength and a Russia worried by Japanese assertiveness. For Britain, imperial competitiveness was a cause of repeated concern, indeed anxiety, not least in the 1900s from Germany, which replaced France as the leading source of worry. Indeed, fear of invasion of Britain itself revived, which altered the relationship between imperial metropole and wider concerns. There was also repeated anxiety about the moves, real or potential, of other powers that might threaten imperial possessions and the links that provided imperial articulation. Thus, increased German influence in the Ottoman (Turkish) empire caused concern, notably about a threat to the Persian Gulf and to routes to India.

In 1912, Rear-Admiral Ernest Troubridge, the Chief of the War Staff of the British Admiralty, in a memorandum on the Italian occupation of some of the Aegean islands, noted of British policy:

> "A cardinal factor has naturally been that no strong naval power should be in effective permanent occupation of any territory or harbor east of Malta, if such harbor be capable of transformation into a fortified naval base. None can foresee the developments of material in warfare, and the occupation of the apparently most useless island should be resisted equally with the occupation of the best. The geographical situation of these islands enable the sovereign power, if enjoying the possession of a navy, to exercise a control over the Levant and Black Sea trade and to threaten our position in Egypt."

Any threat to Egypt entailed also threatening the route to India via the Suez Canal.

There was also economic anxiety, not least due to competition from the rapidly growing economies of America and Germany. This encouraged calls for the replacement of free trade through tariff reform (protectionism). A self-sufficient imperial trading block was seen as economic salve, strategic means and political goal. In 1902, Joseph Chamberlain, the Liberal Unionist Secretary of State for the Colonies from 1895 to 1903 and an advocate of an empire based on cooperation, told the Colonial Conference:

> "The weary Titan staggers under the too vast orb of its fate. We have borne the burden for many years. We think that it is time that our children should assist us to support it.... If you are prepared at any time to take any share in the burdens of Empire, we are prepared to meet you with any proposal for giving you a corresponding vote in the policy of the Empire."

In 1903, Chamberlain resigned from the Cabinet because it would not support his call for tariff reform, which was amplified by the Tariff Reform League also formed that year. Chamberlain sought to win working-class support. The likely outcome of developments was unclear, not least as so much depended on politics, with the elections of 1906 and 1910 leading to a Liberal-Irish Home Rulers alignment with policies very different to those of the Conservatives and Liberal Unionists. Empire itself varied greatly in is character, with the Dominions more autonomous than hitherto but still closely aligned with Britain. The situation in new colonies was very different. In 1904, the Director of Military Operations warned about the precariousness of empire:

> "The fact cannot be too plainly stated that throughout Egypt and the Soudan, and throughout the great Protectorates of Uganda and British East Africa, our whole position depends entirely on prestige. We are governing with a mere handful of white officials vast populations alien to us in race, language and religion, and for the most part but little superior in civilization to savages. Except for the small, and from a military point of view inadequate, British force in Egypt, the authority of these officials is supported only by troops recruited from the subject races, whose obedience to their officers rests on no other basis than a belief in the invincibility of the British government and confidence in its promises. If that belief and confidence be once shaken, the foundations of all British authority between Cairo and Mombasa will be undermined, and at any moment a storm of mutiny and insurrection will sweep us into the sea."[1]

In Kenya, British settler interest had developed from 1902, with the land in the Kenya Highlands regarded as promising and the East Africa Syndicate becoming a key player. The settlers pushed hard for a railway and because settlement was seen as a way to anchor British interests, there was government support for it, which was crucial, as public funds were central. In 1903, the line was opened to Lake Victoria. The line relied in part on local workers and in part on Indian labor, a combination seen more generally.

In World War One (1914–18), the successful articulation of the empire was readily apparent for without the empire Britain would have been unable to mount offensive operations in the Middle East, would have been largely reduced to the use of the navy alone against German colonies in Africa and the Pacific, and would have been forced to introduce conscription, a contentious move, earlier than it did in 1916. The use of imperial forces was helped by the absence of an enemy in East Asia, with the exception of the German base at Tsingtao in China. This was captured by Britain's ally Japan in 1914, although Japanese activity in China contributed to growing British concern about her intentions, which in turn drew on earlier worries, notably in Australia, about Japan, worries in which White racism and demographic anxiety played a role.[2]

More than 800,000 Indian soldiers fought for the British in the war, so that, far from the British having to garrison South Asia, it was a crucial source of manpower for them. Large numbers of Indians were at first used on the Western Front, while others captured Basra in 1914, protecting British oil interests in south-west Persia, and advanced into Mesopotamia (Iraq) the following year—this commitment a continuation of pre-war interest in increasing influence in the Persian Gulf. The impact of raising troops in India in the Punjab was such that it became a virtual and vital "home front" for the British war effort, while India also provided large quantities of products for the war effort, including food and textiles. In Africa, labor conscription was a heavy burden, with large numbers of carriers used to provide the logistics for Allied columns, and due to disease there were very high rates of casualties among the carriers. As Secretary of State for the Colonies, Churchill took the decision that Africans who fought in the lengthy campaign to conquer German East Africa (Tanganyika) would not receive individual named headstones in official cemeteries.

With the path to fighting consistency eased by major pre-war efforts,[3] the Dominions also raised large numbers of men, with the Canadians providing a substantial force for the Western Front. Forty percent of the men of military age (ie. between 19 and 45) in New Zealand, where conscription was introduced in 1916, served overseas, and of this 120,000 men, over 50,000 were injured and 18,000 died. These efforts and losses played a major role in the shared experience of empire, and were also important in developing attitudes toward the British connection. Thus, the war was seen as formative in the nationalism of the Dominions, although, in practice, this process was far more long-term. Heavy Australian losses, including 58,460 dead among the 332,000 troops who served overseas, were to play a potent role in a controversy focused on the argument that British self-interest and incompetence had led to unnecessary sacrifice—especially in the Gallipoli campaign of 1915—although this argument rested on a less than secure reading of that campaign, particularly of the general surprise at the skill of the Turkish defense (and was less important at the time than it was to be subsequently when it became central to hostility toward the British link). During the war, tension in Canada was more evident. Whereas large numbers of Canadians volunteered (and 56,119 men died), the introduction of conscription by the Military Service Act passed in 1917 and its enforcement in 1918 was unpopular in Québec and led to riots that Spring. However, this was an indication of pre-existing strains, as many French Canadians felt only limited commitment to Canada, and did not extend to a fundamental rejection of the empire.

Such a rejection did occur in Ireland in 1916, but the extreme nationalist Easter Rising in Dublin, however much it contributed to wider strands of anti-imperialism, a fashionable topic,[4] was rapidly crushed. It had enjoyed little support,[5] indeed far less than the Irish risings in 1798 let alone 1641. A far larger number of Irish Catholics volunteered to fight for George V on the Western Front and elsewhere. The firm British response to the Rising, however, served to radicalize much of Irish public opinion, although, given the fact that Britain was then at war, the execution of rebel leaders was scarcely surprising, and subsequent criticism reflects a failure to appreciate the embattled nature of the empire at that moment.

Other factors also helped increase nationalist support. Backers of Home Rule were alienated by the hostile role of the Conservatives in the British coalition government, constitutional nationalists increasingly lost their ability to lead the Catholic community, and a proposal to introduce conscription in March 1918 was particularly important in undermining both them and support for the empire, although it was necessary because of opinion in Britain. Contingency was the key factor in Irish independence: The role of the war was crucial in that it destroyed the basis for the Home Rulers who, under John Redmond, the leader of the Irish Parliamentary Party from 1900 until his death in 1918, had been imperialists as well as nationalists. Redmond hoped to be the Irish equivalent of a Canadian or Australian Prime Minister—"local but loyal"—and his brother, Willie, an MP, died in 1917 fighting on the Western Front.[6] Ironically, in the long term, Home Rule was to be advanced for Scotland, Wales and Northern Ireland as a way to address the "British question" in the 1990s.[7]

In some respects, albeit not in Ireland, the collective effort represented by the war led to a strengthening of empire. An Imperial War Cabinet, including representatives of the Dominions, met from 1917 and provided a welcome public sign of cohesion in decision-making that countered the emphasis on distinctive interests. The war also saw a measure of the economic union that had interested Chamberlain in the 1900s: Schemes for an Imperial Customs Union were considered, while Britain's role as a market for imperial goods was fostered by military needs and political preference. The impact of the war on food imports to Britain from Continental Europe ensured that the British market increased for imperial exporters such as South Africa. Other recently-conquered colonies were also affected, such that in Sudan food exports rose to meet wartime demand; but, at the same time, there and elsewhere, the war seriously disrupted established economic patterns, even in areas not well integrated into the imperial economy, leading to both price and wage inflation.

The war gravely damaged Britain's economy, as most foreign investments were sold in order to finance the war effort, while the disruption of trade and the diversion (under state regulation) of manufacturing capacity to war production ensured that the economy was less able to satisfy international (and domestic) demand. This encouraged the growth of manufacturing elsewhere, both in colonies, such as India, and in areas, such as Latin America, that had traditionally taken British imports. Import substitution and industrial expansion was pushed in South Africa under a consolidated tariff for the entire Union introduced in 1914. America, which did not enter the war until 1917, benefited most of all, as the British war effort rapidly became heavily dependent on American financial and industrial resources, while the Americans were well-placed to replace British exports to Canada and Latin America.

At the same time as economic strain, there was, as with the Napoleonic Wars and World War Two, an attempt to remold the international system in order to strengthen the empire. This involved not just extending imperial sway, but also building up allies including with territorial gains, which thus became a means of informal empire for Britain. Thus, Italy was recruited with the promise, under the Treaty of London of 1915, of gains from Austria, including in Dalmatia; and Greece in 1917 by promised gains from Turkey. There was to be British intervention in Italy and Greece anew in 1943–5. Gains from the Turkish empire were also used to win Arab and Jewish support, and in May 1918, Arthur Balfour, the Foreign Secretary, referring to an Arab kingdom in the Hejaz, an Arab state in Iraq, and a Jewish "home" in Palestine, argued that "they will certainly give increased protection to British interests, both in Egypt and in India … buffer states."

Empire, both formal and informal, and for other powers as well as Britain, had, however, to be protected, extended and sustained both during the war and after, and the latter in a difficult situation wherein religion and nationalism were shaped and expressed in part as responses to empire and to state-formation. This process recorded and developed tensions—in particular, imperial consolidation as well as opposition to it highlighted the status and future of those defined as minorities, and their relationship with the imperial power. The extent to which empire could rest on contradictory assumptions was also clear in many contexts. A lack of stability and certainty, however, was always part of the equation of imperial authority, while imperialism generally depended on intermediaries and did not preclude separate political identities, activities and initiatives on the part of the local population.

The war was followed not by a retreat of empire but by its advance, as the imperial ethos remained strong, and the British, in particular, saw the events of the war outside Europe as reflecting the value of empire. The defeat of Germany and its allies indeed carried the British empire to its maximum impact. Britain played a leading role in the peace conferences held in Paris, most importantly that with Germany that led to the Treaty of Versailles of 1919. Britain gained League of Nations' mandates for Tanganyika (German East Africa), part of Togo and a sliver of Cameroon, all conquered German territories in Africa, and for Nauru Island in the Pacific; while Australia, New Zealand and South Africa all made gains: German New Guinea as well as the Bismarck Archipelago; Western Samoa; and South-West Africa respectively. The policies of racial control seen in South Africa were extended to South-West Africa.

The partition of the Turkish empire led to British mandates over Palestine, Transjordan and Iraq; while, in 1914, Britain had already annexed Cyprus and made Egypt a protectorate, and in 1916 Qatar became independent from the Turks under British protection. British power along the Suez Canal route and in the Islamic world was now far stronger, while the British empire had made the greatest gains in Africa.

Ardent imperialists, such as Viscount Milner, Secretary of State for the Colonies in 1919–21 and Leo Amery, Milner's personal secretary at the Colonial Office and Secretary of State for the Colonies in 19254 to 1929, pressed for the further strengthening of the empire—partly in the hope that it would never be dragged into the Continental mire—and there were attempts to extend British influence and control. Hopes that Syria would be ruled by the pro-British Arab Hashemite dynasty, and that Britain would dominate "Arabia" were thwarted, but British influence increased in both Persia and Turkey, in the latter of which the victorious Allies staked out zones of influence. British forces, operating against the Communists in the Russian civil war that followed their coup in 1917, moved into the Caucasus, Central Asia, and the White Sea region, and were deployed in the Baltic and the Black Sea. And in 1919, Curzon, now Foreign Secretary, advocated control over parts of the former Russian empire, a policy seen as a forward-defense for India.

Such ambitions could not be sustained, and the high tide of empire was to ebb very fast. The strain of the war, the men lost, the money spent, and the exhaustion produced by constant effort, was heavy enough, and it had left a burdensome debt, such that Britain had been transformed from the world's leading creditor nation to its greatest debtor. Britain's difficulties were exacerbated by political division, an absence of stable leadership, and the re-emergence of pre-war problems, and as a sign of insecurity (and paranoia) there was also concern that Britain's imperial position was the target of wide-ranging conspiracies, both Communism and pan-Islamicism.[8] The expansion of imperial rule and Britain's international commitments both involved intractable problems. Armed intervention in Russia, which had been supported by Churchill, Secretary of State for War in 1919–21, was a failure and was abandoned in 1919. It had been opposed by left-wingers sympathetic to the Communists, and by conscripts eager for demobilization, but failed, essentially, because of the difficulty of the task.

In the Middle East, revolts in Egypt (1919) and Iraq (1920–1) helped lead Britain to grant their independence in 1922 and 1932, respectively, although maintaining considerable influence in both, in what was to be a successful exercise in informal empire.[9] The Third Afghan War in 1919 underlined the difficult situation on the North-West Frontier, where there was a revolt in Waziristan, while there were also serious disturbances in Punjab that year. British influence collapsed in Persia in 1921, when the pro-British Shah was overthrown by Reza Khan, who exploited nationalist sentiment and was to become the first of the new rulers of the Pahlevi dynasty, while, in the Chanak crisis of 1922, the government backed down in its confrontation with the nationalists in Turkey led by Kemal Ataturk.

Arthur Griffith-Boscawen, Minister of Agriculture, wrote, during the Chanak crisis, "I don't believe the country cares anything about Thrace," and, among the Dominions, only Newfoundland and New Zealand pledged help, a sign that optimistic British assumptions about the attitude of the Dominions—for example, those of Milner—required revision as they increasingly asserted their independence in policy-making. In Britain, the bulk of the Cabinet also rejected the willingness of Lloyd George and Churchill, Secretary of State for the Colonies in 1921–2, to risk war, and the crisis helped precipitate the fall of the coalition government headed by the former. His Conservative successor as Prime

Minister, Andrew Bonar Law, who had been born in New Brunswick (his father was a Presbyterian clergyman from Ulster), argued that Britain "cannot alone act as policeman of the world."[10]

The loss of most of Ireland was also a major blow to imperial self-confidence: The empire began at home. This was not a failure at the periphery, and at the hands of a totally alien population, but right at the center, in what had been a part of Britain for centuries and had been represented at Westminster since the Act of Union of 1800, so that the weakness of British imperialism when confronted by a powerful nationalist movement was cruelly exposed. World War One had destroyed the basis for the Irish Home Rulers, and in the 1918 general election 46.9 percent of the vote and 73 out of the 105 parliamentary seats—including most of those outside Ulster—were won by Sinn Féin party, nationalists who refused to attend Westminster and demanded independence: Unionists won 28.3 percent and the Home Rule Nationalists 21.7 percent. In 1919, a unilateral declaration of independence proclaiming an Irish Republic was issued by the Daíl Eireann, the revolutionary parliament of the Irish Parliament, and fighting broke out. British refusal to accept independence led to a civil war in which republicans were funded by the Irish diaspora, notably in America,[11] a stark instance of the "empire coming home" with harsh consequences. This civil war was ended by the Anglo-Irish Treaty of December 1921, which accepted both partition and effective independence (rather than Home Rule) for the new Irish Free State (Eire), which became the governing body over most of the island, excluding a large part of the province of Ulster in the north that remained part of the United Kingdom.

The Irish Free State became a self-governing Dominion within the empire, with a Governor-General appointed by the Crown, the same status, in the "Community of Nations known as the British Empire," as Australia, Canada, Newfoundland, New Zealand and South Africa. But the new Dominion was far more alienated from Britain and the empire than the others. The new "community" was called the British Commonwealth of Nations.

In India, the war had led to tension in the imperial relationship, in part because of resentment by some Indian soldiers of their treatment, as well as the impact in political and intellectual circles of notions of self-determination; but the disruption integral to war on this scale was more important, and there were also continued communal tensions. After the war, the Amritsar massacre of April 1919, when, in response to disturbances in the Punjab, General Dyer ordered (Indian) troops to fire on a demonstrating crowd, causing nearly 400 fatalities. This affected British authority by suggesting that it was inherently repressive. However, there was no simple duality of independence or control, and indeed, in 1919, under the Montagu-Chelmsford Reforms, a Government of India Act established the principle of diarchy in the provinces—namely, responsible self-government in certain areas of competence by Indian ministers under the supervision of provincial legislatures, while the British government retained finance and policy in its competence; this Act was a product of Liberal aspirations that were not shared by all Conservatives.

Across the range of imperial interests and commitments, despite major efforts, there was a lack of resources and will to sustain international ambitions, particularly schemes for imperial expansion. Such schemes were expensive, but, as after previous wars, retrenchment and judging between commitments were increasingly the order of the day. The cuts recommended by the Geddes Committee in 1922—the "Geddes Axe"—hit military expenditure most heavily. Yet it would be inappropriate to focus only on problems, for, at one level, the picture was one of continued strength, certainly in comparison with the other European powers, France, and, even more, Germany and Russia that had suffered much more from the war. The scuttling of the German High Seas Fleet at Scapa Flow on 21 June 1919 greatly increased the relative strength of the British navy, not least because under the Versailles peace settlement Germany was denied permission to build a new fleet.

America had now replaced Britain as the world's leading creditor, but American isolationism helped to mask the political consequences of the shift of financial and economic predominance, while the commitment to the new international order advocated by President Woodrow Wilson was rejected by the Senate and was unwelcome to his three Republican successors. Britain was able to manage its relations with America without excessive difficulties, in part because Britain accepted American and not Japanese views on relative naval strength. As a minor but indicative imperial instance, longstanding rival British and American claims over the coral atolls of Canton and Enderbury in the Phoenix Islands in the Pacific became a source of serious dispute from 1936, but an agreement of 1939 led to joint administration without prejudice to the claims of either. In 1979, control passed to Kiribati as part of the general process of decolonialization. There was a separate dispute over Hull Island, but it was also brought under the condominium and eventually transferred to Kiribati.

It is also important to put problems in the empire in perspective. As another instance of the process seen in North America in 1783, the loss of the bulk of Ireland did not herald the collapse of other links within the British Isles, nor any serious pressures in them. There were revolutionaries within the area under British rule opposed to empire and there were related imperial concerns, for example about terrorism,[12] but across the breadth of military correspondence, the overall emphasis was rather on external threats, and notably so from 1922. The non-cooperation movement in India led by Mahatma Gandhi ebbed in effectiveness from 1922, the Indian army enabled Britain to discharge its military commitments (especially in Iraq) without conscription, and in Egypt, Britain retained control of the Suez Canal zone, as well as of defense and foreign affairs. In 1923, Britain transferred the Ross Sea Dependency in Antarctica and in 1926 the Tokelau Islands in the Pacific, but to Australia and New Zealand, respectively. Financial strength was suggested by Britain's return to the Gold Standard (convertibility of sterling with gold) in 1925, a measure actively pressed by Churchill, then Chancellor of the Exchequer from 1924 to 1929, as a sign of imperial power, and Britain remained the world's leading shipper.

There was also a strengthening of empire, especially a deepening of imperial control as areas that, earlier, had been often only nominally annexed were brought under at least some colonial government. Thus, in southern Sudan, posts were established by Arab troops under British officers, and military patrols were launched, while road-building improved the British position on the North-West Frontier of India. The more independent, even buccaneering, stage and style of imperialism was ended as state control increased. Thus, a Privy Council decision that Southern Rhodesia belonged to the British Crown and not to the British South

Africa Company led in 1923 to Southern Rhodesia becoming a self-governing colony, while Northern Rhodesia passed in 1924 under the control of the Colonial Office as a protectorate, although the Company continued to control mineral rights and much land.

This deepening of control, however, challenged the processes of accommodation by which Britain had won local support for, or at least compliance with, imperial rule, and added an often unwelcome important political, administrative and military dimension to this rule. Thus, the stationing of a large garrison in Waziristan as part of the pacification that followed the 1919 revolt helped provoke a new, and more intractable, revolt in 1936.

There were also important economic changes in parts of the empire, many of them linked to attempts to control the environment, for example by introducing irrigation schemes, as in Sudan where the drive begun in 1900 to use the Gezira plain for the cultivation of cotton was pressed with the construction of an expensive irrigation scheme that was officially opened in 1926. This served to produce a cash crop designed to further the imperial economy, and was therefore an example of the process by which distant regions were more intensely integrated into the imperial economy. Prior to irrigation, the Gezira had been used to grow grain for the nearby city of Khartoum. There was also extensive investment in Indian irrigation. In the Pacific, the Phoenix Islands Settlement Scheme sought to move people from the Southern Gilbert Islands, where copra was to be cultivated. The project lasted until the settlements were evacuated in 1963.

Much British and imperial foreign investment in the inter-war period took place in the empire, for example copper-mining in Northern Rhodesia where large-scale mining began from 1924, notably by the Anglo-American Corporation of South Africa, and cotton and coffee production in Uganda, while, in Kenya, coffee had been grown commercially near Nairobi from 1901. The annexation of Tanganyika from Germany made possible a line from Cairo to the Cape, a project that had been facilitated in 1905 with the opening of a bridge over the Zambezi River near Victoria Falls. However, the task of extending the network was too great, due to the terrain, the stronger economic need for eastward rail links to Indian Ocean and Red Sea ports—for example from central Sudan to

Port Sudan, the rival possibilities provided by air and road services—and financial considerations.

In Africa, much investment was linked to the imposition of a White settler and company control that had a clear racial dimension, so that in Kenya both the African and the Indian population suffered discrimination, while White settlers extended their control over the land. The continuation in peacetime of the pass system introduced for Africans during the war was both indicative of attitudes and a cause of hostility, while the use of hut taxes to raise revenues, taxes per household, were unpopular, not least as they made it necessary to obtain cash. The annual report of the Colonial Office for Northern Rhodesia for 1924–5 noted that "the native's only means of finding money for his tax is through the service of the European."[13]

In Malaya, in contrast to Kenya, the development of a strong British presence in rubber and tin production was not affected by a White settler presence comparable to that in East Africa. British companies there benefited from the ready availability of investment capital and also from their easy access to international commercial networks, and the British role in industrial technology was also seen with the machinery used in tin production, especially for dredging. Similarly, in Ceylon (Sri Lanka) and Assam, there was no significant settler presence to accompany the developments of tea production successfully focused both on the distant metropolitan market and also benefiting from the demand for tea elsewhere in the empire, especially in the Dominions.

Economic and political integration within the empire was further pressed forward by the extension of new communication systems, including the railways along which the goods already referred to were moved to the ports and the harbor facilities developed there. In Africa, the creation of new links was at a greater scale than had been the case prior to 1914. The war itself had led to the extension of rail links, especially that in 1915 built to link the rail system of South West Africa with that of South Africa. Major Sudanese rivers were affected by sudd (blockages of vegetation), but these were attacked, a process helped after World War One by the use of mechanical dredgers. In Sudan, new port facilities were constructed at Port Sudan on the Red Sea and on the rivers, while the railway system, initially built to help the conquest, was greatly extended.

New air routes pioneered by Imperial Airways, a company founded with government support in 1924, linked the empire to Britain, and the Britain to Australia airmail service began in 1932: It owed much to the development of the Cairo to Baghdad Air Mail Service by the Royal Air Force in the early 1920s. Weekly flights from London began to Cape Town (1932), Brisbane (1934) and Hong Kong (1936). It took nine days to fly to Cape Town in 1936, and fourteen for Adelaide, but these were far shorter than sailing times. However, liner services were also very important to imperial links, while the Empire Air Mail Scheme launched by Imperial Airways with the support of the Air Ministry, with the first service to Alexandria, beginning December 1936, required subsidies and was reliant on flying boats that were readily damaged.[14]

Air and sea services helped further the integration of British and colonial élites, sustaining mutual interest, and ensuring the neo-Britishness that was characteristic of settler life. Thus, these services were used by sports teams and touring theatrical companies, as well as officials and businessmen. This partial integration of élites was also seen in India where, by the 1930s, tennis parties, some of the less exclusive clubs, and horse-racing provided venues where the upper levels of Anglo-Indian society mingled easily with their Indian counterparts.[15]

As a reminder of the continual need to approach topics carefully, air power was also an aspect of a focus of empire on control through force. Aircrafts were used against Afghanistan in 1919 and to help suppress opposition in both British Somaliland and Iraq in 1920, a policy very much encouraged by Churchill, successively as Secretary for War and Air (1918–21) and for the Colonies (1921–2). So also with operations in Jordan, Sudan, Aden, Iraq, and on the Northwest Frontier in 1921–31. The cause of "air control" was pushed hard. In 1921, the Gold Medal Prize essay of Britain's prominent Royal United Services Institute (RUSI) went to Flight Lieutenant C.J. Mackay for "The Influence in the Future of Aircraft upon Problems of Imperial defense." Published in the *RUSI Journal* the following year, this contribution was followed by numerous articles, especially in that leading periodical, on the potential of aircraft, including on their ability to bring rapid victory by the use of gas.[16] The policy was enacted for the British public notably in the mock bombing attack on an "enemy village" at the Hendon Air Display of

1921. This was an aspect of empire as drawing psychological energy and a sense of possibility from technology, something seen earlier with ocean-going wooden warships, steamships, railways and telegraph lines.[17]

A different social dimension of official British imperialism was captured by the Antarctic Place Names Committee established in 1932 in order to ensure that British maps at least reflected official views. Among categories excluded were names of existing territories, towns or islands, names in any foreign language, names of sledge dogs, "names in low taste," and "names with obscure origins."[18]

More prominent institutions sought to foster imperial links, as well as the empire in British consciousness. On Empire Day every year, schools staged pageants and displays, souvenirs were issued, and large parades were held in Hyde Park. The British Empire Exhibition in 1924–5, for which Wembley Stadium (with its trademark towers demolished in 2003) was built in 1923, was a major public occasion, celebrated in the press and the newsreels, and by a set of stamps, and another Empire Exhibition followed in Glasgow in 1938. The Empire Marketing Board, established in 1926 by Leo Amery, the Colonial Secretary, sought to encourage trade within the empire as a substitute for Protectionism, but was abolished in 1933 when imperial preference replaced free trade.[19]

Other links included assisted emigration, especially by the Oversea Settlement Committee and the Society for the Oversea Settlement of British Women; it was hoped that these women would marry and produce children in whom a love of Britain would be instilled, and that they would ensure the purchase of British goods.[20] The settlement of demobilized soldiers in the empire was seen as a means to reduce pressure on jobs in Britain. Child emigration schemes, which continued until 1967, and led to a formal governmental apology in 2010, made sense in terms of a "Greater Britain" conceptualization of imperial nationhood.[21]

In relative terms, emigration to the empire became more important, in part because of American restrictions on immigration enacted in 1921 and 1924; which also hit trans-Atlantic passenger traffic, and encouraged the passenger lines to try to develop cruising. In New Zealand, assisted immigration resumed after World War One and continued until 1927, with the two categories most in demand being men ready to act as farm laborers and women ready to be domestic servants. Meanwhile, in Canada, immigration revived after World War One, although it did not reach its 1909–13 peak, and anyway collapsed with the Great Depression of the 1930s. However, in South Africa immigration from the Commonwealth was greater outweighed by the consequences of a high birthrate among Afrikaners.[22]

The awarding of British university degrees through extension courses, with London University external degrees being the award in many university colleges across the empire, was another significant link that was particularly important for those seeking to use education in order to better themselves. Other educational links included the use of British school examination boards, the role of British publishers in the empire, and the hiring of teachers and academics trained in Britain, and these combined to focus educational advancement in British models and to ensure that what was seen as British civilization was actively studied at schools as well as accepted and endorsed by officials, businessmen and academics.[23] The British Whiggish notion of organic constitutional development and political change in stages could then by extension be applied to change within the empire.

The royal family was a potent symbol of imperial partnership, and the accessions to the throne of Edward VIII and George VI successively in 1936, the first since that of George V in 1910, provided powerful images of continuity, and were also used to define the empire as a distinct political form. Imperial tours by members of the royal family—such as that by George VI to Canada in 1939, the first to Canada and Newfoundland by a reigning sovereign—were seen as important ways to sustain the spirit of empire. Another link with the empire was provided by the Governors-General of the Dominions, such as John, Viscount Jellicoe, who served in New Zealand in 1920–4, and John Buchan, Lord Tweedsmuir, who served in Canada in 1935–40.

Imperial federation was an influential idea in this period. Its origins can be traced back to the late-nineteenth century, and the development of the notion of a Commonwealth—unity in independence—proved useful in maintaining the support of the Dominions. Aside from Canada, Newfoundland, Australia (1901) and New Zealand (1907), this group had been expanded when the search for reconciliation after the Boer War led to the formation of the Union of South Africa in 1910. The constitution gave power over the whole of South Africa to the Afrikaners, a form of responsible government that was very much a "White" solution, and which bitterly disappointed the hopes in the British Crown held by some Black leaders. In contrast, in the 1920s, Māori leaders had greater success in obtaining redress for grievances when they approached the Crown, several, such as Tahupōtiki Wiremu Rātana in 1924, traveling to London.

An imperial conference in 1926 defined the Commonwealth as "the group of self-governing communities composed of Great Britain and the Dominions," and this formed the basis for the Statute of Westminster (1931), which determined that Commonwealth countries could now amend or repeal "any existing or future act of the United Kingdom Parliament ... in so far as the same is part of the law of this Dominion." "A common allegiance to the Crown" was seen as characteristic of the "freely associated members of the British Commonwealth of Nations."

This notion of devolved empire did not, however, settle the question of India, which was not a Dominion, while Irish national sentiment was not satisfied with the Dominion status that followed the treaty of 1921. Ireland was a prime instance of the extent to which, alongside the pretense of imperial coherence and consistency, there was much in the form of exceptions, ambiguities, and a response to circumstances on the ground, not least in the form of the complexity of the definition, framework and practice of British nationality and of the demands placed upon them.[24]

These disparate elements interacted to create not only an awareness of imperial identity but also a sense of imperial partnership, camaraderie, even nationalism. When on 11 October 1924, a *Times* editorial criticized the British government of Ramsay Macdonald, the first Labor Prime Minister, it referred to the need to "place first and foremost the interests of the British empire." Rudyard Kipling, a keen defender of empire, found the celebration at Westminster Abbey in 1927 of the Diamond Jubilee of the Canadian Confederation a positive "step on the threshold of a new life and self-knowledge for the Dominion and the Empire."[25]

Imperial partnership, however, was not free from tensions and the impact of other identities. These tensions varied, many stemming from activities that otherwise provided imperial links, not least the crisis in Anglo-Australian relations in 1932–3 over the "bodyline" cricket tour, as aggressive English bowling aroused Australian anger. However, the spread of cricket not only to the Dominions, but also to South Asia and the West Indies, in both of which there were few White settlers and where the sport lastingly spread beyond their number, indicated the way in which empire served to disseminate cultural norms and models.[26] More generally, acculturation worked best at the level of colonial élites, but was not only effective at that level.

Defense was an area of imperial cooperation, although it was not without tension. Visiting Australia in 1919, Jellicoe, who had been First Sea Lord, was made aware of opposition to subsuming the Australian navy into an imperial force and of Australian reluctance to spend more on the navy. Indeed, the Dominions benefited from the cover provided by British military strength, which enabled them to feel safe with only modest expenditure on defense, so that the Canadian navy was greatly run down after World War One. At the Imperial Conferences of 1923 and 1926, the Canadian Prime Minister, William Mackenzie King, made it clear that his country would not fight in a war simply at Britain's behest, but, instead, that its interests had to be at stake and that the Canadian Parliament would play a crucial role in validating this.

The limited provision by the Dominions for defense contributed greatly to the more general military vulnerability of the empire that became apparent in the 1930s. Moreover, the Commonwealth failed to develop workable processes for effective cooperation on defense and international relations. Although the threat posed by rising Japanese power was appreciated in the 1930s, there was no effective response by the Dominions.

Meanwhile, economic relations between Britain and the Dominions were a major source of disagreement, not least because economic problems were encouraging a general move toward protectionism. This was seen as a way to develop the Commonwealth, and lobby groups, such as the Empire Industries Association launched in 1925, pushed the case for protectionism, but the relationship between Britain and the Dominions within such a system was a matter for controversy, as the latter wished to protect their industries from British competition, and were concerned that free trade within the empire would harm them. This was seen in shipping where non-Australian ships were banned from Australia's coastal trade.

The response was Imperial Preference, a cause championed from 1929 by the Canadian-born press baron Lord Beaverbrook in his "Crusade" for Empire Free Trade, and eventually established in agreements reached at the Imperial Economic Conference held at Ottawa in 1932. These involved bilateral understandings on a large number of products; although British exporters benefited less than Dominion producers, because while the Dominions raised tariffs on non-British imports, they were unwilling to cut tariffs on British imports as they feared the impact on Dominion producers. The Ottawa agreement was a cautious arrangement that contrasted with the bold views of Leo Amery who pressed for a common economic policy and currency, but was not to return to office until 1940. Nevertheless, the agreement was promising, especially in light of rising protectionism elsewhere during the Depression of the 1930s, while the tension and lack of warmth shown at Ottawa—an Imperial Conference that was far less harmonious than those of the 1920s––suggested that it would be difficult to achieve more. The protectionism introduced in Britain with the general 10 percent tariff under the Import Duties Act of 1932 that brought an end to free trade was made more politically acceptable by Imperial Preference; but its essential thrust was concern about the economic position in Britain.

Thanks to Imperial Preference, the empire became more important to Britain, although the important growth of motor car and white goods manufacture in Britain in the 1920s and 1930s did not depend on colonial products or markets. Import substitution in some colonies, such as India, hit British export markets,[27] while in Canada this was related to the spread of American-owned branch-plant operations,[28] and British exports to the empire fell in value; but, as those to the remainder of the world fell even more during the Depression, the empire took 49 percent of British exports in 1935–9, compared with 42 percent a decade earlier. In the late 1930s, the British exported more to South Africa than to the more self-sufficient and protectionist America.

Instead of thinking primarily in terms of the global economy theoretically made possible by free trade, British policymakers were increasingly thinking in terms of an economic bloc led by Britain, in which the Dominions played a major role, and that operated as a sterling area. Stanley Baldwin, Conservative Prime Minister in 1935–7, and Neville Chamberlain, his successor in 1937–40, and the Chancellor of the Exchequer in 1931–7, both thought in these terms. Until the 1967 devaluation of sterling, the currencies of most Commonwealth countries, bar Canada, were fixed in value relative to sterling, and they conducted their international trade in sterling, and many of these states held large sterling balances, which helped support the currency and thus the financial stability of Britain and its government. This emphasis on the empire was linked to a political assertiveness that presented the British empire as a leading world power that enjoyed coherence and had distinct political interests. The economic benefits of empire helped justify the strategic consequence of imperial commitments, not least the need to consider how best to defend the interests in the Middle East, the presence in South-East Asia, and the route to Australasia; these commitments also potentially represented a serious overreach that would pose a major problem in responding to particular crises.

The value of imperial control and association was indicated by the degree to which economic ties in the "informal empire" faced serious difficulties in the inter-war period. In Latin America, American businesses made major inroads, while in China British cotton goods exports were hit by Japanese competition and by the development of Chinese production. China had already become more assertive as a republic, with the rise of nationalism making foreign interests a conspicuous target and was also harder to manage because of its acute divisions. In 1927, the British played a major role in the international deployment of warships and troops to protect the International Concession at Shanghai from Chinese nationalists, but the concessions in Hankou and Jiujiang were abandoned in 1927 after massive public protests overawed the local British military presence: a Chinese trade unionist was killed in each city by British troops, but, whereas, in 1925, the position in Hankou had been underpinned by local warlords, in 1927 there was no such backing.[29] In Saudi Arabia, the negotiation in 1933 of an agreement with the American company Standard Oil was a vital step in the development of a powerful American presence.

There were also significant political issues in some parts of the empire, although these were not necessarily a matter of hostility or even resistance, but often of the reconciliation of differing views. Thus, the Dominions had their own territorial interests, notably Australia and South Africa.[30] In certain colonies, there was a growth or revival of anti-imperial feeling that was related to indigenous notions of identity and practices of resistance, many of them central to a peasant culture of non-compliance with ruling groups. New organizations, such as the All-India Muslim League, founded in 1906, the National Congress of British West Africa (1920), the Young Kikuyu Association in Kenya (1921), and the African National Congress in South Africa (1923), fostered demands for change, and drew on the activism of individuals educated in new institutions established by the government, in part to provide officials. In colonies such as India and Jamaica, administrators and officers had for a long time been concerned as to how best to control populous territories with very small forces; and the military strength available was seen as the crucial support of a moral authority on which rule and control rested. The extent to which this authority was accepted by the colonized in the nineteenth century should not be exaggerated, but there is little doubt that it was far more under challenge by the inter-war years.

British rule confronted serious problems in a number of colonies. In part, this was an aspect of the way in which empire was never a pacified or finished product, so that, and notably for colonies gained from the late nineteenth century, the imperial project and decolonization were concurrent, or at least greatly overlapped. In addition, the combination of opposition in the colonies and financial problems in Britain ensured that colonies became harder to administer and difficult to provide sufficient resources for. The Saya San rebellion in Burma of 1930–2 owed much to the impact of the Depression on rice production and to a drive to introduce Buddhist control.[31] There was also considerable trouble along and near the axis of British empire in the Mediterranean. Greek Cypriot nationalists rioted in 1931. In Malta, where self-government was granted in 1921, the British were opposed by the Nationalist Party, the constitution suspended in 1930–2, and withdrawn in 1933, rendering Malta again a Crown Colony. Arab action in Palestine—a pogrom in 1929, a general strike in 1936, and a rebellion in 1937—were largely directed against Jewish immigration. The rebellion was suppressed and did not have political consequences in Britain comparable to the question of the future of India. However, there was concern about the impact of growing Arab nationalism, and in 1939 anxiety about the developing international crisis led to the issue of a White Paper designed to defuse this nationalism by rejecting the idea of partition for Palestine between Jews and Arabs. The use of force and of surveillance in Palestine indicated the extent to which policies of divide and rule, and the co-option of élites were not sufficient to ensure political control,[32] and, to a varying extent, the same was true in other colonies.

The differing ability of local societies to cope with the pressures of change and economic difficulties exacerbated contrasts within and between colonies and created a range of problems for colonial governments. Economic developments and tensions helped cause political problems across society. In India, as elsewhere, rent disputes provided a close link between economic troubles and political division. The Depression of the 1930s reduced investment for colonial development, limiting the resources available to provide jobs at all levels, while the decline in markets for colonial goods—minerals, food and plantation products—hit local financial systems, cutting off credit and investment. As a result, social tensions became more potent: In the Gold Coast (modern Ghana), there were agrarian disputes linked to cocoa production in 1930–1 and 1937–8, and in Jamaica, where unemployment was high, labor tensions were linked to activism by the League of Coloured Peoples and, in 1938, helped cause a serious crisis.[33] In both the formal and the informal empire (for example, Argentina) there was an anti-liberal nationalism that criticized Britain's economic role for allegedly causing serious problems.

The growing strength of the non-violent Indian National Party created the most serious political problem. Gandhi's non-violent criticism of British rule, in particular his flouting of the tax on salt in 1930, led, in Britain, to uneasiness about the imperial position; although visual confidence was expressed in the majestic buildings designed by Sir Edwin Lutyens and Sir Herbert Baker for the official quarter in New Delhi finished in the 1930s, these buildings are now the focus of socio-cultural criticism by the Modi government.

There was a general sense among policymakers that empire had to change, and that reform of the government of India was, alongside Imperial Trade Preference and more equal relations with the Dominions, the best means to strengthen the empire. It was to that end that Amery, an ardent imperialist, supported the Government of India Act in 1935, while Lord Irwin (later Earl of Halifax), the Viceroy of India, backed eventual Dominion status for India.

The British government sought a legislative response to pressures for change in India, and although designed to ensure British retention of the substance of power, the Act of 1935 moved toward self-government. Dyarchy was extended to central government, while, as an aspect of modernization, the Act proposed the creation of an All-India Federation, an incorporation of the hitherto autonomous princely states, although opposition by most of the princes ensured that this was not implemented. A section of the Conservative Party, led by Churchill (excluded from office from 1929) bitterly opposed the 1935 Act, seeing the moves toward self-government as a crucial step to the abandonment of empire. For Churchill, the new policy on India was more than a tactical step, and he offered an apocalyptic vision of its consequences that, however, appeared impractical and out of place to many.[34] Churchill was not alone. The Indian Empire Society, under the presidency of John, Viscount Sumner (1859–1934), a key spokesman of the Conservative diehards, who had voiced unpopular views on the Amritsar massacre of 1919 and the Irish settlement of 1921, campaigned vigorously; but Baldwin, the Conservative leader, was no friend of the diehards. The Viceroy of India described Churchill as an "Imperialist in the 1890–1900 sense of the word," and that sense now appeared less relevant. The bitterness of the parliamentary rebellion against the 1935 Act was a testimony to the continued pull of traditional notions of empire and the rebels' sense of danger, but also to their failure. Ultimately, the provincial elections of 1937 in India were a success for the Indian National Congress.[35]

Another sign of changing attitudes was provided by sensitivity to Indian opinion in the films shown there. In 1938, *The Relief of Lucknow*, a proposed film dealing with an iconic episode in the Indian Mutiny, was banned by the India Office, as were later moves to film stories from the Mutiny, and, in 1939, the American film *Gunga Din* was prohibited following opposition to its showing by Indian newspapers. This led to the issue of guidelines by the India Office that banned films based on episodes in the history of British India, adaptations of Kipling, and films that presented Indians as villains.[36] However, the continued market for empire among the British public was seen with films such as *Sanders of the River* (1935), an account of a heroic District Commissioner in Nigeria who aligns with a benign tribal chief, *The Drum* (1938), which was based on A.E.W. Mason's 1937 novel of that name in which rebellion on the North-West Frontier is thwarted with the help of a loyal Indian prince, and *The Four Feathers* (1939), the last based on A.E.W. Mason's novel of 1902, with empire a place of redemption.

Empire was changing at its closest point. In Ireland, relations between the Free State and Britain remained good and offered another aspect of the co-ownership of empire until the Fianna Fáil party under Éamon de Valera gained power after the 1932 election. He successfully pressed the British to recall the Governor-General James McNeill, and the new one, Domhnall Ua Buachalla, a veteran of the Easter Rising, nominated by de Valera, undertook no public duties; while the Executive Authority (External Relations) Act of 1936 limited the role of the Crown in the Free State to diplomatic formalities, and then only as advised by the Executive Council. After coming to power, de Valera set off an "Economic War" with Britain by suspending the payment of land annuities from Irish farmers to the British government. A cycle of retaliation led to protectionism by both sides, hitting Irish agricultural exports to Britain, and the "war" was ended by agreement in 1938, as part of which the three deep-water treaty ports Britain had continued to control were handed over. This was criticized by Churchill who correctly presented the ports as essential to the security of the Atlantic trade routes. The previous year, a new constitution, passed after a referendum, asserted the Irish state's territorial claim to Northern Ireland, while the oath of allegiance to the Crown that MPs had been obliged to take under the Anglo-Irish Treaty of 1921 was abolished. The constitution was republican, described the Irish State, now rechristened Eire (Ireland), as a "sovereign independent, democratic state," and stipulated that the head of state was to be a directly-elected President; and Irish was to be the first language, an important declaration of cultural independence.

In September 1938, conscious of numerous British global commitments, the Chiefs of Staff warned about the dangers of becoming entangled in major military action on the continent against Germany.[37] In the event, in World War Two, it was the empire that repeatedly provided vital assistance for embattled Britain, especially before American entry in December 1941 but also thereafter. The outbreak of war had been followed by the convoying of Australasian troops to Egypt, providing a crucial fill-up to the British strategic reserve in the Middle East. The convoys were escorted by Australian warships, while the five destroyers in the Australian fleet had been sent to join the British fleet in the Mediterranean at the outset of the war. In 1940, at a time of threatened German invasion, the presence of Canadian forces, successfully convoyed across the Atlantic the previous winter, greatly strengthened the ability to repel attack. Canadian and New Zealand pilots played an important role in the Battle of Britain, while the Canadian navy also took the major role in convoying ships in the western Atlantic. Over five million fighting troops were raised by the empire during the war, the largest number in India; while the absence of large-scale sustained opposition within the colonies to British rule ensured that military resources could be concentrated on war with the Axis.

The empire also provided strategic depth. When, in the House of Commons on 4 June 1940, Churchill pledged to fight on, he added that, even if Britain was conquered, "our Empire beyond the seas, armed and guarded by the British Fleet, would carry on the struggle" until America joined in. This echoed the assurance offered by Edward Gibbon in his *History of the Decline and Fall of the Roman Empire* (1776–88) that, in the unlikely event of civilization collapsing in Europe before new barbarian inroads, it would be sustained "in the American world."[38]

Dominion and empire forces were given a bigger role as a result of Italy's entry into the war on 10 June 1940 and Japan's on 7 December 1941. Benito Mussolini, Italy's Fascist dictator, sought gains from the British empire, as well as from France and in the Balkans, and Admiral Domenico Cavagnari, the Chief of the Italian naval staff, had planned a fleet able to seize control of both ends of the Mediterranean, so that it would operate on the oceans. Mussolini's ambitions, however, were not based on a reasonable assessment of the capabilities of the Italian military machine, and Dominion and empire forces played a major role in resisting Italian attacks, and then in invading Italian colonies. In East Africa, larger Italian forces overran British Somaliland in August 1940, but on a larger scale a poorly-prepared and commanded invasion of Egypt from the Italian colony of Libya was mounted hesitantly, stalled, and was then routed in December 1940 by the British forces. The Italians were then driven out of Egypt, before the British went on to conquer Cyrenaica (eastern Libya), taking large numbers of prisoners. The Australians played a prominent role in the operations in Libya, while the decision of Churchill to send tanks (that were a key part of Britain's strategic reserve) to Egypt was important to the success of operations in North Africa, and, like the movement of Dominion and empire forces there, it reflected the benefit of controlling the sea-lanes. This was also seen in East Africa. In February 1941, British forces (mostly from East, South and West Africa) outfought the more numerous Italians in British and Italian Somaliland, and this was followed by the conquest of Ethiopia.

This was part of the expansion of British imperial influence and power, direct and indirect, that was seen in the war, and notably so before America's entry into the conflict. With neutral Denmark rapidly conquered by the Germans in April 1940, Iceland, a sovereign kingdom in personal union with Denmark, declared neutrality, but the British occupied Iceland next month to pre-empt German moves. So also with the conquest of Lebanon, Syria, Iraq and southern Iran,[39] and with the consideration of moves to occupy the Canaries, the Azores and the Cape Verde Islands. Here were echoes of British conduct during the French Revolutionary and Napoleonic Wars.

If victory over Japan in 1942–5, particularly at sea and in the air, was primarily an American triumph, and a key aspect of the way in which America dominated the Anglo-American alliance,[40] this had important implications for Australasia and the British colonies in the Pacific as the war saw a marked increase in the American military presence in the Dominions and the colonies. This was a matter not only of bases and the presence of troops, warships and planes, but also of defense-planning. Although there was tension, not least over the role of America in the South-West Pacific,[41] the war ended with closer strategic relations between America and both Australia and Canada, while economic and strategic links between the Dominions and Britain became less important. The development of industries in Canada and Australasia was linked to a longer-term decline in dependence on imports of British manufactures, while, more generally, their economies and societies changed. Although this stemmed from the imperial war, the growing size of the economies and governments of the Dominions lessened the role of Britain. War also brought a fluidity in assumptions and relations and a decline in deference in the latter that affected attitudes toward imperial links. The pressures of the war were felt differently across the empire, with "Home Fronts" registering the fortunes and exigencies of the war in a way that could encourage irritation and anger as well as fellow-feeling and cooperation, and sometimes at the same time.[42]

More seriously for Britain, the Roosevelt administration was opposed to colonial rule and, instead, in favor of a system of "trusteeship" as a prelude to independence. Roosevelt pressed Churchill on the status of both Hong Kong (which he wanted returned to China) and India, and British officials were made well aware of a fundamental contradiction in attitudes. In 1943, at the Tehran conference, Roosevelt told Churchill that Britain had to adjust to a "new period" in global history and to turn their back on "400 years of acquisitive blood in your veins."[43] This was an aspect of a different national ideology as well as a competitive imperialism aimed at supplanting Britain.

There were indeed major changes in the colonies. In India, which provided the bulk of the troops for the Malaya and Burma campaigns, there was an upsurge in volunteering and the Indian Army became a million strong in 1942, and two and a half million strong by 1945, the largest volunteer army in history. The British changed their military policies to encourage both the recruitment of traditional "non-martial" races, notably from southern India, and a degree of Indianization of the officer corps. At the same time, the war witnessed an increase in agitation for independence.

The Quit India movement of 1942 spearheaded by the Congress Party (the Indian National Congress) was a serious crisis for British rule, with a series of rural rebellions, mainly in eastern India. The British responded by arresting senior Congress leaders, after which the movement became more violent, hindering the operation of British authority. However, the Quit India movement did not encompass all of India, and it was suppressed. India in 1942–5 was no repeat of the Thirteen Colonies in 1775–83: There was less dissidence, and the Japanese could not play the role of the French. The Japanese-backed Provisional Government of Free India that was formed by the Indian nationalist Subhas Chandra Bose in October 1943, was granted administrative control of the Andaman and Nicobar islands the following month; while a pro-Japanese government was granted titular independence in Burma in August 1943, but Bose's Indian National Army made little impact.[44] The Viceroy, Field Marshal Archibald Wavell, who had responded promptly to serious food shortages, wrote in July 1944: "On the whole, India is getting along reasonably well in spite of the lack of interest in it on the part of the War Cabinet.... Once the Japanese war is over, our troubles out here really will begin."[45] As a sign of changing values, the canopy at India Gate in Delhi, which until 1968 had been occupied by a statue of George V installed in 1936, features since 2022 a statue of Bose, the Prime Minister Narendra Modi declaring at its dedication that it was an "example of the abandonment of a slavery mentality."

Aside from active dissidence, if not on occasion, as with Bose, treason, war more generally encouraged native politicization in colonies, for example Sudan. Furthermore, the experience of military service expanded horizons. The range of such service saw the repetition of accustomed tasks that in many respects affirmed racial and social hierarchies, for example the use of Basuto mule drivers for British mountain-artillery units in Italy, and, at the same time, a challenging of such hierarchies. Thus, officers from Bechuanaland found that their orders could be ignored by British NCOs, but such discrepancies led to tension and pressure for change,[46] as was also seen with demands that racist recruiting practices by the Royal Navy were ended.[47]

More generally, participation in the war altered relations within the empire, those between Britain and the Dominions and colonies, and those within each of these. This encouraged British leaders—political and military, army and navy—to argue that it was necessary to plot the course of operations in part to affirm the role of the empire and, in particular, that of Britain within it.[48]

The "informal empire" was also greatly affected by the war. The assertive British role in Egypt, which included the military intimidation of King Farouk in 1942, in order to make him accept a change in government, increased hostility to Britain's role. On 6 August 1945, Mahmoud El Nokrashy Pasha, the Prime Minister, pressed in the Senate for the withdrawal of British troops and the removal of restrictions on Egyptian independence. Meanwhile, Japan had destroyed the treaty port system in China and, thereafter, Communist triumph in the Chinese Civil War (1946–9) cemented the rejection of Western influence. In Latin America, British economic and political influence lessened as America became more powerful, while the war led to the slackening of British economic links, which encouraged a measure of industrialization.

Alongside the argument that Japanese success helped ensure the redundancy of the British imperial strategy in Asia (as well as that of the Dutch and French empires) and, crucially destroyed the empire's prestige, it is necessary to focus on the overall political and resource costs of the two world wars; as a result, Britain's post-war decision to abandon its colonial presence in South Asia can be seen as stemming in part from conflict within the European system, rather than as simply a response to the war with Japan or to growing indigenous pressure on Britain to "Quit India." Shrewd observers at the end of World War Two saw the weaknesses of empire, especially as Britain was financially exhausted.

Britain's empire was largely to have disappeared within two decades of the end of World War Two in 1945, one of the most important shifts of authority in global history, as well as an important aspect of the more general decline of Europe's place in the world; but such a result had seemed far from obvious, for just as World War One had ended with an expansion of empire, so it appeared likely that World War Two would be followed by the same, and, at least, that most of the empire would be retained. During the war, the French feared British designs on their empire, America was concerned that British military planning was overly directed to imperial goals, and the British occupied Italian Somaliland and Libya, both of which were seen as important for protecting the route to India. Churchill indeed considered the annexation of the latter (as well as the Kra isthmus from Thailand in order to protect Malaya), and there were hopes that it would be able to maintain wartime gains under the equivalent of League of Nation mandates. Italian Somaliland remained under British administration until 1950, while çontrol over Libya was partitioned between Britain and France with Britain gaining the lion's share: Cyrenaica and Tripolitania, which both gave Britain a military presence to the west of Egypt and extended her control over the shores of the Mediterranean to a greater extent than hitherto. Had the Germans had overseas colonies they would doubtless have met with a similar fate.

There were also hopes of a recovery of imperial military greatness, as the surrender of Japan was followed by the reimposition of control in occupied areas, including Malaya, Singapore and Hong Kong, and the return of the navy to Chinese waters[49]; while Britain joined Australia, India and New Zealand in contributing troops to the American-dominated occupation of Japan. British power in Asian waters also ensured that the British played a major role in the reintroduction of Dutch and French power into the Dutch East Indies and Vietnam, respectively, although the former commitment, which lasted until November 1946, led to conflict with Indonesian nationalists. Similarly, in 1944 the British had sent troops to Greece, in part to prevent a Communist takeover, and British support of the royalist government continued after the war.

British policy in Antarctica and the South Atlantic also indicated a continued desire to act as an imperial power: The creation of the Falkland Islands Dependencies Survey in 1945 signalled a determination to use scientists to consolidate influence, and the mapping of the Antarctic Peninsula and nearby areas carried out by the Survey was designed to underline Britain's title to the area. British maps omitted names found on Argentine and Chilean maps of the Antarctic Peninsula, and the cruiser HMS *Nigeria* was dispatched to Antarctic waters in 1948 in order to support British claims.

There were also plans for the extension of British power in South Asia. In 1946, Sir Francis Tucker, Head of Eastern Command in India, who was concerned about threats to India from the north, proposed a British protectorate over what he termed Mongol territory from Nepal to Bhutan. Sir Claude Auchinleck, Commander-in-Chief in India, had to explain that the idea was not realistic[50]; and this was also true of ideas about extending British influence in Tibet, and even Xinjiang, in order to maintain them as buffers between India and China; the China then seen as a threat was Kuomintang (Nationalist) China.[51]

Imperial expansion, indeed, now seemed anachronistic; at least when practiced overseas by Western European powers. The dominant role in the victorious coalition had been taken by America and the Soviet Union, both of which, albeit from different perspectives, had anti-colonial ideologies to match their imperialist policies and saw no reason to view the retention, still more expansion, of the British empire with any favor. Churchill's imperial perspectives had enabled him in 1943–5 to see the danger of Soviet domination of Eastern Europe, but Roosevelt could not grasp this and he thwarted Churchill's largely unrealistic call for Allied military advances into Southeast Europe. Under American pressure, the Atlantic Charter, issued by Churchill and Roosevelt in the Placentia Bay conference in August 1941, had declared "the right of all people to choose the form of government under which they will live," and the United Nations, which was founded in 1945, was to show favor for the notion of national self-determination.

The British empire was also challenged by internationalism from a different direction. The new international economic order was American-directed and a challenge to the "Imperial Preference" protectionism of the sterling bloc, and deliberately so. The Bretton Woods conference, held in America in 1944, produced plans for post-war cooperation that led to the foundation of the International Monetary Fund and the International Bank for Reconstruction and Development (World Bank), both of which had American headquarters. Free trade was also actively supported as part of an American-directed liberal economic order, and the General Agreement on Tariffs and Trade (GATT), signed in 1947, began a major cut in tariffs that slowly re-established free trade.

Despite these challenges, there was an attempt to protect, if not revive, the British empire, although this was more a matter of an imperial regionalism and geopolitical survivalism than the global vision the Americans were pursuing.[52] Empire was seen in the late 1940s as a crucial economic sphere and resource: Oil from the Middle East was increasingly valuable to the economy, the discriminatory tariffs of "Imperial Preference" were important to trade, and financial links helped maintain sterling.[53] Ernest Bevin, the influential Foreign Secretary in the Labor government from 1945 until 1951, was determined to preserve British military strength in the Middle East and hoped to use imperial resources to make Britain a less unequal partner in the Anglo-American alliance. There was an attempt to develop the economy of Tanganyika (now mainland Tanzania), with an ambitious—but totally misconceived, and consistently unsuccessful—Groundnuts Scheme designed to increase the supply of vegetable oils and fats within the sterling area, in order to cut imports from non-sterling countries, and thus to help maintain the level of the currency.[54] Similar hopes were built on African mineral resources, and these encouraged the belief that Britain did not need to join schemes for economic cooperation in Western Europe.

There was also an ethical dimension to the furtherance of empire. Although support for Indian independence played an important role in Labor Party circles, there was also a conviction, which drew on aspects of the liberal tradition—not least the nonconformist belief that there was a duty of care to protect the less fortunate—that imperial rule could serve the interests of the colonial peoples. Most were not regarded as developed and as ready for independence as the Indians.

The late 1940s became a struggle over control of the British system of empire, both formal and informal, notably in South Asia and the Middle East. In India, World War Two had helped undermine British rule, and post-war political volatility made it impossible to provide a level of stability sufficient to serve as the basis for a restoration of the processes of accommodation that ensured widespread consent. The rise of the Congress Party had challenged the British position, not least by hitting the effectiveness, business and morale of government, while the increased sectarianism of Indian politics, particularly with the rise of the Muslim League, made imperial crisis-management, let alone control, impossible. To the Muslims, in turn, the cause of Indian independence was compromised by Hindu sectarianism, and they called for partition. In response to the Muslim League's "Direct Action Day" of 16 August 1946, Wavell, the Viceroy, pressed for a show of consistency—namely, a commitment to ten more years of rule, or the fixing of a date for withdrawal. His replacement, Lord Louis Mountbatten, concurred, and it was agreed, in early 1947, that the British would transfer power in June 1948. The British hope for a quasi-federation of Muslim and Hindu India fell victim to an inability to reach compromises, leading to a reluctant agreement to partition; and the decision to bring forward withdrawal to August

1947 made it harder to contain communal violence. The end of empire in South Asia was marked by large-scale violence, and left a lasting dispute over Kashmir; although it is too easy to blame deep sectarian divides on British rule.

India had been the most populous and important part of the empire, and the area that most engaged the imaginative attention of the British, although it was not important to British emigration; and, once India had been granted independence, it was difficult to summon up much popular interest in the retention of the remainder of the empire. There had been talk of India only being given independence if it agreed to help in the defense of other imperial possessions, specifically Aden, Burma and Malaya, and an expectation that an independent India would accept a continued presence by British forces, or at least cooperate closely in military matters, but such hopes were totally misplaced. Indeed, unlike Britain, India was to be neutral in the Korean War (1950–3). In 1944, when post-war Indian independence seemed already likely, there had been consideration of separating off the Andaman Islands in the Bay of Bengal, so that imperial control and a naval base could be retained there, but this option was not pursued; as Britain still had bases at Mombasa and Singapore, it scarcely seemed necessary. There was postwar consideration of moving Anglo-Indians to the Andaman Islands, but this was not pursued and the islands were transferred to India in 1950.

Indian independence greatly affected British military options. India was important to British trade routes, especially to the Persian Gulf and the Strait of Malacca, but more significantly, Indian troops were important to Britain's expeditionary capacity around the Indian Ocean and in the Middle East. The loss of those troops removed an important mainstay of the military dimension of the empire. Whereas, in 1941, Indian forces had played a major role in the successful invasion of Iraq, a decade later, when Britain was in dispute with the nationalist government in Iran over its nationalization of British oil interests, Plan Y—the plan for a military intervention by the seizure of Abadan, the center of these interests—was not pursued, in large part because without Indian troops and with British forces committed in Germany and Korea it no longer seemed militarily viable.

Independence was also granted to Burma and Ceylon in 1948, as, with India independent, it seemed pointless to hang on to either. The result in Burma was unhappy from the British point of view, with regional separatism, political instability, military rule, and poor relations with Britain all rapidly following independence. The situation was happier in Ceylon (Sri Lanka), as democratic rule was established and British interests maintained by the Anglo-Ceylonese 1947 defense Agreement. Ceylon was subsequently held up as a model of decolonization, although, by the 1990s, Tamil separatism had undermined this conviction.

In Palestine, it proved impossible to suppress violence and to negotiate a peaceful end to the mandate, and the British presence was brought to a close in 1948, with the government keen to get an embarrassing problem off its hands. Tensions between Arabs and Jews, which the British were unable to contain, were made harder to manage by pressure on Britain from the pro-Zionist American government.

Less controversially, Crown Colony status for Newfoundland ended the following year; and a small majority in a referendum led to union with Canada. Also in 1949, Eire became a republic: The previous year, vestigial British authority had been tackled by the Republic of Ireland Act, which repealed the External Relations Act of 1936 and took Eire out of the Commonwealth. Proposing the Bill in the *Dáil*, John Costello, the Prime Minister, claimed it would "end forever, in a simple, clear and unequivocal way this country's long and tragic association with the institutions of the British Crown."

Unlike after the loss of America in 1783, that of India was not to be followed by imperial recovery, and, instead, the weakness of Britain as an imperial power was readily apparent. The war had exhausted her public finances and seriously damaged the economy, and this left her in a weaker position to sustain imperial commitments, while the wartime sale of overseas investments ensured that it would not be possible to use "invisible exports" in order to finance the serious trade deficit. In addition to these sales, the heavy costs of the war, like those of the conflicts in 1793–1815, had largely been financed on credit; but, unlike after 1815, there was to be no period of maritime dominance, imperial hegemony, and the absence of an expensive foreign challenge, to help ensure renewed fiscal stability. Instead, after 1945 there were a series of imperial crises and a confrontation with the Soviet Union in the "Cold War," both of which posed serious financial burdens. Furthermore, the American loan given to assist Britain when wartime Lend-Lease help ended in 1945 had been provided on condition that the pound be made convertible into the dollar, a measure that put pressure on the Bank of England's reserves. The sterling crises of 1947, when the currency's convertibility was hit hard, and April 1949 when there was a devaluation of 30 percent, underlined British weakness.

Due to these problems, the British had little to offer those whose cooperation they sought, for example in the Middle East, and it was felt necessary to seek American assistance in resisting Communist pressure in Greece and Turkey in 1947, and in Southeast Asia in 1949. The foundation of NATO (North Atlantic Treaty Organization) in 1949 was similarly a response to the need to rely on America in the face of Britain's concern to resist Soviet expansionism in the absence of effective Western European assistance.

Pushed onto the defensive, the British were also not in a good position to reassert themselves in areas of earlier imperial influence, such as China, although there the destruction of the Kuomintang (Nationalists) by the Communists in the Civil War of 1946–9 was the key element. That conflict involved the navy in the familiar task of protecting nationals and other interests. The frigate *Amethyst* was fired upon in the Yangzi River by Communist forces in 1949, but the British response was restricted to refloating the ship, which had run aground, and escaping downriver to the sea—a dramatic escape, but not one that maintained economic or political interests. The response offered to the provocation that had led to the First Opium War in 1839 seemed a world away.

Indeed, there had been a fundamental shift in Britain's political attitudes and military capability; and in the international context. A British national identity became stronger with empire ceasing to play a key role within it,[55] and with Greater Britain becoming less significant to the national image.[56] As a result, the recent world war was misleadingly seen by many as being a case of Britain alone, which represented a failure to give the empire the central role it had taken.[57]

When Churchill regained power at the head of a Conservative government in 1951 (the year in which the British withdrew from Libya), he had no intention of dismantling the empire, and, indeed, the Conservatives had fought the earlier 1950 election by urging the electors to "make Britain great again." In 1952, Britain became a nuclear power, as a policy initiated by the Labor government to give Britain an independent nuclear role was brought to fruition. More generally, there was a sense of greatness. The accession in 1952 and coronation in 1953 of Queen Elizabeth II led to talk of a "New Elizabethan Age," which was celebrated with a Coronation Review of the fleet. The Queen's broadcast to the Commonwealth after the coronation referred to

> "my peoples, spread far and wide throughout every Continent and ocean in the world ... united to support me ... the living strength and majesty of the Commonwealth and Empire, of societies old and new, of lands and races different in history and origins, but all, by God's will, united in spirit and in aim."

The ascent of hitherto unclimbed Mount Everest in 1953 by an imperial team contributed to this excitement, not least because the planned coincidence of timing ensured that the achievement was focused on the new monarch and reign. Separately, mountaineering in the Himalayas was linked to attempts to keep an eye on Chinese moves in Tibet, another stage of the Great Game.

Although global commitments were reduced in some areas in the early 1950s, elsewhere they were maintained, and even expanded, in order to demonstrate that Britain was not weak, to protect British interests and to enhance military capability in the event of war with the Soviet Union. However, these commitments put serious pressure on Britain's ability to maintain force levels in Europe, a goal that, in turn, challenged Britain's role as a military power outside Europe. From 1948, a major and successful military effort was made to resist a Communist insurrection in the economically crucial colony of Malaya, which it was hoped would serve as the basis for a Dominion of South-East Asia that would also include Sarawak, Singapore and North Borneo. British interest in Malaya owed much to the geopolitics of the conflict with Communism, but also to the importance of Malayan rubber and tin exports to America and the consequent value of the colony to the maintenance of the strengthening of the Sterling Area through dollar inflows.[58] Holding

Malaya was also a matter of protecting Singapore, which alongside Hong Kong continued to be significant for British strategy.[59]

British assertiveness also included, in late 1952, RAF overflights of Buraimi oasis, an oil-rich part of the Arabian peninsula, then in dispute between the British-backed Sultan Said bin Taimur of Oman and Saudi Arabia, which looked to American support, while, in Antarctica, the Churchill government funded expeditions to consolidate territorial claims.

No more colonies were granted independence under the Churchill ministry (1951–5), although in 1954 the government abandoned its military commitment over Buraimi, while, that year, British troops were withdrawn from the Suez Canal Zone after fighting two years earlier had indicated the cost of staying on. Also in 1954, Britain had to accept the liquidation of its oil interests in Iran, but further east Britain underlined its willingness to take an active role in collective defense when it became a founder member—with America, Australia, New Zealand, Pakistan, France, Thailand and the Philippines—of the South-East Asia Treaty Organization (SEATO).

In 1955, Britain agreed to transfer the Simon's Town naval base from British to South African control, a measure that Churchill had strongly opposed. Under the agreement, however, Britain retained important naval advantages, including South African agreement to make the base available to Britain in war, even if South Africa itself was neutral, as well as South African responsibility for the maintenance of the base, orders for warships from British yards, and acceptance of British views on the development of the South African navy. Significantly, the British had earlier hoped to win a South African commitment to the defense of the Middle East, but this did not play a role in the agreement.

The assertive British policy in the Middle East, directed against the Soviets and the challenge from Arab nationalism, and intended to impress the Americans, led to the creation of the British-backed Baghdad Pact in 1955 that, by the end of the year, linked Britain, Iran, Iraq, Pakistan and Turkey. This policy also led to plans for intelligence operations designed to overthrow the governments of Egypt, Syria and Saudi Arabia, plans that culminated with the unsuccessful Suez invasion of 1956 directed against Egypt.

In sub-Saharan Africa, the most important confrontation occurred in Kenya, where the British suppressed the Mau-Mau uprising in 1952–7. In this, the British benefited from a wide-ranging social reform policy, including land reform, in which the government distanced itself from the White colonists, as well as in their use of force from effective counter-insurgency techniques and from the assistance of loyal Africans, including former insurgents. Force was also applied in Cyprus from 1955, in response to communal tensions between Greek and Turkish communities, and the development among the former of the EOKA Greek Cypriot terrorist movement that sought union with Greece. The new governor, Field-Marshal Sir John Harding (who had replaced a civilian), saw the situation in large part in a military light, a response that appears anachronistic from the perspective of imminent decolonization, but that did not seem so to many in the 1950s; indeed there was a parallel between policies then and those in the inter-war period.

Security policies meanwhile were increasingly set without reference to empire. Canada was a founder member of NATO, but it was a security framework for Western Europe, not one focused on the empire, and although both Britain and Canada wanted NATO to have a North Atlantic identity, this goal was undermined by successive enlargements: Greece and Turkey in 1952, and West Germany in 1955. As a more obvious sign of Britain's lesser role and prestige for the Dominions, in 1951, Australia and New Zealand, concerned about possible challenges from China, Indonesia and Japan, independently entered into a defense pact with America: ANZUS. Four years later, the Vice-President and Vice-Chairman of the Migration Council wrote to the Daily Telegraph to complain about government inaction in the face of the decline of commonwealth cohesion, more particularly the partnership with Australia.

In the event, America was unwilling to heed the views of Australia and New Zealand: It wanted the alliance to be part of a range of security agreements, not a partnership, and this helped to maintain Australian and New Zealand interest in continued good relations with Britain. At the same time, South Africa unsuccessfully sought to supplement its naval links with Britain by others with Western powers.

The Americans were unwilling to let Britain join ANZUS because, in 1950, the British government had recognized the Communist government of China, beginning a pattern of difference with American over policy toward China that, in part, reflected clashing conceptions of the role of ideology and the nature of pragmatism in international politics. This was not the limit of differences between the two powers, for the British wish to preserve the empire—seen by both the Labor and Conservative leaderships as the basis for Britain's international and economic position—contrasted with American interest in a new world order of capitalist democracies, an order that challenged imperial rule as much as Communism. For example, the CIA-supported "Asia Foundation" produced anti-imperialist propaganda in Singapore on the model of the anti-Soviet "Radio Free Europe". While British governments saw the empire as a way to demonstrate to America the value of the "Special Relationship", the Americans both encouraged what they saw as orderly decolonization and sought to manage it as a means of thwarting Communism and increasing informal American control. Thus, former colonies received American military assistance, as Pakistan did from 1953. There were also different views between Britain and America on the liberalization of trade and air routes, while America had taken an unwelcome position on Palestine, and had helped to weaken Britain's position in Iran.

Nevertheless, the two powers were united in opposition to Communism, especially in the establishment of NATO, while, in 1950, the British contributed the second largest foreign contingent (after the Americans) to the American-led United Nations army that resisted the Communist North Korean invasion of South Korea, a departure from pre-war imperial geopolitics and one that was expensive. The cost of the military build-up of these years lessened the resources available both for economic development and for social welfare, while Britain lacked the resources to sustain the Colonial Office policies outlined in the successive Colonial Development and Welfare Acts of 1940, 1945, 1949, 1950 and 1959. Government action was able to provide only a portion of the investment necessary for colonial economic development. In 1956, Harold Macmillan, the Chancellor of the Exchequer, revealed anxiety about the cost of colonial aid; while other ministries opposed colonial industrialization as a threat to British economic interests.

1956 saw a major crisis for British imperialism, as well as independence for the largest remaining colony, Sudan. The weakness of the imperial response to challenges and the limited domestic popularity of empire were exposed in the Suez Crisis. Britain and France attacked Egypt, in an intervention publicly justified as a way of safeguarding the Suez Canal, which had been nationalized by the aggressive Egyptian leader, Gamal Abdel Nasser. His Arab nationalism was also seen as a threat to Britain's Arab allies, and to the French position in Algeria, while the Prime Minister, Anthony Eden, saw Nasser as another Fascist dictator. Although poorly planned, the invasion saw a major display of military power, but was abandoned in large part because of American opposition. President Eisenhower was already dubious about many aspects of the "Special Relationship" between Britain and America, especially in the Middle East, and had made this clear to Churchill in 1953. Concerned about the impact of the invasion on attitudes in the Third World, the American government refused to extend any credits to support sterling, blocked British access to the International Monetary Fund until she withdrew her troops from Suez, and refused to provide oil to compensate for interrupted supplies from the Middle East.

American opposition, which underlined the vulnerability of the British economy, was crucial in weakening British resolve and led to a humiliating withdrawal. The Suez Crisis can be seen as marking the end of Britain's ability, or at least resolve, to act independently, and has been aptly termed the lion's last roar; from then on, there was an implicit reliance on American acceptance, as in the Falklands War of 1982.[60] The crisis also strained British relations with other powers, both commonwealth, such as Canada, and non-aligned. As at the time of the Munich crisis of 1938, the British government, in 1956, displayed a failure to understand the nature of political opinion in the Dominions, and the decline in their relations with Britain was apparent in the crisis and was accentuated by it; although the Canadian role in organizing the United Nations Emergency Force helped ensure a successful close to the Suez Crisis.

Eden's successor as Prime Minister, Macmillan, set out to restore relations with America, rather than to preserve, let alone try to strengthen, the empire. He put much effort into this task, but he was a suppliant, as American policy over the provision of missiles for Britain's nuclear bombs was to demonstrate, and, in 1960, Macmillan described the British "as Greeks in the Roman Empire of the Americans," in other words providers of wisdom, not power. In Ian Fleming's short story "The Hildebrand Rarity," published that year, James Bond is told by Milton Krest, an obnoxious and brutal American,

> "Nowadays there were only three powers—America, Russia and China. That was the big poker game and no other country had either the chips or the cards to come into it. Occasionally some pleasant little country … like England would be lent some money so that they could take a hand with the grown-ups. But that was just being polite like one sometimes had to be to a chum in one's club who'd gone broke."

In the story, however, it was still possible to present Britain as an imperial power, as Bond was in the Seychelles to check out security conditions, because the Admiralty needed a safe fall-back position in the Indian Ocean for the naval facilities at Gan (established in 1941) in the Maldives which in fact gained independence in 1965.

When he became Prime Minister in 1957, Macmillan sought a profit and loss assessment for each of the colonies, an instrumentalist approach that summed up a lack of conviction in the imperial idea, and while he was Prime Minister (1957–63) there was a wave of decolonization and much of the empire was dismantled, especially in Africa, but also in South East Asia. Churchill and Eden (1955–7) would have been far less willing to abandon the empire at this rate, for, to them, independence was gradual, an organic process that was, in large part, unwelcome, or in which the unwelcome process could be lessened by dilution over a long timescale, an approach that was very much taken toward the African colonies.

Decolonization, which brought to an end all the Western European territorial empires, was a very varied process, with the British government having very different plans for particular colonies, and the context and chronology were often determined by local and regional factors, rather than a common drive. Nevertheless, decolonization was hastened by a strong upsurge in colonial nationalist movements, particularly in the Gold Coast (Ghana), which policy-makers did not know how to confront, as the educated local élites, which had become more prominent, proved far more eager to embrace change than the tribal chiefs that the British had had close relations with. In addition, nationalism caused problems in countries where Britain was influential: The overthrow of the pro-British Iraqi government in 1958 underlined the limitations of British power, and was followed by Britain encouraging America to help with or take over some of its former responsibilities in the Middle East; although Britain did act militarily to support its ally Jordan when it was threatened by Egyptian pressure in 1958.

By departing from colonies, the British were also able to abandon their position as unwilling mediators of local divisions, as was the situation in Palestine. In Malaya, tension between the prosperous Chinese minority and the Malay majority burst into violence in 1969, but Britain had ceased to be the colonial power in 1957, not least because it was felt (correctly) that independence offered the best way to resist Communism there. In contrast, the continued commitment to Northern Ireland ensured that sectarian tensions there had far less happy consequences for Britain.

Decolonization proceeded on the assumption that Britain would withdraw from those areas that it could no longer control, or where the cost of maintaining a presence was prohibitive. Although criticized by some right-wing Conservatives committed to empire, especially the Suez Group and Robert, 5th Marquess of Salisbury, Secretary of State for Dominion Affairs in 1940–2 and 1943–5, for the Colonies in 1942, and for Commonwealth Relations in 1952, Chairman of the Cabinet Colonial Policy Committee, who resigned in 1957 over the issue,[61] decolonization was not a central issue in British politics, in part because the empire was seen as being transformed into the commonwealth, so that the management and presentation of colonial withdrawal lessened both the controversial possibilities of decolonization and reduced the domestic perception of decline. The British view of empire was important, as the proclaimed logic of Britain's imperial mission, bringing civilization to backward areas of the globe, allowed Britain to present the granting of self-government as the inevitable terminus of empire, and this view was shared in the Dominions, the contribution of which to British interests remained readily apparent in Canada's membership of NATO. The retention of the role of the Crown also made it seem as if the empire was being maintained, in the shape of daughter nations within the commonwealth, rather than ended.

The British hoped they could manage decolonization in order to wield renewed influence and to maintain their reach well beyond the confines of NATO. As a result, in 1956, the government advanced the idea of a free trade area for manufactured goods that would encompass Western Europe and the Commonwealth, and therefore preserve both agricultural imports from the Commonwealth to Britain and an economic basis to imperial links. Rejected by the French President, Charles de Gaulle, in November 1958, this scheme was an aspect of the British determination to retain an identity and role outside Europe.

The contraction of empire was relatively painless at the imperial center because public interest in much of it, and support for its retention, was limited, although the absence of consultation within the British political system was such that this limit was not tested. The Colonial Office and the Ministry of Defense were keener to retain empire than the Foreign Office and the Treasury, but this debate was not tested by the electorate. Some traditional Conservative interests, such as the military, were concerned about empire, but this was less the case with much of the Party's middle-class support, and the latter was increasingly prominent in constituency associations and at party conferences. Although the link between imperial sentiment and working-class support is largely suggestive, it is significant that, in Scotland, Conservative support declined from the 1959 election and that working-class Scottish Conservatism/Unionism was particularly badly hit, but Labor, which, instead, rose to dominance, was opposed to Scottish Home Rule.[62] The possible implication of continued imperial control or, alternatively, decolonization for large-scale immigration were scarcely considered.

Fearful for their position, White settlers and landowners in the colonies, in contrast, were vociferous critics of decolonization. Settlement had increased after 1945, in part because the high tax regime of the Labor governments of 1945–51 encouraged emigration, and the dominant position of White settlers in Southern Rhodesia (now Zimbabwe) helped make contentious the future of the Central African Federation (of Rhodesia, Northern and Southern, and Nyasaland) created in 1953. Godfrey, 1st Viscount Malvern, who had been Prime Minister of

Southern Rhodesia from 1933 to 1953 and in 1953–6, was the first Prime Minister of the Federation, made threatening reference in the House of Lords to the local army and air force. This tension looked toward the eventual Unilateral Declaration of Independence by Southern Rhodesia in 1965.

Criticisms by settlers and their supporters in the Lords simply underlined the importance of an absence of colonial representation in the Commons, as, whereas thanks to its representation there Ireland had played a crucial role in the arithmetic of parliamentary power prior to independence, there was no equivalence for any other colony. Furthermore, the pattern of earlier emigration was important. There were far more "kith and kin" in America and the Dominions, than in the African colonies, and many of the latter, for example in Kenya, were landowners, and did not strike a popular resonance in British politics. There was no equivalent to the major French presence in Algerian or that of the Portuguese in Angola. Within the commonwealth, South Africa, a state based on White-minority rule, was isolated, and its departure in 1961 did not lead to the collapse of that body. The failure of federation in Central Africa was matched by that in the West Indies: political and economic rivalries between the colonies could not be overcome; and Britain's plan to include Singapore in Malaysia was also to fail. The Central African Federation collapsed in 1963 in large part due to African nationalist pressure and Southern Rhodesian White racism.

Decolonization was also encouraged by defense issues, particularly the commitment to NATO, that led to British criticism of the implications for alliance strength of the French focus on their retention of Algeria. Moreover, colonies now appeared less necessary in defense terms, not least because Britain had, in 1957, added the hydrogen to the atomic bomb. The declining role of the colonies in the British economy was also important: Many of them appeared less valuable than the areas where informal empire, in the shape of influence tipped with military power, continued, particularly the Persian Gulf and South-East Asia.

In Malaya, where the British did not allow the struggle with Communist insurgents to deter them from their political course, independence was granted in 1957, while in West Africa, the Gold Coast, which had a troublesome nationalist movement and a buoyant export economy based on world demand for cocoa, gained independence the same year under the name Ghana, the first British African colony other than South Africa to gain independence. This reflected the relative wealth of the colony and the absence of a powerful White settler community. In contrast, in colonies with such communities, notably Kenya and Southern Rhodesia, there was interest in ways to retain an important political role for the settlers, although it was also hoped that economic growth and constitutional provisions would ease racial differences.

In 1960, British Somaliland, Nigeria (the most populous of the African colonies), and Cyprus followed, the last especially significant, as it had been said that Cyprus would "never" be independent, and because, with a small population, it set the precedent for the cession of independence for such territories. Independence was granted in the aftermath of a bitter struggle with EOKA, and the confusion and violence of this process reflected the degree to which the British were not always able to manage decolonization effectively. Indeed, there was at least a sub-current in violence to much of decolonization. The granting of independence by France to its remaining sub-Saharan colonies in 1960 drove forward the process of decolonization, and its pace was particularly rapid in the early 1960s, which helped to make it normative. Sierra Leone, Southern Cameroon (as part of Cameroon), and Tanganyika gained independence in 1961, Jamaica, Trinidad (with Tobago), and Uganda in 1962, British North Borneo (as Sabah), Sarawak, Singapore, Zanzibar, and Kenya in 1963, and Malawi, Zambia, and Malta in 1964. In Kenya, the Whites were too few to prevent independence on the basis of majority (African) rule, and the British government supported a multiracial settlement in the shape of the Kenya African Democratic Union formed in 1960, although, in the event, the more nationalist Kenya African National Union which sought immediate independence proved far more powerful, won the 1961 and 1963 general elections, and gained power. The passage of the Kenya Independence Act in Parliament faced criticism there from Conservative MPs, notably on the treatment of White settlers.

Direct representation for Malta in Westminster had been considered, but this course was followed neither there nor in Gibraltar, despite a large majority in favour of integration in the referendum held in Malta.

There was thus no comparison with the representation used by the French for territories such as Martinique. Nevertheless, there were areas where popular support for remaining part of the empire was expressed, and, in 1959, the Cayman Islands, which were officially part of Jamaica, voted in a plebiscite to remain a colony, as, having been separated from Jamaica, they still are.

The list of colonies granted independence should not lead to a neglect of those areas where imperial rule or influence remained important, especially South West Asia, with both formal empire in Aden and informal in the Persian Gulf. In 1955, 1957 and 1959, rebellions in Oman, an allied state where British influence was strong, were put down with the help of British troops, and, in 1962, the government declared that British troops would be based in Aden "permanently," although, in 1964, independence there was promised for 1968. As late as 1970, the British played a key role in the change of ruler in Oman, where they also made a major effort to help suppress the separatist Dhofari rebellion. Informal imperialism proved a difficult option for a declining power, but it ensured a measure of post-imperial continuity. Thus, to take the University of Exeter, in the 1960s, it offered an Advanced Diploma in Public Administration, which was taken almost exclusively by overseas students, mostly from Commonwealth countries, particularly Nigeria. There were also various contractual links with several Nigerian universities involving members of staff teaching in Ibadan and Ife, while Alan Bartlett, the Academic Registrar, took leave of absence in late 1961 to advise University College, Ibadan on developing an academic office. The university was associated with the Diploma course in Government and Administration at the Nigerian College of Arts, Science and Technology. In 1963, the Liaison Committee was willing to offer leave of absence of up to three years for secondment to overseas universities. The committee supported twinning Departments with equivalent Departments in overseas universities, and mentioned Kwame Nkrumah University (Ghana), the University of the West Indies, and the University of Ibadan (Nigeria).[63] Moreover, as other reflections of African interests, there was concern about the situation in South Africa as apartheid became more entrenched.

James Cook, the Vice Chancellor, recommended the consideration for vacancies of academics dismissed for opposing apartheid.[64] In addition, Exeter was designated as the official UK repository of materials on Ghana.

Students from the empire and from former colonies could be found on the campus. So also with staff. In 1952, Sir Thomas Taylor moved from the University College of the West Indies to be Principal, only to die on holiday in 1953.

Cook, in 1955, was appointed by the Inter-University Council for Higher Education Overseas to be its representative on the Council of the new University College of Rhodesia and Nyasaland. Once retired, Cook went on to be Vice-Chancellor of the University of East Africa.

In part, with the empire, past and present, links carried forward earlier arrangements, such as the Diploma in English Studies for Egyptian students that was offered by the University College in the early 1950s.

The end, as a result of the Suez Crisis, of the course hit hard in 1957–8.[65] The republican coup in Iraq in 1958 affected links there, while those with Nigeria largely ended with the 1966 coup and the subsequent Biafran War (1967–70). In the early 1970s, government policy on raising fees for overseas students hit Commonwealth links with fewer students for example from India,[66] and led, instead, to a focus on Arab states, notably the United Arab Emirates.

The departure from empire lent added force to Macmillan's unsuccessful bid to join the European Economic Community (EEC) in 1961–2 and was encouraged by it—much like the Labor government's decision in 1967 to reapply for membership preceded the decision to withdraw from "East of Suez." Anglo-American relations were more important to Macmillan than imperial links, and he wished to preserve the "Special Relationship" by showing that Britain could play a key role in Europe.

The departure from empire also provided one of the might-have-beens of post-war British history. There was fighting in the last stages of empire, including in Malaya, Kenya and Aden, but nothing on the scale that the French and Portuguese confronted in their colonies: the heroic defense of imperial pretensions depicted in *Zulu*, a popular film in 1964, was an incident from 1879. It is unclear how far a major nationalist rising in a British colony, or a foreign invasion of one, would have led to a substantial response that might have proved bitterly divisive within Britain, but neither occurred until Aden (1967) and the

Falklands (1982), respectively, and these episodes did not lead to a serious questioning of government policy. Certainly, decolonization did not prove as divisive for the Conservatives as relations with the European Union were to be from the late 1980s.

The abandonment of empire also entailed conflict in protecting the newly-independent commonwealth, and other overseas interests. In 1961, in Operation Vantage, the British successfully deployed forces to dissuade the Iraqis from invading Kuwait, with which relations remained very close after the end of the British protectorate.[67] In 1991, however, the liberation of Kuwait from Iraq occupation was very much as part of an American-led coalition.

Operation Vantage was followed, in 1963–6, by a successful confrontation with Indonesia in support of Malaysia which had been formed from Malaya, Singapore, Sarawak and British North Borneo (now Sabah), in part as a way to group together for security after the end of imperial control. The creation of Malaysia was seen as a way to manage the process of British withdrawal, and thus to maintain British interests while cutting defense costs. The military commitment to Malaysia showed the "East of Suez" policy providing political and economic value. An additional sign was provided in 1964 when mutinies by military units in newly-independent Kenya, Tanganyika and Uganda led to a successful British response, which included the transport of troops by sea from Aden and their helicopter landing at Dars-es-Salaam in Tanganyika, modern technology in the service of empire.

Harold Wilson, who came to power as head of a Labor government in 1964, hoped to maintain Britain's role as a major independent power, and sought to act as a leading figure on the international stage. In support of India against China, and, reflecting concern about the consequences of China's easy victory over India in their border war of 1962, Wilson declared that "Britain's frontiers are on the Himalayas." The possibility that this victory would be followed up appeared to threaten the stability of the Indian Ocean rim and, with it, British interests in South-West and South-East Asia and in the Indian Ocean. British strategic thinking, which owed much to the earlier geopolitical ideas of Halford Mackinder, discerned a tension between the Eurasian heartland and the oceanic rim, and thus saw the stability of South Asia and the Indian Ocean, in which

Britain was the leading naval power, as closely linked. Already, in 1960, the carrier HMS *Victorious* had joined the Far East station with a complement of aircraft capable of dropping nuclear bombs and a few nuclear bombs abroad; this in furtherance of a decision to have two carriers "East of Suez." Subsequent planning called for the use of a carrier in the Indian Ocean for nuclear strikes on southern China and for a second carrier to be deployed in 1964. These carriers were to complement RAF planes based in Singapore. In contrast, the American role in the Indian Ocean in the early 1960s was minor, with only a small squadron showing the flag in the Persian Gulf, while, until the late 1960s, the Indian navy was equipped with surplus British warships, and links between the two navies were close. This was an aspect of the use of arms sales and military training in order to maintain imperial links, a process that was particularly prominent in Africa, so that, in the Nigerian Civil War of 1967–70, the British provided the federal government with weaponry.

Wilson initially maintained the "East of Suez" commitment, thus both underlining Britain's claim to be a power in South Asia and supporting American interests in maintaining stability in the Indian Ocean and the Persian Gulf. Planning for the new submarines armed with nuclear missiles included firing stations in the Indian Ocean designed both to block Himalayan passes, through which the Chinese could advance on India, and to reach targets in southern Russia. Wilson also sought to be a peacemaker in Vietnam, South Asia and Rhodesia, to try to ease Cold War tensions, the last following a course set by Churchill, Eden and Macmillan.

However, Britain lacked the necessary diplomatic strength to further its goals, and the varied commitments to Europe, represented by NATO and by the wish to join the EEC, affected the consideration of other interests. Wilson failed to end the Vietnam War, and Pakistan and India turned to Soviet mediation. The commonwealth, which had changed greatly with the entry of newly-independent former colonies, was not able or willing to provide support for Britain's international goals; the rival to the European Economic Community, the European Free Trade Association (EFTA), of which Britain was the leading member, was not intended as a political force, and in any event was weak; and intractable problems, including a Southern Rhodesian government unwilling to abandon White supremacy. The British government was insistent that independence there was not an option unless the democracy that permitted Black majority rule was established, the line earlier taken in Kenya. The bulk of the White settlers, however, preferred to look to South Africa's apartheid government as a model, and, in 1965, announced an unilateral declaration of independence (UDI). British diplomatic efforts failed to end the Rhodesian crisis, and the use of the navy to impose "sanctions"—prohibitions on trade, particularly in oil—also failed.

More generally, Britain's attempt to act as a major power had to be abandoned in the face of the country's severe financial problems, which led to a major devaluation of sterling in 1967, gravely weakening Britain's prestige and also hitting her position as a major power. As a result, under pressure from the Chiefs of Staff, who were concerned about the mismatch between commitments and resources, the government decided in 1968 to abandon Britain's military position "East of Suez." Forces were withdrawn from Aden when independence was granted in November 1967, from the Persian Gulf in 1971, and from Singapore in 1975 (they had been much scaled down in 1971). The withdrawal from the Gulf took place against the wishes of the local sheikhs, but, to the British government, it no longer seemed a viable presence, not least because of the withdrawal from Aden and the sterling crisis, but also due to disillusionment with Britain's imperial position. The Conservative opposition criticised the decision to withdraw from the Gulf, and this encouraged Lee Kuan Yew of Singapore to persuade the Labor government to delay the withdrawal from Singapore until 1971, but he was disappointed, as once in power under Edward Heath in 1970–4, the Conservatives pursued the policy of withdrawal. Although, under the Commonwealth Five-Power Defense Arrangement (which replaced the Anglo-Malaysian Defense Agreement), Britain joined Australia and New Zealand in a limited commitment to Malaysia and Singapore, this proved only a transitional arrangement.

As a consequence of withdrawal, Britain became less important in the Indian Ocean,[68] while the concern that had been expressed in 1947 that partition would weaken India's potential as an ally had been doubly vindicated, for the rivalry between Pakistan and India, which led to war again in 1971, provided opportunities for both China and Russia to win local support. Britain sought to counter this by encouraging the American naval build-up in the Indian Ocean, and making Diego Garcia available to America as a base. In 1974, an American carrier entered the Persian Gulf, the first such deployment since 1948.

Unlike Australia and New Zealand, Britain did not come to the assistance of America in Vietnam: for Britain, Vietnam was to be no second Korea. Instead, Australia and New Zealand fought without Britain, which, combined with the withdrawal from "East of Suez," represented a major shift. Britain became increasingly less relevant to Pacific states. When, in 1985, there was a major crisis within the ANZUS alliance over the New Zealand government forbidding the visit of an American warship that might carry nuclear arms, this was not a dispute in which there was any role for Britain.

There was also a major shift in British defense planning with the cancellation in 1966 of a planned 50,300 ton fleet carrier, the CVA-01 and the sister ship that had also been projected. These had been seen as crucial to maintaining British military viability "East of Suez," not least because bases on land had been lost or compromised by independence or instability, the fate in particular of bases in Kenya and Aden.

Decolonization continued with Gambia and the Maldives gaining independence in 1965, Bechuanaland (as Botswana), Basutoland (as Lesotho) and British Guiana (as Guyana) in 1966, Aden in 1967, Mauritius, Nauru and Swaziland in 1969, and Tonga and Fiji in 1970. In most cases, this process posed few problems for Britain, but the withdrawal from Aden was far from bloodless and, from the British perspective, there was a failure to create an acceptable successor government. Nevertheless, Aden was no longer a key point on shipping routes and, by delaying their departure until after Egypt had been defeated by Israel in the Six Day War in 1967, the British lessened their concern about exploitation of this move by Egypt, then the leader of pan-Arab nationalism.

In the face of disparate interests, the West Indies Federation established in 1958 had failed in 1962. This was principally due to tensions over the degree to which a federation meant a powerful federal government, as Trinidad, the site of its headquarters, sought, or not, as the other major player, Jamaica, argued. In addition, there were economic and financial issues, as well as differences of personality. In 1961, with opinion there hardening against federation, the Jamaican government held a referendum that decided on secession from the Federation, and that led Trinidad to decide to do likewise.

This failure was followed by independence for Jamaica in 1962, Trinidad and Tobago in 1962 and Barbados in 1966; and separate militaries accordingly. Under the Associated Statehood Act of 1967, Antigua, Dominica, Grenada, St. Kitts-Nevis-Anguilla, St. Lucia and St. Vincent gained full self-government, while Britain remained responsible for external affairs and defense. Cohesion was limited and the states moved to full independence: Grenada in 1974, Dominica in 1978, St. Lucia in 1979, St. Vincent in 1979, Antigua and Barbuda in 1981, and St. Kitts and Nevis in 1983. After independence, the former colonies were linked in the organization of Eastern Caribbean States, which was established in 1981 and has more members and associate members, including the French territories of Guadeloupe and Martinique. Meanwhile, the Bahamas had gained independence in 1973 and British Honduras, as Belize, in 1981, although, in the face of territorial claims from Guatemala, the British provided a resident army and air force garrison for Belize.

There was soon little left in the empire, apart from such far-flung outposts as the Falkland Islands, Gibraltar, and Hong Kong. The last was the only colony with a substantial population not *en route* for independence; and this was largely due to Chinese irridentinist interest in the colony, which compromised the possibility of independence, and to poor British relations with Communist China. The New Territories of the peninsula were, by treaty, due for return in 1997. Completed in 1985, the Hong Kong and Shanghai Banking Corporation building was then the world's most expensive building, and one that easily played a major role in a compendium of British imperial buildings that began with Dublin Castle in the Middle Ages.[69] Hong Kong, as a whole and not just the New Territories, was returned to China in 1997.

A sense of empire as anachronistic was captured in the public reaction in 1969 when the Wilson government sent two frigates, a detachment of parachutists, and a group of London policemen to invade the Caribbean island of Anguilla, which in 1967 had rejected membership in the St. Kitts-Nevis-Anguilla federation. There was governmental concern that the island would become a base for drug smugglers, but the bloodless invasion was treated as a farce by much of the British press. Anguilla was allowed to remain as a British colony, which is still the situation. In 1967, the plan to create an airfield on the uninhabited Indian Ocean island of Aldabra (part of the Seychelles) was thwarted by environmentalists concerned about giant tortoises.

The attitudes surrounding empire were very different to those of two decades earlier. Northern Ireland, though part of the legacy of empire and regarded as such by separatist Catholics, was seen in Britain and by the mostly Protestant Unionists in Northern Ireland as an essentially domestic issue. Changing slowly as the percentage of Catholics neared a majority, in contrast to the 2:1 ratio of Protestants to Catholics when Northern Ireland was established in 1922, the situation in Northern Ireland was transformed in 2016 by Brexit, for the majority there (56 percent) voted against, and the settlement approved in 2019 created an economic border in the Irish Sea, between Northern Ireland and Britain, even as Ireland remained united for trade in goods. The prospect of unification with the South became stronger, not least as the South came to seem a less alien place to Northern Irish Protestants. The 1998 Good Friday agreement ending the sectarian disorder of the Northern Ireland "Troubles" that had started in 1968, included a route to this in terms of a referendum in both North and South, the former once the British government thought a majority in the North likely to favour reunification. Meanwhile, Eire/Ireland moved past being postcolonial, and developed as a mature and effective society with an economy stronger in many respects than that of Britain.[70]

Ireland was seen as different, but with the legislation in 1997 for a Scottish Parliament and Executive the drift became very much away from a British identity, not least as separatism became an incremental process. Just as this identity was created by Act of Parliament so it may well be dissolved by another, with yet again, Parliaments in Edinburgh and London playing the key role. On 24 September 2009, indeed, BBC Radio 4's flagship *Today* program referred to "our devolved nations." Two years earlier, Radio 4 had dropped the UK-themed music until then played at the 6.30 am start of broadcasts. In 2014, 44.7 percent of those who voted in a referendum on Scottish independence supported the proposal, while in 2016, 62 percent of the Scots who voted opted to remain in the EU, and in 2019 the SNP won 45 percent of the vote and 48 out of the 59 Scottish seats in the British general election, albeit without winning a comparable percentage of the vote; while in 2024, the SNP won only 30 percent and nine seats.

In recent decades, the long tradition of British history that prevailed for a quarter-millennium from the Act of Union with Scotland has largely collapsed. Empire disappeared, particularly from the granting of independence to India in 1947, as, soon after, did Britain's leading maritime role, and it became apparent that British history in many respects had meant British empire history, and much of it passed with the loss of empire. Until 1947, Britishness was quintessentially Imperial, and empire was a transoceanic Britishness, and not simply an island one.

Conversely, the late 1940s saw the beginning of a new, provincialized state which, as "Great Britain," came into being to run a global colonial and trading system that has since disintegrated. Legislation in 1962, 1968 and 1971 sought to limit the implications of the British Nationality Act of 1948 that had given rights of residence to all "citizens," and notably by limiting the ability of South Asians living in Kenya and Uganda to settle. Despite this and other attempts to contain if not restrict immigration, it became large-scale and influenced the character of Britain, its society, its culture and, particularly, its cities.[71] The "Little Britishness" characteristic of the post-war period, and associated in particular with Margaret Thatcher, Conservative Prime Minister 1979 to 1990, is of very recent origin and not as deeply-rooted as is generally implied. Looked at differently, there is still a great deal of point in England, but it is unclear how far there still is in Britain. Indeed, from the Scottish perspective, Scotland has been regionalised from the 1940s as "Great Britain" is no longer seen as a multinational polity. There is certainly less English interest now in Scottish culture than was the case in the Victorian period. In the nineteenth century, and even the 1930s, Robert Burns and Walter Scott were very significant writers for English school curricula, but, by the 1960s, both had been discarded. Moreover, cultural and religious continuity was greatly compromised in the 1960s, notably with the decline in the position, popularity and relevance of the Established Churches. In addition, Americanism and globalization challenged native styles, whether in food or in diction, with all that they meant for national distinctiveness and continuity.

Meanwhile, as part of the decline of empire, Britain's informal empire had been getting steadily weaker, in part due to changes in Britain itself, notably economic decline. There were also major problems due to economic and political nationalism in other countries. Thus, in 1948, the nationalization of the railways in Argentina led to the end of ten British rail companies there. A similar process was seen elsewhere, with political developments, such as anti-Western regime changes in Egypt in 1952, Iran in 1958, Iraq in 1958, and Iran in 1979, also seeing the seizure of British assets and the loss of influence. A very different form of influence, however, was presented by the commonwealth, which in 2024 had a combined population of 2.7 billion people, albeit 1.45 billion of them being inhabitants of just one country—namely, India.

A process of apparently immutable decline had been challenged by a greater international assertion from 1982. The Falklands War of that year saw a successful defense of empire[72] in the shape of the determination of the settlers to preserve British rule in the face of Argentinean aggression. From 1990, when sending forces to the Persian Gulf as part of a practice of international coalition warfulness that was presented by supporters as humanitarian, progressive and opposed to aggression, and by critics as an aspect of a neo-liberal imperialism. From the 1991 Gulf War with Iraq over Kuwait on, Britain very much returned east of Suez and in the 2000s the process led to an active military presence in both Iraq and Afghanistan. The echoes of the past appeared very strong, but British action was now in large part in response to American initiatives. If this situation was "co-empire," it was an aspect of Britain very much in the shadow of America. Indeed, to critics, this was Britain as part of the American empire.

8. PRESENT DISCONTENTS

> "You committed genocide against our people. Give us our land back. Give us what you stole from us. Our bones, our skulls, our babies, our people. You destroyed our land. Give us a treaty. We want a treaty. This is not your land. This is not your land. You are not my King. You are not my King."

The heckling of Charles III at Australia's Parliament House on 20 October 2024 by Lidia Thorpe, a Senator for Victoria, was an abrupt display of the continued anger of some of the indigenous population of Australia; but also a reminder that most of the Australian people are not descended from this population. Indeed, the complaint is really as much about internal Australian politics and culture as about the link with Britain. This politics had been seen with the 2023 Australian Indigenous Voice referendum, in which the proposal for a constitutional referendum to prescribe a body called the Aboriginal and Torres Strait Islander Voice was rejected, with 60 percent of those voting opposing the proposal. As so often, discussion of empire was largely really about post-imperial politics.

Meanwhile, back in Britain, the 2024 exhibition at Tate Britain for the Turner Prize included a display by Pio Abad on the legacy of empire, looting and ill-gotten gains, not least a sequence of screenprints in which drawings of Benin bronzes seized by British forces in 1897 and now held in the British Museum[1] sat side by side with objects from Abad's flat that also have origins overseas, for example Tate and Lyle sugar. The question of return is one that invites differing views as does the assessment of British policy toward Benin which became a part of Nigeria. Economic motives played a major role in policy, notably a determination to control palm oil production, while the British abolition of slavery was matched by the establishment of forced labor practices. The character of Benin itself invites consideration, not least the killing of people as an aspect of rituals, a killing represented in some of the art.

In turn, the 2024 Tate Britain exhibition "The 80s: Photographing Britain" claims that photography was a valuable tool for imperialism, creating racist stereotypes, only to have its "colonial gaze" and "sexist and racist past" challenged by its account of the period 1976 to 1993.[2] In other genres, such as cinema or travelogues, there is now a far more hostile account of empire.[3]

Less vivid, but as pointed was the Royal Historical Society's Race, Ethnicity and Equality Report in 2018 which claimed a serious bias in the teaching and practice of history in British universities. Works on Black British history also repeatedly argued a case for White neglect and hypocrisy.[4] There were frequent calls for "a conversation" about empire but this is rarely a conversation being usually a one-sided diatribe, as in the 2024–5 British Museum exhibition "What Have We Here?" or in pressure to "diversify" the curriculum.[5]

Such a critique drew on an approach to the past that sees it as inevitably bad because the past, as well as on related patterns of Black and White criticism within Britain and its former empire. This criticism is of both imperialism and aspects of modern Britain.[6] The criticism was more than replicated within government, as in the report on the official gov.uk website "The Historical Roots of the Windrush Scandal: Independent research report," a piece commissioned by the Home Office that presents Britain as pursuing hostile immigration policies based on historical White Supremacy. In 2003, Jack Straw, the Labor Foreign Secretary from 2001 to 2006, blamed British colonialism for many of the world's international disputes.

The idea of humanitarian governance as an aspect of past British imperialism is now one that is criticized more than discerned. In part, this criticism is an aspect of an attacks on liberalism and Christianity from the stance of modern identity politics. Indeed, a criticism of empire is central to the latter and notably so with the presentation of empire as an inherently racist project and one that deployed knowledge-formation accordingly.[7] Linked to this are the totally mistaken, but oft-repeated, views that Western imperialism somehow created capitalism and the slave-trade, and that its settler-colonialism was inherently genocidal with slavery an important driver of the Industrial Revolution.[8]

This critique replaced a former type of progressivism. These were Whiggish accounts of imperial rationale, development and justification, accounts that had played an important role in the "national story" of Britain. They now can be presented as liberal and reactionary, or as liberal or reactionary, with liberal now treated as a critical description referring to international capital flows and free trade.

A problem, however, with this "either … or" account remains that it underplays greatly the diversity of factors involved in imperialism, notably the drive for security and religious factors, as well, as a related matter, as the need to focus on particular conjunctures when assessing imperial motivation and activity. The latter were a matter not only of chronology but also of geography: It is a mistake to argue that imperialism had a common drive, because it meant so many different things in particular areas and to specific communities. A later parallel is the alleged role of the "national security state" in accounting for what to others is "American imperialism." The terrorist attacks on New York and Washington in 2001 drove intervention in Afghanistan and encouraged action against Iraq, but critics found it easier to allege other "neo-imperialist" reasons including, in the latter case, a determination to control oil production.

Then, and at other times, the emphasis on materialist factors needs to be qualified. For example, missionaries were not always the assistants of empire that they can be seen as, and sometimes complicated matters for imperial rulers. Missionaries helped to develop the notion of universal human rights,[9] and left much good in their wake, especially in the domain of education, literacy, and the establishment of standard written languages, in part as a consequence of publishing the Bible. All of this is an important corrective to crudely drawn materialist accounts of empire and is an issue that recovers something easily forgotten in our increasingly secular societies: Religion really mattered to people and religious values greatly affected institutions, national identities and politics.

Criticism of the British empire, however, is incessant as well as an aspect of a wider critique of Western imperial links. Thus, in 2021, Andrés López Obrador, the Mexican President, repeated his 2019 demand for a formal apology by both Spain and the papacy for the conquest of the Aztec empire in 1519–21 and for the subsequent colonial rule by Spain. Spain's Foreign Ministry rejected the demand, arguing that the conquest should not be "judged in light of contemporary considerations." Discussion of the British empire in practice feeds into these considerations and is affected by them, and this contextualizes all writing about British imperialism.[10]

As a related, but also different, matter, there are also the tensions between the (very varied) approaches to the past offered by historians, however defined, and those that derive from other subject specialists. This is very much the case with the politicized debates of the present. Yet, rather than blaming these other specialists, it would be foolish to ignore the direction of historical work, particularly the move of much of popular history from being celebratory of empire to being aggressively critical.

Take, for example, as indicative of a wider tendency, William Dalrymple's *The Anarchy. The Relentless Rise of the East India Company* (2019), "a timely cautionary tale of the first global corporate power," published by Bloomsbury, a major publisher, at a very reasonable price, which betoken the pricing economics of confidence, advertising, and a large print run. The book was extensively and largely favourably reviewed, and was selected as a book of the year. The profits that arose from Company activity and the disruption that resulted attracted repeated attention in the book. That, however, is an approach that tells us very little about the general tendency in eighteenth-century imperial activity, and particularly what was distinctive about that of the British. Thus, the EIC (East India Company) was one of a series of "national" East India companies, including those of France, the Netherlands and Sweden. Moreover, for Britain, there was the Hudson Bay Company, the Royal African Company, and the chartered companies involved in North America, as well, for example, as the Bank of England. Delegated authority in this form, or shared state/private activities more generally, were a major part of governance. To assume from the modern perspective of state authority that this was necessarily inadequate is misleading as well as teleological. Was Portuguese India, where the state had a larger role, "better"?

In India, after the death of the mighty Mughal Emperor Aurangzeb (r. 1658–1707), there was, under his weaker successors, the development of a tier of powers within the sub-continent, for example the Nizam of Hyderabad. In the latter perspective, the EIC emerged as one and, eventually, the most successful of the successor powers. This raises questions of comparative efficiency, notably how the EIC succeeded in the Indian military labor market, this helping in defeating the Marathas in the 1800s and 1810s.[11] An Indian power, the EIC was also a "foreign" one; although foreignness should not be understood in modern terms, and the EIC, in practice, was an Anglo-Indian hybrid entity. The EIC was not alone among the successful players, and was not even particularly successful in India, other than against marginal players, until the 1760s. Compared to the invading Nadir Shah of Persia in the late 1730s, or the Afghans from the late 1750s, the EIC was limited on land. Moreover its activity was part of a longstanding pattern of the invasion of India. This is a context that generally receives inadequate attention or is presented as if the other invaders brought benefits and the British disadvantages.[12]

So also for eighteenth-century Asia as a whole. Dalrymple and others can be highly critical of the form of capitalism the EIC represented; but it was less destructive than the Manchu conquest of Xinjiang in the 1750s, or, indeed, the Afghan destruction of Safavid rule in Persia in the early 1720s. Such comparative points raise questions about the conceptualization and methodologies of cross-cultural and diachronic comparison, but also show the selectivity involved in the criticism of the British empire, a selectivity that is partly based on ignorance.

Focusing anew on India, the extent to which the Mughal achievement in subjugating the Deccan in the late seventeenth century was itself transient might be underlined, and, alongside consideration of the Maratha-Mughal struggle in the late seventeenth century, that provides another perspective on subsequent developments. The disruptive character of British activity can again be contextualized. The extent to which Bengal, for example, did not know much peace prior to takeover by the EIC from 1757 is also worthy of consideration. It helps explain why so many local interests, there and elsewhere, found it appropriate, as well as convenient, to ally with the EIC which brought a degree of protection for the regional economy and offered defense against Maratha, Afghan, and other, attacks and/or exactions. Furthermore, the terms of entry into a British-led global economy were less unwelcome than later nationalist writers might suggest.

In current debates relating to imperial conquest, imperial rule, decolonization and post-colonial problems, there is a clear emphasis on resistance to empire, from without and within,[13] as well as a critique of the rhetorics and practices of British imperialism.[14] Many works reflect a strong anger at a form of disempowering humiliation, almost a kind of historicized castration. This, however, is present-day narcissism masquerading as historical judgment and certainly a flawed response to the more complex and interactive processes of empire. Indeed, with reference to the latter, emphases on agency, transnationalism and co-ownership, as well as on the attempt by the British to legalize an order opposed to despotism,[15] challenge this anger and the related demands for reparations.

The latter is an aspect of a wider strand of pressure for "equality, diversity and inclusion" that in practice entails wealth redistribution with a smokescreen of diversity. As a contemporary instance of the fluidity of interests, assumptions and attitudes, there was a tendency to underplay the wider implications for the understanding of empire of the increasing role of ethnic minorities in modern Britain. In 1987 three Black Britons entered the House of Commons and in 2002 Paul Boateng became the first Black Cabinet Minister. By 2019, there were six Black and Asian Cabinet ministers and in 2022–4 Rishi Sunak became the first British Asian to be Prime Minister: his parents were of Indian descent and emigrated to Britain in 1966 from East Africa.

Emphases on agency, transnationalism and co-ownership are unwelcome because of history's place at the fore of culture wars, part of a total assault on the past, one that is explicitly designed to lead the present, and determine the future. This assault is a long-term process that owed much to the Marxist side in the "Cold War" that began in 1917 and continued until the fall of the Soviet bloc in 1989–91. However, the attack on empire was by no means limited to Marxists. Thus, on 22 November 1962, Arthur Bottomley, leading for the Labor opposition in the House of Commons in supporting the Kenya Independence Bill, referred to "the burden which belongs to all of us Europeans who first invented racial discrimination," an inaccurate remark that he linked to his more understandable criticism of White settlers there, notably their "privileged position in the past." A trade unionist, Bottomley had been Parliamentary

Under-Secretary of State for Dominion Affairs (1946–7) and then Commonwealth Relations (1947), and was to go on to Secretary of State for the latter in 1964–6.

This process has been revived and given new direction in recent years. The relentlessness of the struggle, the Leninist approach, that the core true believers and committed will lead the rest, that there is to be no compromise, no genuine debate, and that the end-result must be power for its own sake, attacks in part through prejudging groups as inherently racist and treats imperialism accordingly. The "long march through the institutions," culminating in a Cultural Revolution, succeeded, in part because conservatives devoted insufficient attention to trying to contest this march.

In particular, the degree to which institutions controlled by, and for, the "soft left" could become the means for propaganda, indeed indoctrination, by the "hard left," while appreciated by many right-wing commentators, was given far too little attention by conservative governments. This was true of Reagan/Thatcher/Bush senior, all of whom understandably focused on international relations and economic affairs, including the development of neoliberalism, and then again of Bush junior/Cameron and their successors. Other issues thus came to the fore, but so also did an understandable wish, drawing on both conservative and liberal principles, not to use the power of the state in order to limit the autonomy of institutions such as museums and universities, or to affect freedom of speech.

This situation was very much of concern before the storm of protest and aggressive virtue-signalling associated with the "Black Lives Matter" movement of 2020. However, the latter helped rapidly to drive forward the pre-existing tendency, not least by leading many organizations, institutions and companies to endorse and adopt attitudes and policies that were at best tendentious and at worst extremely damaging to any practice of rational enquiry. Thus, a survey circulated by Oxfam in June 2021 to its staff in Britain stated that racism was deeply embedded in society and that "all echelons of power, to some degree, exist to serve whiteness (whether by legacy, the presence of neo-colonialism or cultural imperialism)." The past was thereby defined in terms of a hostile legacy. The emphasis throughout was on Whiteness and Blackness in oppositional terms and with a clear primacy for both across time. This is fundamentally ahistorical as it acts to downplay all other identities and causes of tension, most notably rivalry within these supposed opposites, for example the conflicts within both Africa and the West both of which were so important to imperial history and to non-imperial history.

The abandonment of any support for rational enquiry was unsurprising, as there was an explicitly anti-Enlightenment argument at play, and notably and aggressively so with Critical Race Theory. This theory acted to deny rationality, presenting it somehow as racist and an imperializing project, whatever that was held to mean. In a resumption of the postmodernist hash, objectivity became a term of abuse and objection. The wash of protest in 2020 was given concrete form by being taken on board in mission statements, hiring policies, and other such mutually-supporting practices that were backed by the designation and filling of new posts. Thus, ideology was focused accordingly. Decolonization was theme and means, policy and rhetoric.

In Britain as a result, historical issues, such as the slave trade, empire and the reputation of Churchill, received critical attention to an unaccustomed degree, and history of a type was thrust into public debate. However, the conceptual, methodological and empirical bases for criticism were flawed and, in particular, there is a tendency among critics, for example of empire, to write in terms of undifferentiated blocs of supposed alignment, to move freely back and forth across the centuries without a due awareness of context, and readily to ascribe causes in a somewhat reductionist fashion.

Thus, Dalrymple, writing in *The Guardian* on 11 June 2020, linked the continued presence in Central London of John Tweed's statue (unveiled in 1912) of Robert Clive, a valiant as well as self-interested hero and maker of empire, to the Brexit vote: "a vicious asset-stripper. His statue has no place on Whitehall … a testament to British ignorance of our imperial past…. Its presence outside the Foreign Office encourages dangerous neo-imperial fantasies among the descendants of the colonisers…. Removing the statue of Clive from the back of Downing Street would give us an opportunity finally to begin the process of education and atonement."[16]

This idea, that education has to lead to atonement, captures the extent to which those writing were not interested in critical debate, nor indeed in the previous mantra of reconciliation or indeed the concept of "conversation." For Dalrymple and many others, Brexit was a consequence of an imperial mentality that has never been confronted.[17] Leave aside the extent to which Dalrymple was strong here on assertion rather than evidence, and that "Little Englanders" and specific issues of the moment, such as Cameron's lack of popularity, were of far more consequence in the 2016 referendum than any supposed hankering after empire. What, instead, you get is a running together of past and present with the modern British supposedly trapped by the past. This was differently seen on 19 November 2024 when Vasily Nebenzya, the Russian representative to the United Nations, cast Britain as a malign power seeking to ensure that the Ukraine war continue, because, allegedly, it was a former colonial power affected by "phantom pains for the empire over which the Sun never used to set" that sought to meddle in the war out of a "longing for lost dominion." The British Foreign Secretary, David Lammy, presiding at that session of the Security Council, criticised Russia for "Imperialism" and for waging an "imperialist war of conquest," while Nebenzya referred to malign British imperial actions in Ireland, South Africa and Kenya.

In rejecting a supposedly malign past, the statues have to fall, and the reading lists and libraries must be reordered, and, indeed, renamed. "Decolonization" becomes a catch-all that can be employed to castigate whatever is disliked and then to demand support for a purging. In August 2024, in addressing the "dominant paradigm of whiteness," Welsh librarians were advised by the Chartered Institute of Library and Information Professionals to avoid holding meetings in "racist" buildings, as part of the effort to conform with the Welsh Labor government's 2022 Anti-racist Wales Action Plan, which pledged to "eradicate" systemic racism by 2030 and to provide a "decolonized account of the past."

Academic historians and museum directors, the majority of whom ironically are clearly on the Left, themselves find they are subject, as part of "History Wars," not to the usual rational and empirical conventions and constraints of intellectual debate, but to an increasingly more intrusive and even controlling attitude on the part of colleagues as well as the broader world, not least the "university authorities." Those who set policy in the latter do so by the finger-in-air method, one that senses what is fashionable among those who will affirm their prejudices. That, indeed, threatens a closure of the space for free thought and expression. Demands for "anti-racist" affirmation and/or training can compound the latter issue. In 2024, teachers on school trips to the International Slavery Museum in Liverpool were advised online by the museum to acknowledge their limitations "especially if you come from a white privileged background."

Given the bullying approach, tone and stance adopted by some universities, not least anonymous denunciations, those thus attacked will be anxious. In part, this is a struggle for mastery within the Left, but conservative academics are frequently attacked. With some universities apparently endorsing the idea that the workplace is the mission field, there is the language of impatient revivalism, as in concepts and rhetorical claims such as needing to grasp the moment, condemnation, and the endlessly reiterated language and idea of decolonization.

This issue pushes to the fore the question of whether some stages and types of British imperialism were more benign or less malign than others. In particular, alongside the ending of the slave trade and then slavery, the empire from the nineteenth century was less maritime and commercial in character and more a matter of territorial conquest, racial ideology and imperial mission. This was an empire that presented as much more hierarchical, exploitative and destructive, and therefore often wasteful and non-instrumental. That left many conquered societies with a set of conditions unfavourable to post-imperial peace and prosperity. Whereas some countries profited from imperial tutelage, many more were badly hurt. Informal empire would have been a better option, for the British and the conquered, in Africa and much of Asia. In part, success bread hubris and smugness, in part there was a concern about the imperial drive of other powers, notably France and Russia, in part a militarization of imperial governance, one seen with the decline of the political role of trading companies. At any rate, the character of empire changed, although that was very differently the case in Latin America and, separately, the settlement colonies.

The biggest problem in the teaching of Humanities according to Catherine Hall, Professor Emerita of Modern British Social and Cultural

History at University College London, in a notice sent to History UK subscribing departments on 6 June 2019, was that "the discipline urgently needs decolonization!" History Workshop published a blog in 2019 in its learning and teaching section: Radhika Natarajan's "Imperial History Now," which claimed that "calls to decolonise curricula are more than a matter of addition, subtraction, or replacement of authors and texts. Instead, they are calls to address the relationship between the forms of knowledge we value in the classroom and the inequities and violence that exist on our campuses and in the world.... Decolonising the curriculum is not an end, but the beginning of a longer process of transformation."

History as a subject proves particularly important, as the past is used as a necessary basis for the "decolonizing mantra." Unfounded claims, such as genocide by Europeans in Africa and the Americas, are repeated. Old ideas, such as World Systems Theory, are taken out of storage, given a racist dimension and thus anti-racist value, and deployed without care or context. The latter is particularly regrettable as world or global history, which became more active as a field from the 1960s,[18] was a qualification of earlier Eurocentric models, and one on which much effort was expended. It proved particularly valuable in demonstrating links between civilizations and in undermining any "zero-sum-game" of cultures. Instead, empires were presented as collective undertakings in which those who were subjects had a significant role and indeed to a considerable extent agency or semi-independent action. Similar points were made about the slave trade.[19] These approaches are now rejected. As a related point, it is striking how few commentators on the British empire or the Atlantic slave trade are able seriously to compare their development and activities with those of non-Western empires and slave trade of the period. The latter are an aspect of world history, but most commentators prefer simply to focus on British.

There are many contextual aspects that deserve thought. The historian will note that the direction of travel, the apparent attack on White male "privilege," has little to do with the most obvious and persistent "bias" in university entry in Britain, that toward a pronounced majority of female students, and notably so in the humanities, including history, whether state or private schools are the issue. A middle-class background to the British undergraduate population is also far more noticeable than any supposed "White supremacism." As far as staff is concerned, and notably so in the Humanities and Social Sciences, the lack of "diversity" and "inclusion" are also most obviously the case as far as the representation of conservative staff are concerned as this representation is very limited and generally a case of "getting in under the radar."

What is possibly most striking is the apparent suspension of any real sense of critique of the new intellectual order. Those who hold contrasting views are readily dismissed and shunned: if you do not think you are a "White supremacist," which is the subtext of the term White "privilege," that means that you are inherently guilty. If you feel uncomfortable about being accused of being a White supremacist—that means you are guilty. This is like a blatantly constructed trap; as is the reference to having "a conversation," when, of course, that is the very last thing that is intended. And notably so in terms of the past, for there is no attempt to understand the values of the past, and, without understanding, there can be scant rational discussion of it. Perish the thought that empire might be explained and contextualized, an approach that is regarded as a symptom of colonial "denial."

In practical terms, we are seeing a bringing to fruition of the attack on positivism that has been so insistent from the Left since the 1960s, an attack that is bridging from academic circles to a wider public. In particular, there was, and continues to be, a critique of subordinating scholarship and the scholar to the evidence; and a preference, instead, for an assertion of convenient evidence that was derived essentially from theory. Empiricism from then was discarded, or at least downplayed, as both method and value. Instead, there was a cult of faddish intellectualism heavily based on post-modernist concepts, and that despite the weakness of the latter, a weakness that is conceptual, methodological, empirical and historiographical, all liberating the present from the past.

Divorcing the Arts and Social Sciences from empirical methods and the constraints of understanding past contexts meant less work for the staff and no real standards other than those of virtue-signalling. This approach invited a confusion that some sought to reshape in terms of a set of values and methods equating to argument by assertion and proof by sentiment: "I feel therefore I am correct," and, in a world of calling out whatever is presented as micro-aggression, it is apparently oppression to be told otherwise.

This is a one-dimensional history, a simpleton's uni-directional account of heroes and villains. Whether or not you welcome the specifics of contemporary one-dimensional history, that is history simply as propaganda. It is a world away from debate. The conventional academic spaces, the geopolitics of academic hierarchy and method, from the lecture hall to the curriculum, have all been repurposed to this political end, and very deliberately so. And so also with public spaces, notably museums, while the statues that are unwelcome are treated not as isolated residues of allegedly outdated and nefarious glories, but as a quasi-living reproach to the new order in a culture wars of the present[20] in which there is scant space for neutrality, non-commitment, or, it might seem, tolerance and understanding. The pursuit and punishment of so-called "microaggression" represents the triumph of academic Maoism.

In part, possibly, and as an aspect of "decolonization," the legitimacy of opposing views is dismissed, indeed discredited, as allegedly racist and anti-intellectual because there is an unwillingness to ask awkward questions and to ignore evidence which does not fit into the answer wanted and already asserted. Examples of the latter might include the extent of enslavement and the slave trade prior to the European arrival in Africa; or the major role of European powers and America in eventually ending enslavement and the slave trade on land as well as at sea. Indeed, the extension of British imperialism was frequently linked, as in Nigeria and Sudan between 1860 and 1905, with the ending of slavery.

In contrast, much of the resistance to imperialism in these areas was linked with slaving interests. This does not make imperialism or resistance "good" or "bad," but should ensure that complexity is offered when explaining the past. Complexity does not prevent the opportunity to offer judgment, but that requires a degree of contextualization that is too often absent. Such questioning is crucial to understanding the past, which is the key aspect of history as an intellectual pursuit, rather than as the sphere for political engagement. As such, the theory described as "decolonization" has absolutely no place other than as a proposition and one that emerged in a particular conjuncture and to specific ends.

Historians need to understand why practices we now believe or argue to be wrong and have made illegal, such as enslavement, or (differently) making children work or marrying them, or conquest, were legitimate in the past. It is not enough, in doing so, to present only one side of, and on, the past simply because that conforms to present-day values. Nor is it pertinent to refuse to recognize debate in earlier, plural societies. (Some) people in the past believed that they were right for reasons that were legitimate in terms of their own times, experience, and general view of the world. These elements deserve consideration and should not be written away solely in terms of a somewhat mechanistic account of economic self-interest.

The answer clearly will not be provided in the "decolonization" approach, which is explicitly antithetical to academic methods in that it proclaims its engagement as its rationale. In a classic instance of Herbert Butterfield's definition of anachronism—making the study of the past a ratification or attack on the present,[21] the past is to be used, in the form of a supposedly exemplary "decolonization," as part to an attempt to recast ideas to match an account of society designed to provide an exemplary future; or at least to defend the role of universities and the careers of particular academics.[22]

The accompanying view of being an historian appears to be of spending their time wishing that people in the past did not think as they in fact did, and converting this into a platform for socio-political activism in the present. This approach has no analytical substance, and, indeed, both threatens to dissolve the discipline and leaves the student not so much short-changed as totally cheated intellectually and pedagogically, which indeed is an aspect of a current-day civilizational malaise.

Imposing anachronistic value-judgments is antithetical to the historical mindset of the scholar. The practice is also inherently transient, and in every respect, as the fullness of time will, in turn, bring in fresh critiques of present-day values, which, possibly, will also be wrenched out of their historical context, not least by ignoring inconvenient evidence. There is a somewhat fantasist approach at present in academe in the assertion of present-day values and, even more, definitions, as if these are transcendent universals, but, maybe, that approach is part of a religious imperative in a secular milieu, one very much seen with "mission statements."

In practice, the supposed universal verities are reduced to a particular conjuncture. Fuelled by a grievance of the past, they amount to a quest for utopian outcomes alongside an abject failure to understand the granulated and historical character of the world as it is. This account could be sharpened in terms of political tensions at present, not least within the British Left. At the same time, there is room for an analysis of a shared spoils system in the shape of jobs, promotion, grants and status. The degree of "sharing" causes tenson and helps fuel differences.

"Decolonization" might sound good to some and silly to others, but it is certainly a programme, and a requirement for change, one that is authoritarian in its methods and totalitarian in its objectives. Moreover, it has become more potent due to the way in which institutions seek to determine the parameters of thought within which society is perceived. This approach has a corrosive effect on society and politics in general as in growing British public criticism of the past. The British Attitudes Survey found 86 percent of respondents in 2013 "proud" or "very proud" of Britain's history but only 64 percent in 2023.

The significance of the issue can be seen in the furore in Britain in the summer of 2021 when the government sought to offer some, rather modest, pushback. It was variously accused of meddling for political advantage, provoking a culture war, *et al.* In practical terms, the governmental response in Britain has been patchy, whereas, in France, President Macron in 2021 was more robust in stigmatizing what he has presented as a challenge to French identity, an issue to which he later returned not least in criticizing antisemitism.

For both "sides," there is a civilizational dimension, whether against "racism," which has become a universal catch-all, or in defending continuity. The historical connections can go very far. The Oxford University debate about the commemoration of Cecil Rhodes centered on criticism of the retention of that legacy, notably the Rhodes' statue erected in 1911, Daniel Dorling, Halford Mackinder Professor of Geography, gave an interview with *Spiegel Online* on 31 May 2019 in which he made a number of simply erroneous remarks, as in "He [Rhodes] happily watched thousands of young black children die in his mines. …

[W]e depopulated almost the entire continent of Africa." Praised earlier in 2010 in a *Guardian* editorial, Dorling had written in 2016 in support of Jeremy Corbyn's "moral clarity." For *Spiegel Online*, he mused that a German invasion of Britain in World War Two would have "helped us get rid of the empire idea of greatness,"[23] which somewhat ignores the extent to which, at a key moment of civilizational conflict, the empire gave Britain the strength to continue to oppose the Axis powers.

Western liberals who do not see views such as those of Dorling as a serious challenge to their civilization are foolish in the extreme. While that civilization has always encouraged debate, which indeed is part of its strength, the type of criticism that is now at play is deliberately intended as revolutionary. It is not debate, but aims at the end of discussion, and should be treated accordingly. Thus, "history wars" are not some opt-out from the real issues of the present.

Indeed, they are doubly a challenge because the West, its liberal humanism, and the very concept of humane reason, is under a grave threat from external changes, notably the rapid rise of the Chinese system and China's energetic attempt to propagate its views around the world. China's path is greatly eased by the stigmatization of the West as racist and imperial, a stigmatization made more damaging by the extent to which domestic audiences within leading former colonial powers are willing to endorse this approach and to ignore China's imperial past and present. This situation is a clear indication of a cultural geopolitics that has important political consequences. For the West to take debate so far as to institutionalize the trashing of its culture, institutions, civilization and legacy, is very serious.

For some parts of the current empire, if that is not too anachronistic a term, the British link is what preserves their difference, most obviously the Falklands and Gibraltar. Bermuda voted against independence in 1995. In Britain, however, the empire, both past and surviving, is no longer seen as a community. Instead, there is a degree of amnesia, so that, for example, in 2008, when Liverpool was European capital of culture, the major role of empire in its history (for good and ill) was largely ignored.[24] When empire is addressed, the ambiguities of its past and heritage are increasingly stressed, and with the tone generally hostile. There is scant public interest in the assets, strategic and economic, it offers, though Gibraltar and Falklands each have a public resonance. The British bases in Cyprus, sovereign territories, have a significance in Middle Eastern power politics, but most colonies are of scant interest to government. The commitment, instead, frequently reflects contemporary concerns that are refashioned for particular colonies as in 2016 when a marine reserve was announced for Pitcairn Island n the south-east Pacific, while in the Atlantic there were the same for South Georgia and the South Sandwich Islands (2012), Ascension (2019) and Tristan da Cunha (2020).

At the same time, there continues to be a process of imperial recessional, within former colonies, however acquired and whenever granted independence, and with the commitment to existing colonies. There was a political dimension with this, with the Conservatives more inclined to stick to empire and the Labor Party far less so. Thus, in October 2024, Britain announced it would cede sovereignty over the Chagos archipelago to distant Mauritius, and that the treaty would also "address wrongs of the past and demonstrate the commitment of both parties to support the welfare of Chagossians."[25] Prominent Conservatives criticized the decision, James Cleverly, a former Foreign Secretary, calling it "weak, weak, weak"; although, in office, the Conservative position had been more ambivalent and the process had been set in motion.

Complicated by the American-run military base on Diego Garcia, the dispute itself reflected the problem of agreeing parties, as the Chagossians, who preferred to remain British, themselves were not principles in the negotiations. Indeed, the outcome threatened a new iteration of colonial rule (now from Mauritius) and geopolitical competition (with China), each key elements in imperial history. So also with the revival in 2024, thanks to this settlement, of the Argentinean claim to the Falklands.

Criticism of empire in its former parts varies greatly in type, intensity, chronology and consequences. Thanks to the introduction of "power-sharing," the Irish situation became less violent from the late 1990s. In Scotland, "power-sharing" was introduced, with the Scottish Parliament established in 1998 following a 1997 referendum. This did not stop a Scottish nationalism that rejected Britishness as much as the English from flourishing in the 2010s. However, the Scottish National

Party and its support for independence failed in the 2014 independence referendum and, more dramatically, in the Westminster Parliamentary elections of 2024.

These were instances of the co-ownership seen with empire in the British Isles and more generally. That, however, was never an easy process, and this was true of imperial acquisition, rule, departure and post-imperial relations, as well as such co-owned processes as enslavement (by African rulers) and the maritime slave trade (by British shippers). British attempts during decolonization to establish systems, forms and practices of post-colonial cooperation that would ensure stability as well as the continuance of British influence, often proved fruitless or short-term. In part, this involved the rejection of British wishes, as with independent India and, later, the refusal of former colonies to provide the use of naval bases during and after the Suez Crisis. Yet, the failure to get federations to work as part of the departure from empire, notably in Central Africa and the West Indies, was more than a rejection of British wishes, but, also, reflected the strong tensions between interests and identities as British authority waned and ended.

Brexit in 2016 and thereafter provoked a discussion of empire that was more problematic than the consideration of particular territorial fragments. Critics of Brexit argued that departure from the European Union was a matter of imperial nostalgia, and used that to produce a grim account of the rationale and context of assumptions and policies.[26] This approach served to condemn both empire and Brexit, a process of joining and guilt by association, which was a standard rhetorical theme in the discussion of empire. In practice, Brexit was a projection more of a "little Englander" approach than a "Greater Britain" one, though the latter played a role. Moreover, in so far as empire was implicitly referred to in the discussion, it was as an anti-imperialist argument directed against the European Union, however implausible that description might appear. This argument indicated the malleability of understandings of imperialism, but also the degree to which anti-imperialism was strongly entrenched, which is a key aspect at, and of the close of, a history of British imperialisms.

In this context, it does not help that more Welshmen fought for Edward I than against him in 1277, the same with Scots and William, Duke of Cumberland at Culloden in 1746, with Irish for and against George V in 1916, that the enslaved from West Africa were provided and sold by local rulers and merchants and as part of a broader pattern of enslavement and the slave trade, and that much of the Indian Army did not rebel in 1857. The investment in a politics of grievance and a rhetoric of anti-imperialism is simply too strong to accept a more complex account of cooperation and resistance, achievement and cruelty, and a whole antiphonal range of other phrases and approaches. So, more generally for history as a whole,[27] but imperial history appears to arouse particular anger, and not least when directed against the West. This acts as a salve for postcolonial failures and is a key constituent in "culture wars" within the West and more widely. As a result, it is particularly necessary to assess the issue and consider the arguments as attempted in this book.

9. CONCLUSIONS

Empire and the imperial experience are at the close as much about the impact on other peoples as that on Britain. Manifestations range from the trivial to the more profound; the former including hobbies and foodstuffs, whether playing cricket in the Ionian Islands, or drinking gin on Minorca. Most of the legacy of imperial products is long forgotten, however, for example Craven Empire De Luxe Mixture Tobacco, which was advertised with the picture of a serviceman.[1]

The more profound effects of the British empire vary. They include the spread of English, major and lasting demographic movements, and the creation of states. The growth of English as the global language of business and of international political and cultural links has been of key importance in global integration, and has also helped disseminate not only English-language culture, but also political, economic and social suppositions. This owed much to British imperial rule, especially in Africa, the Middle East and South Asia.

The impact of language is one also of the many ways in which it is appropriate to think of a symbiotic transfer of imperial hegemony from Britain to America. Symbiosis and transfer do not, however, mean sameness. Whereas much of the spread of the English language prior to the mid-twentieth century arose as a result of territorial control, and its impact on government and education, since then, under American influence and, to a degree, hegemony, this spread has largely been due to economic advantage outside the context of any such control.

However, in the case of the British empire, it is repeatedly difficult to differentiate between the impact of empire, in the shape of territorial control, and that of external influence during the period of imperial dominance. The latter would have been profound without formal control, as the role of America today indicates. To use informal empire as a term to describe this is not without considerable value. Yet, aside from the somewhat elastic, if not, at times, nebulous and rhetorical meaning and application, there is a problem that the idea focuses on one power, rather than the range of external influences that might well exist in specific terms.

Thus, for example, while Britain was the most important external force commercially in China in the 1920s, and was dominant in Chinese external and coastal shipping, it was not the sole non-Chinese power wielding influence and also able to apply pressure. So, also, with Britain's Atlantic economy. Britain was not the sole power drawing on the value of Atlantic trade (including the slave trade) nor of the gains to be gained from controlling New World hinterlands. The latter were a major source of prosperity, providing good soils and weaker Native opposition than was the case for China in its relationship with its landward hinterland. This contrast was important to British success but it is always necessary to avoid monocausal explanations, and, indeed descriptions; and, as already noted, Britain was not alone.

Now, in contrast, it is China that is influential and not least in the former British empire where, to a degree, it is competing well in the struggle for post-imperial influence, if not "control," and dong well in, for example, Myanmar, Pakistan and the Solomon Islands. In the former British Caribbean, Antigua and Barbuda, Dominica, Grenada, and Trinidad and Tobago signed up to China's Belt and Road infrastructure initiative in 2018, and Barbados, Jamaica and Guyana in 2019.

More generally, a revision of our understanding of the British empire is an aspect of the reconsideration of global history. Thus, the misleading "Military Revolution" account of the rise of the global military power of European powers that this has led to a relative neglect of the continued strength of Asian powers in the period 1500–1750. In particular, there is a highly misleading tendency to read the outcomes of the late nineteenth century back into the earlier period.[2] A revision of this account leads to a more convincing presentation of European imperial power as syncretic. The dependence of Europeans on others, albeit in very different contexts, emerges as central in the discussion of the period 1500–1800. Indeed, the slave trade and its wrenching and miserable power relationship confirms this picture, an insight that deserves more attention given the significance of this trade for the assessment of empire.

In the nineteenth century, the military decline of China and the Ottomans should be traced in terms of deep underlying domestic political and fiscal factors rather than any technological triumphalism of Western militarism: Non-military technology, politics, and logistics were more important in the nineteenth century than more advanced weapons. Related to this, care is needed before adopting survival-of-the-fittest interpretations of international security competition, interpretations that have often been employed in a somewhat glib fashion.

The fall of European empires in the twentieth century can be brought in by suggesting that the role of the declining legitimacy of empires reinforces the earlier conclusion about the importance of culture and ideas in the making and remaking of the international system as distinct from the rational pursuit of power and wealth and the use of technology. In so far as there is a current return to a multipolar global international order in which Asian states play a major role, the context will of course be very different to 1700. Yet again, caveats about such a return can be offered from the empirical—for example, India as the core element of Britain's Asian empire was a key part of that order until 1947, to the conceptual in terms of the changing nature of power, not least with reference to less disparate fiscal and information systems that are aligned on the global level by commercial links.[3] Formal or informal, pragmatic cooperation, within and between empires,[4] was both goal and means to a greater extent than is often appreciated. There were quasi-contracts between the metropolitan government and its colonists, but with politics and ideologies aspects of the relationships.[5] Pragmatic cooperation remained the situation in 1815–1939 when Britain was not only the leading naval power but also the dominant empire across much of the globe. This was the period of the onset of modernity, as defined by such criteria as large-scale industrialization, urbanization, and the spread of literacy.

The pressures and problems stemming from this process of modernization, notably under the strain of war, could be accentuated by foreign rule (whether transoceanic or within the West), but this rule was not the root cause of change. This is not a welcoming reflection for many, not only because it challenges the facile habit of blaming outsiders for unwelcome developments, but also because this approach questions the ability of post-imperial regimes to cope with the continued affects of globalization.

If the British empire is blamed for many of the aspects of modernization and globalization, it also serves as a way of offering historical depth to a critique of American power; and, in part, this is at issue when British imperialism is criticized. As with the British, particularly in the nineteenth century, American global policy developed with a pursuit of liberal morality linked to the furtherance of imperial goals.[6] There was a quest for an open world, in the shape of free trade and the unfettered movement of money, and a confidence that technology endorses as much as it underlines a privileged position in the international order. The power of the British and American empires can be presented in instrumental terms, as protection systems for economic practices.

However, for both Britain and America, the idea of empire included the pursuit of a benign and mutually-beneficial world order, and, in each case, there was a willingness to use major efforts to engage with rival empires that were also, correctly, seen as tyrannies: Napoleonic France, Wilhelmine and Nazi Germany, and World War Two Japan. Imperial history involved rivalry and competition between empires alongside a measure of alliance and cooperation, as in those conflicts. Turning to the level of the imperial government and of local élites and populations within particular parts of empire, cooperation could be far more important than the question of the formal domestic character of this government, in so far as these were different. It is instructive that there has been a change in emphasis from the international competition to domestic nature in the modern discussion of empire, as well as from power to culture. This may be an aspect of an intellectual presentism that is misleading as a guide to the past, although cultural elements are part of the practices and politics of cooperation that were important to successful imperial governance.

Nevertheless, the terms of the mutual benefit offered by the British and American empires were unwelcome to many, more particularly in the British case as its empire rested more clearly on conquest, control, constraint and coercion. In contrast, there was a democratic objective at the heart of American capitalism that was seen as in America's and the world's interest, and that helped foster American opposition to the

European colonial empires, notably that of Britain.[7] The Americans hoped that newly-independent peoples would support democratic capitalism and thus look to America. They wanted an empire by invitation,[8] which, however, raised the questions, as in Latin America, of "whose invitation?" and "by how secured?"

If the British empire is both alien and redundant from this perspective (and, as a minor echo, British accents and actors seemed obvious trademarks of villainy through the democratizing lens of Hollywood), that has not prevented a conflation of British and American imperialism in some quarters. This offers another way in which the experience of British rule can be seen as unwelcome. More generally, criticism, if not caricature, of the British empire are freely offered, and few defenders are to be seen, in Britain or elsewhere.

This criticism would be more impressive if it could be shown that the British were worse than other imperialists. Although it was not alone in being seaborne, the seaborne character, global range and, association with particular commercial, and, eventually, industrial developments, of the British empires over the last half-millennium, gave it a particular character. Yet, the British scarcely invented long-distance commerce, enslavement, war, external rule and racism.

Instead, imperial pretensions and power, not self-determination, were the norm, and still are in parts of the world such as Tibet and Xinkiang, both still under Chinese control as they have been from the eighteenth century. In place of the North-West Frontier of British India, there is the North-West Frontier of modern India, with Kashmir occupied by large numbers of Indian troops and paramilitaries, and in 2019 the constitutional provisions giving the majority-Muslim region a degree of autonomy removed, while the federal government also replaced the status of Kashmir, Ladakh and Jammu as a status with that of two territories ruled directly by Delhi. Moreover, Hindu settlement has been encouraged, which raises the issue of settler colonization.

Furthermore, "the underlying centrality of slavery in the historical relationship between Egypt and the Sudan" was such that anti-colonial nationalism in Egypt was fully compatible with a determination to regain power over Sudan,[9] as in Nokrashy Pasha's speech in the Egyptian Senate in August 1945 in favor of Egyptian independence. Indeed, the national projects of former colonies notably Africanization policies of Kenya and Uganda, the Arabization ones of Egypt, and the Malayanization and other counterparts, all had had brutal consequences for many; and, as a result, cast a more positive light on the polyglot nature of British imperialism.

At this level of abstraction, it can be too easy to forget that people were involved in making empire and in the web of connections and relationships that sustained it. At the time, their reputation could be very mixed, as with Robert Clive, Warren Hastings and Cecil Rhodes, and modern discussion of all three in part has echoes of contemporary debate. And so for many who have been largely forgotten. Frederic Shelford, the consulting engineer to the Crown Agents for the West African Railways, was criticized in 1904 by name and at length in Parliament by Newton, 6th Earl of Portsmouth, for incompetence if not corruption. Crucially, Shelford's father-in-law was Permanent Under-Secretary at the Colonial Office. British commentators presented their colonial administrators as opposed to indigenous corruption, but there was much corruption in this administration.[10]

If the British empire is central to much of world history over the last four centuries, that was in part because its character stemmed from all the peoples and countries that were affected, including not only colonial subjects, but also other expansionist powers, both Western and non-Western. The interrelationships were multifocal and far from unidirectional. Indeed, it is a mistake to present England/Britain as necessarily the main player in the developments from which it profited. For example, the struggle between England and the Dutch in 1652–74 was central to the English/British dominance of the "Middle Colonies" of North America until 1775. However, Dutch failure in this struggle was in part due to the earlier Dutch mid-seventeenth century defeat by Portugal in the South and Mid-Atlantic notably in Brazil, but also in Atlantic Africa. This exemplifies the extent to which it is not always clear what is an expansionist power, for the same state might be such in one area but not in another.

The mistaken assumption that Western powers were the ones responsible, only or largely, for imperialism and supposedly related crimes such as enslavement is underlined by the case of the Pacific, which tends to receive less attention than is merited in the discussion of British imperialism. For example, the Chatham Islands were invaded by Māori from New Zealand in 1835. To blame this expansionism solely on guns obtained by trade with Europeans is in part to make the means the cause. Instead, there was the migration and movement of Māori tribes to avoid attacks by neighbors with muskets. Rather than a deliberate conquest, the tribes Ngati Tama and Ngati Mutunga escaped to the Chathams as a safe refuge. But after initial good relations with the Moriori people, Polynesians of Māori descent, who had settled in about 1500, misunderstandings multiplied and the newcomers brutally attacked the Moriori, who were pacifists. They were largely slaughtered, with the survivors enslaved. There could have been 1,600 of them in 1800 and they were reduced to only 100. In 1842, the islands officially became part of the colony of New Zealand and, in 1863, the enslaved were freed by the resident magistrate.

In Fiji, British influence, and then control, was welcome locally not only as a way to limit American pressure, but also to deter Tongan expansionism, as well as to ensure order within Fiji. The annexation of Fiji in 1874 in part reflected a parliamentary campaign pressing for it as a means to end slavery. This, plus the Pacific Islanders Protection Act of 1872 and the establishment of the Western Pacific High Commission in 1877, were regarded as ways to protect the indigenous people. Charles Morris Woodford, a naturalist who learned local languages, became the first Resident Commissioner of the Solomon Islands Protectorate, serving from 1896 until 1914 and trying, with few resources, mostly Fijian policemen and episodic help from the Royal Navy, to stop headhunting, fight smallpox, support Anglican missionaries, and create a civil administration.

The contrast between lines of imperial control on the map and small administrations was more generally apparent. Even if willing, colonial administrations were not in a good position to regulate commercial companies. Instead, they tended to share power, with the companies, as with the British on the Solomons, and/or with existing chiefs, as with the British on Fiji, and also with the local representatives of the Western military.

Such cooperation and protection, nevertheless, was on terms. Taxation for example could force islanders into wage labor. Partly as a result, islanders worked as indentured labor, for example in Queensland, labor that was voluntary, but could involve coercion and/or deceit.

Meanwhile, in North America, the Native Americans did very badly in the United States when the protective presence of the British Crown was removed. Differently, in Canada, the position of the First Nations deteriorated with Canadian nationhood, as government regulation was established and enforced, notably by the Indian Acts of 1876, 1880, and 1884. In 1884, the *potlatch* ceremony, central to the coastal cultures, was banned, a measure not reversed until 1960. Tribal governance was overthrown, resources seized, and British/Canadian/settler/White (the choice of adjective is instructive) systems of marriage, parenthood and land tenure all enforced. Reserves were regulated by the Department of Indian Affairs. As in Australia, indigenous children were forced into residential schools in order to break traditional links, while indigenous communities were sometimes moved. There was no right to vote in federal elections until 1960.

In many countries, the end of British rule or influence was frequently followed not by democracy but by the interplay and impact of international geopolitical competition and, on the national level, the entrenchment of one-faction governmental systems. These were often authoritarian.

In Egypt, the republican coup in 1952 was followed in 1953 by an abolition of democracy, in the shape of the 1923 liberal constitution, and of political parties, and by the harsh treatment of rivals by special tribunals. Charges of treason were widely distributed as the military seized total control, which it used to its own profit. Meanwhile, the state socialism followed by the Egyptian government did not produce significant economic improvement. Religious and ethnic minorities were badly treated.

Moreover, as in Burma/Myanmar from the late 1940s and in Zimbabwe in the 1980s, post-imperial systems could be very violent toward particular groups. Nigeria became an envelopment for Hausa control, and the Igibo suffered very greatly in the Biafran War of 1967–70. Moreover, post-British rule was frequently unstable. Coups included in Pakistan in 1958, 1971, 1977, and 1999, Ghana in 1966, 1972, 1978, 1979 and 1981, Sierra Leone in 1967 and 1997, Nigeria in 1966, 1985 and

1993, and Grenada in 1979 and 1983. Since independence in 1956, Sudan has had 19 coup attempts, 7 of them successful. Unsuccessful coups included Pakistan in 1951, 1973, 1980, 1984 and 1995, Ghana in 1983, 1984, 1985, 1986, and 1987, Gambia in 1981 and Nigeria in 1990.

The limited extent of popular support for national government in the post-imperial Middle East was to be suggested in the "Arab Springs" of the 2010s and 2020s, while civil wars in Sudan in 1955 to 1972, 1983 to 2005, 2003 to 2020, and 2023 to the present, were scarcely an advertisement for the end of the British empire. The glumness of the present, which includes Russian imperialism in Ukraine and Chinese informal empire, does not excuse the harshness and problems of past imperialism, British and other. Nevertheless, the present situation should possibly encourage an assessment that is more alive to the contexts and character both of that imperialism and of the modern world.

Endnotes

Preface Endnote

1 Enclosed in Ashley Dodge to Jeremy Black, 7 Oct. 2024.

Chapter 1 Endnotes

1 A particularly poor recent instance, but coming from a major publisher, is S. Sanghera, *Empireworld: How British Imperialism Shaped the Globe* (London, 2023).
2 I. Hampsher-Monk, "Edmund Burke and Empire," in *Proceedings of the British Academy*, 155 (2009): 117–25; P. Woodfine, "'Suspicious Latitudes': Commerce, Colonies, and Patriotism in the 1730s," in *Studies in Eighteenth-Century Culture*, 27 (1998): 45–6; D. Armitage, "The Cromwellian Protectorate and the Languages of Empire," in *Historical Journal*, 35 (1992): 553–5.
3 A. Burton, *The Trouble with Empire: Challenges to Modern British Imperialism* (Oxford, 2015).
4 See, for example, E. Downey, T. Hulme and M. Vandrei, "The *Mayflower* and Historical Culture in Britain, 1620–2020," in *EHR*, 138 (2023): 898–932.
5 H. Hoock, *Empires of the Imagination: Politics, War, and the Arts in the British World, 1750–1850* (London, 2010).
6 F. Furedi, *The War Against the Past* (London, 2024).
7 K. Kumar, *Visions of Empire: How Five Imperial Regimes Shaped the World* (Princeton, NJ, 2017).
8 S. Sivasundaram, *Waves Across the South: A New History of Revolution and Empire* (London, 2020).
9 *David Copperfield* (London, 1849–50), chapter 4.
10 *Our Mutual Friend*, chapter 25.
11 *David Copperfield*, chapter 1.
12 *David Copperfield*, chapter 36.
13 M. House and G. Story (eds.), *The Letters of Charles Dickens* (12 vols, Oxford, 1965–2002), V, 622.
14 *A Tale of Two Cities*, chapter 7.

15 *Little Dorrit*, chapter 21.
16 *Bleak House*, chapter 4.
17 *Letters*, X, 53.
18 A poor part of London.
10 *Letters*, XI, 115–16.
20 *Edwin Drood*, chapter 16.
21 See, amongst a massive literature, A.M. Burton (ed.), *After the Imperial Turn: Thinking with and through the Nation* (Durham, NC, 2003) and S. Howe (ed.), *The New Imperial Histories Reader* (London, 2010).

Chapter 2 Endnotes

1 L. Brady, *The Origin Legends of Early Medieval Britain and Ireland* (Cambridge, 2022).
2 L. Ashe and E.J. Ward (eds.), *Conquests in Eleventh-Century England: 1016, 1066* (Woodbridge, 2020).
3 D. Bates (ed.), *1066 in Perspective* (Leeds, 2018).
4 R. Frame, *The Political Development of the British Isles, 1100–1400* (Oxford, 1990).
5 I.A. MacInnes, *Scotland's Second War of Independence, 1332–1357* (Woodbridge, 2016).
6 S.T. Ambler, "The Dark Trophies of the Battle of Evesham, the Northumbrian Cult of Simon de Montfort and the War of the Welsh Marches, 1264–1265," in *EHR*, 149 (2024): 57–9; K.J. Stringer and A.J.L. Winchester (eds.), *Northern England and Southern Scotland in the Central Middle Ages* (Woodbridge, 2017).

Chapter 3 Endnotes

1 G.P. Baker and C. Lambert, "'William Fowler,' Sir William Garrard, Sir John Hawkins and the Sixteenth-Century Atlantic Slave Trade," in *EHR*, 139 (2024): 680–714.

Chapter 4 Endnotes

1 V. Bernhard, *Slaves and Slaveholders in Bermuda, 1616–1782* (Columbia, MS., 1999); M.J. Jarvis, *Isle of Devils, Isle of Saints: An Atlantic History of Bermuda, 1609–1684* (Baltimore, MD, 2022).
2 L.H. Roper, *Advancing Empire: English Interests and Overseas Expansion, 1613–1688* (Cambridge, 2017).

3 L. Working, *The Making of an Imperial Polity: Civility and America in the Jacobean Metropolis* (Cambridge, 2020).

4 J.G. Turner, *They Knew They Were Pilgrims: Plymouth Colony and the Contest for American Liberty* (New Haven, CT, 2020).

5 P. Brown, "'This Thing of Darkness I Acknowledge Mine,' *The Tempest* and the Discourse of Colonialism," in *Political Shakespeare: New Essays in Cultural Materialism*, edited by J. Dollimore and A. Sinfield (1985): 48–71.

6 C.G. Pestana, *The English Conquest of Jamaica: Oliver Cromwell's Bid for Empire* (Cambridge, MA, 2017).

7 J.D. Drake, *King Philip's War. Civil War in New England, 1675–1676* (Amherst, MA, 1999).

8 N. Das, *Courting India: England, Mughal India, and the Origins of Empire* (London, 2023).

9 P.J. Stern, *Empire, Incorporated: The Corporations that Built British Colonialism* (Cambridge, MA, 2023).

10 W. Pettigrew and M. Gopalan (eds.), *The East India Company, 1600–1857: Essays on Anglo-Indian Connection* (London, 2017).

11 D. Veevers, *The Origins of the British Empire in Asia, 1600–1750* (Cambridge, 2020) and "Building Borders in a Borderless Land: English Colonialism and the Alam Minangkabau of Sumatra, 1680–1730," in *Journal of the British Academy*, 9 (2021): 58–89.

12 D. Ormrod and G. Rommelse (eds.), *War, Trade and the State. Anglo-Dutch Conflict 1652–89* (Woodbridge, 2020).

13 S. Fullerton, "New England in the Royalist Imagination, 1637–89," in *EHR*, 137 (2022): 1373–6.

14 P. Gauci, *The Politics of Trade. The Overseas Merchant in State and Society, 1660–1720* (Oxford, 2001); N. Glaisyer, *The Culture of Commerce in England, 1660–1720* (Woodbridge, 2006).

15 H. Bromley, "England's Mercantilism: Trading Companies, Employment and the Politics of Trade in Global History, 1688–1704," in *EHR*, 138 (2023): 744–72.

16 G. Pizzoni, *British Catholic Merchants in the Commercial Age, 1670–1714* (Woodbridge, 2020).

17 J.M. Schultz, *National Identity and the Anglo-Scottish Borderlands, 1552–1652* (Woodbridge, 2019).

Chapter 5 Endnotes

1 Historical Manuscripts Commission Reports, *Egmont Diary* I, 220; BL. Add. 51417 folio 77.

2 R. Wodrow, *Analecta* (4 vols., Edinburgh, 1842–43): 280.
3 Cobbett, *Parliamentary History* XIII, 354.
4 R. Taylor, "The Politics of Goldsmith's Journalism," in *Philological Quarterly*, 69 (1990): 71, 83–86.
5 Molesworth's memorial, 20 November 1750, BL. Add. 51378 folios 87–89.
6 A. Murdock, *"The People Above." Politics and Administration in Mid-Eighteenth Century Scotland* (Edinburgh, 1980).
7 BL. Blakeney Mss I, p. 64.
8 F.W. Freeman, *Robert Fergusson and the Scots Humanist Compromise* (Edinburgh, 1984).
9 A. Smith, *Jacobite Estates of the Forty-Five* (Edinburgh, 1982).
10 Eg. *Contrast*, 6, 20 July; *Monitor*, 16 July 1763.
11 *St James's Chronicle*, 14 February 1765.
12 A. Doig, J.P.S. Ferguson, I.A. Milne and R. Passmore (eds.), *William Cullen and the Eighteenth-Century Medical World* (Edinburgh, 1993).
13 E. Jones (ed.), *The Welsh in London, 1500–2000* (Cardiff, 2001).
14 K. Morgan (ed.), *An American Quaker in the British Isles: The Travel Journals of Jabez Maud Fisher, 1775–1779* (Oxford, 1992), 264.
15 John to Pryse Campbell, 28 October 1735, Carmarthen, Dyfed Archive Service, Cawdor Muniments, Box 138.
16 P. Langford, *Englishness Identified. Manners and Character 1650–1850* (Oxford, 2000).
17 T.D. Watt, *Popular Protest and Policing in Ascendancy Ireland, 1691–1761* (Woodbridge, 2018).
18 Ridpath to Count Bothmer, Hanoverian minister, 2 Dec. 1713, HL. HM. 44710.
19 J. Jack, *"A New Voyage Round the World*; Defoe's *Roman à These,*" *Huntington Library Quarterly*, 24 (1961): 322–36.
20 D. Carey, "Reading Contrapuntally: *Robinson Crusoe*, Slavery and Postcolonial Theory," in Carey and L. Festa (eds.), *The Postcolonial Enlightenment: Eighteenth-Century Colonialism and Postcolonial Theory* (Oxford, 2009).
21 John Tucker MP to Richard Tucker, 10 Mar. 1744, Bod. Ms. Don. C. 107 f. 18; L. Colley, *Britons: Forging the Nation, 1707–1837* (New Haven, CT, 1992); T. Devine, *Scotland's Empire and the Shaping of America, 1600–1815* (Washington, 2004).
22 S. Kinkel, *Disciplining the Empire: Politics, Governance, and the Rise of the British Navy* (Cambridge, MA, 2018).
23 Johnstone to James Balmain, 23 Dec. 1761, HL., Pulteney papers, no. 671.
24 *Bath Chronicle*, 1 Jan. 1761; *Gentleman's Magazine*, 31 (1761): 123–4.
25 Arthur Dobbs to John, 3rd Earl of Bute, 2 June 1762,Mount Stuart, papers

from Cardiff, 2/74. See also, D. Clarke, *Arthur Dobbs, Esq., 1689–176* (London, 1958).

26 Molesworth to Bute, 8 Oct. 1765, MS 4/121.

27 *Travels*, chapters 26, 30.

28 M.N. McConnell, *Army and Empire. British Soldiers on the American Frontier, 1758–1775* (Lincoln, NE, 2005).

29 R. Travers, *Empires of Complaint: Mughal Law and the Making of British India, 1765–1793* (Cambridge, 2022).

30 S. Sen, *Empire of Free Trade. The East India Company and the Making of the Colonial Marketplace* (Philadelphia, 1998); P.J. Stern, *The Company State: Corporate Sovereignty and the Early Modern Foundations of the British Empire in India* (2011).

31 H.V. Bowen, "Sinews of trade and empire: the supply of commodity exports to the East India Company during the late eighteenth century," in *EcHR*, 55 (2002): 466–86.

32 Bowen, *Revenue and Reform. The Indian Problem in British Politics 1757–1773* (Cambridge, 1991), and "Tea, Tribute and the East India Company c. 1750–c. 1775," in S. Taylor, R. Connors and C. Jones (eds.), *Hanoverian Britain and Empire* (Woodbridge, 1998), pp. 158–76.

33 Marshall, *The Making and Unmaking of Empires. Britain, India, and America c. 1750–1783* (Oxford, 2005), eg. p. 378.

34 R. Scobie, *Celebrity Culture and the Myth of Oceania in Britain, 1770–1823* (Woodbridge, 2019).

35 J. Thomas, *The East India Company and the Provinces in the Eighteenth Century. I Portsmouth and the East India Company 1700–1815* (Lampeter, 1999).

36 M. Knights, *Trust and Distrust: Corruption in Public Office in Britain and its Empire, 1600–1850* (2021).

37 Cambridge, University Library, Cholmondeley Houghton papers, Mss. 88/139.

38 Liverpool to Sylvester Douglas, 11 Sept. 1798, BL. Add. 38310 f. 234.

39 R.B. Sheridan, "The Commercial and Financial Organization of the British Slave Trade, 1750–1807," in *EcHR*, 2nd series, 11 (1958–9): 249–63, esp. p. 263; J.A. Rawley, *London: Metropolis of the Slave Trade* (2003).

40 J.E. Inikori, *Africans and the Industrial Revolution in England: A Study in International Trade and Economic Development* (2002), pp. 407–8, 416, 513, 518–19.

41 M.D. Mitchell, "Three English Cloth Towns and the Royal African Company," in *Journal of the Historical Society*, 13 (2013): 447.

42 Crookshanks to Thomas, Duke of Newcastle, Secretary of State for the Southern Department, 10 Mar. 1731, BL. Add. 32687 f. 395.

43 J.L. Bullion, *A Great and Necessary Measure. George Grenville and the*

Genesis of the Stamp Act, 1763–1765 (Columbia, MS, 1982); W.B. Kerr, "The Stamp Act in Nova Scotia," in *New England Quarterly*, 6 (1933): 552–66; A.J. O'Shaughnessy, "The Stamp Act Crisis in the British Caribbean," in *William and Mary Quarterly*, 3rd Ser., 51 (1994): 203–26.

44 T.G. Burnard, "'Prodigious riches': the wealth of Jamaica before the American Revolution," in *EcHR*, 44 (2001): 520–2.

45 O'Shaughnessy, *An Empire Divided. The American Revolution and the British Caribbean* (Philadelphia, 2000), pp. 104–5.

46 R. Grassby, *The Business Community of Seventeenth-Century England* (Cambridge, 1995).

47 J.D. Grainger, *The Battle of Yorktown, 1781: A Reassessment* (Woodbridge, 2005).

48 E. Gould, *The Persistence of Empire. British Political Culture in the Age of the American Revolution* (Chapel Hill, NC, 2000).

49 Liston to John, 3rd Duke of Dorset, 19 Ap. 1786, Maidstone, KAO. U269 C184.

50 Pitt to Eden, 7 Jan. 1788, NA. PRO. 30/8/102 fol. 115.

51 G.H. Gerzina (ed.), *Britain's Black Past* (Liverpool, 2020).

52 *Sotheby's Sale*, 6–7 Dec. 1984, item 477.

53 Fox to Duke of Portland, 18 Nov. 1786, BL. Add. 47561 fol. 87.

Chapter 6 Endnotes

1 E. Ingram, *Commitment to Empire: Prophecies of the Great Game in Asia, 1797–1800* (Oxford, 1981); P. Mackesy, *British Victor in Egypt, 1801* (London, 1995).

2 L. Ford, *The King's Peace: Law and Order in the British Empire* (Cambridge, MA, 2021).

3 A. Forrest, *The Death of the French Atlantic: Trade, War, and Slavery in the Age of Revolution* (Oxford, 2020).

4 Lines 189–200. See also C. Bolton, *Writing the Empire: Robert Southey and Romantic Colonialism* (London, 2007).

5 C. Bolton, *Writing the Empire: Robert Southey and Romantic Colonialism* (London, 2007).

6 J.A. Auerbach, *Imperial Boredom: Monotony and the British Empire* (Oxford, 2018).

7 S. Makdisi, *Making England Western: Occidentalism, Race and Imperial Culture* (Chicago, IL, 2014).

8 A.S. Mlambo and N. Parsons, *A History of Southern Africa* (London, 2023), p. 117.

9 R. Cheriau, *Imperial Powers and Humanitarian Intervention: The Zanzibar*

Sultanate, Britain, and France in the Indian Ocean, 1862–1905 (Abingdon, 2021).

10 M. Horswell, *The Rise and Fall of British Crusader Medievalism c.1825–1945* (London, 2018).

11 B. Kingsburg, *An Imperial Disaster: The Bengal Cyclone of 1876* (London, 2018).

12 J. Fradera, *The Imperial Nation: Citizens and Subjects in the British, French, Spanish, and American empires* (Princeton, NJ, 2018).

13 Bruce to Edward, Lord Stanley, Foreign Secretary, 12 Jan. 1867, NA. FO. 5/1104 f. 40–2.

14 C. Wright, *Wellington's Men in Australia: Peninsular War Veterans and the Making of Empire c.1820–40* (Basingstoke, 2011).

15 C. Kinealy and G. Moran (eds), *Irish Famines before and after the Great Famine* (Hamden, CT, 2020).

16 E. Malcolm and D. Hall, *A New History of the Irish in Australia* (Sydney, 2018).

17 A.K. Chatterjee, *Indians in London: From the Birth of the East India Company to Independent India* (New Delhi, 2021).

18 D.I. Salesa, *Racial Crossings. Race, Intermarriage, and the Victorian British Empire* (Oxford, 2011).

19 G.J. Heuman, *"The Killing Time": The Morant Bay Rebellion in Jamaica* Knoxville, TN, 1994); J. Evans, "Re-reading Edward Eyre—Race, resistance and repression in Australia and the Caribbean," in *Australian Historical Studies*, 33 (2002): 175–98.

20 J. Greenland's *Uprising: Morant Bay, 1865 and its Afterlives* (2015).

21 The Miskito position was very much infringed from the 1960s, leading in the 1980s to large-scale violence. This is an instance of the degree to which the post-imperial situation has frequently been disadvantageous for minority peoples, some of whom had cooperated with Britain.

22 W. Mulligan, "Decisions for Empire: Revisiting the 1882 Occupation of Egypt," in *EHR*, 135 (2020): 94–126.

23 R. Owen, *Lord Cromer: Victorian Imperialist, Edwardian Proconsul* (Oxford, 2004).

24 K. Roy, *The Indian Rebellion, 1857–1859: A Military History in the Global Context* (Abingdon, 2025).

25 G. Paquette, "Anglo-Portuguese Relations in the Mid-Nineteenth Century: Informal Empire, Arbitration and the Durability of an Asymmetrical Alliance," in *EHR*, 135 (2020).

26 J. Bangura, *The Temne of Sierra Leone: African Agency in the Making of a British Colony* (Cambridge, 2017).

27 B. Porter, *The Absent-Minded Imperialists: Empire, Society, and Culture in Britain* (Oxford, 2004).

28 Eg. E.M. Spiers, "Military correspondence in the late nineteenth-century press," in *Archives*, 32 (2007): 39–40.

29 J.S. Bratton et al, *Acts of Supremacy: The British Empire and the Stage, 1790–1903* (Manchester: Manchester University Press, 1991); P. Hoffenberg, *An Empire on Display: English, Indian, and Australian Exhibitions from the Crystal Palace to the Great War* (Berkeley, CA, 2001).

30 *Julian Browning Autographs and Manuscripts*, catalogue 24 (London, 2001), p. 7, item 55.

31 For the BBC changing the presentation of Doyle's *The Lost World* (1912): "BBC will strip Conan Doyle of racial overtones," in *Daily Telegraph*, 12 November 2000.

32 J.C. Bender, *The 1857 Indian Uprising and the British Empire* (Cambridge, 2017).

33 M. Taylor, *Empress: Queen Victoria and India* (New Haven, CT, 2018).

34 J. Kestner, *The Edwardian Detective 1901–15* (Farnham, 2000).

35 B. English, "The Kanpur Massacres in India in the Revolt of 1857," in *Past and Present*, 142 no. 1 (1994): 169–78.

36 B. Robson (ed.), "The Kandahar Letters of the Reverend Alfred Cane," in *Journal of the Society for Army Historical Research*, 69 (1991): 215.

37 A reference to Hell.

38 P.A. Townend, *The Road to Home Rule: Anti-Imperialism and the Irish National Movement* (Madison, WI, 2016).

39 R. Toye, *Churchill's Empire: The World that Made Him and the World He Made* (Oxford, 2010).

40 G. Wilkinson, *Depictions and Images of War in Edwardian Newspapers, 1899–1914* (Basingstoke, 2003); P. Donaldson, *Remembering the South African War: Britain and the Memory of the Anglo-Boer War, from 1899 to the Present* (Liverpool, 2013).

41 *Hansard, House of Commons Debates*, March 15, 1883, vol. 277 column 617.

42 *Hansard, House of Commons Debates*, May 7, 1883, vol. 279, columns 125–26.

43 B. Cesario, *New Crusade: The Royal Navy and British Navalism, 1884–1914* (Berlin, 2021).

44 W.K. Storey, *The Colonialist: The Vision of Cecil Rhodes* (Oxford, 2025).

45 D. Bell, *The Idea of Great Britain: Empire and the Future of World Order, 1860–1900* (Princeton, 2007).

46 M. Peel and C. Twomey, *A History of Australia* (2nd ed., London, 2021), p. 146.

47 J. Barnes, *Arthur and George* (London, 2005); S. Basu, *The Mystery of the Parsee Lawyer: Arthur Conan Doyle, George Edalji and the Case of the Foreigner in the English Village* (London, 2021).

48 M. Lake and H. Reynolds, *Drawing the Global Colour Line: White Men's Countries and the International Challenge of Racial Equality* (Cambridge, 2008).
49 J.L. Thompson, *Forgotten Patriot: A Life of Alfred, Viscount Milner of St James's and Cape Town, 1854–1925* (Madison, NJ, 2007).
50 I. Smith, *The Origins of the South African War, 1899–1902* (Harlow, 1996).
51 T. McMahon, M. de Nie and P. Townend (eds.), *Ireland and the Imperial World: Citizenship, Opportunism and Subversion* (London, 2017).

Chapter 7 Endnotes

1 BL. Add. 50300 fol. 176.
2 C. Heere, *Empire Ascendant: The British World, Race, and the Rise of Japan, 1894–1914* (Oxford, 2020).
3 D.E. Delaney, *The Imperial Army Project: Britain and the Land Forces of the Dominions and India, 1902–1945* (Oxford, 2017).
4 E. Dal Lago, R. Healy and G. Barry (eds), *1916 in Global Context: An Anti-Imperial Moment* (London, 2018).
5 N. Gallagher, *Ireland and the Great War: A Social and Political History* (London, 2020).
6 K. Jeffery, *Ireland and the Great War* (Cambridge, 2000); A. Gregory and S. Pašeta (eds.), *Ireland and the Great War. "A War To Unite Us All"?* (Manchester, 2002).
7 A. Jackson, *Home Rule: An Irish History, 1800–2000* (Oxford, 2004).
8 J. Fisher, "Major Norman Bray and Eastern Unrest in the British Empire in the Aftermath of World War I," *Archives*, 27 (2002): 39–56, esp. 45–52.
9 E. Monroe, *Britain's Moment in the Middle East, 1914–1956* (Baltimore, MD, 1963); B.C. Busch, *Britain, India and the Arabs, 1914–21* (London, 1971); J. Darwin, *Britain, Egypt and the Middle East: Imperial Policy in the Aftermath of War 1918–1922* (London, 1981); B. Westrate, *The Arab Bureau: British Policy in the Middle East, 1916–1920* (University Park, PA, 1992).
10 K.O. Morgan, *Consensus and Disunity: The Lloyd George Coalition Government 1918–1922* (Oxford, 1979), pp. 323, 325, 342.
11 R.J.C. Adams, *The Shadow of a Taxman: Who Funded the Irish Revolution* (Oxford, 2022); F.M. Carroll, *America and the Making of an Independent Ireland* (New York, 2021).
12 T. Harper, *Underground Asia. Global Revolutionaries and the Assault on Empire* (London, 2020).
13 Colonial Office, *Colonial Reports – Annual. No. 1292. Northern Rhodesia. Report for 1924–25* (London, 1926), p. 14.

14 P. Ewer, "A Gentlemen's Club in the Clouds: Re-assessing the Empire Air Mail Scheme, 1933–1939," in *Journal of Transport History*, 28 (2007), corrects the more positive account in R. Higham, *Britain's Imperial Air Routes, 1918–1939* (Hamden, CT, 1960).

15 E.M. Collingham, *Imperial Bodies: The Physical Experience of the Raj, c. 1800–1947* (Cambridge, 2001).

16 Damian P. O'Connor, "The Twenty Year Armistice. RUSI between the wars," in *RUSI Journal*, 154, 1 (Feb. 2009): 86–9.

17 D.R. Headrick, *Power Over Peoples: Technology, Environments, and Western Imperialism, 1400 to the Present* (Princeton, NJ, 2010).

18 K. Dodds, *Pink Ice. Britain and the South Atlantic Empire* (2002), pp. 26–7.

19 D. Higgins and B. Varian, "Britain's Empire Marketing Board and the failure of soft trade policy, 1926–33," in *European Review of Economic History*, 25 (2021): 780–805.

20 D. Kennedy, "Empire Migration in Post-War Reconstruction: The Role of the Oversea Settlement Committee, 1919–1922," and B.L. Blakeley, "The Society for the Oversea Settlement of British Women and the Problems of Empire Settlement, 1917–1936," in *Albion*, 20 (1988): 403–44, esp. 432–3.

21 E. Boucher, *Empire's Children: Child Emigration, Welfare, and the Decline of the British World, 1869–1967* (Cambridge, 2014).

22 A. Thompson, "The Languages of Loyalism in Southern Africa, *c.* 1870–1939," in *EHR*, 118 (2003): 648.

23 T. Pietsch, *Empire of Scholars: Universities, Networks and the British Academic World, 1850–1939* (2013).

24 A. Waldie, "Contesting an Elastic Constitution: British Nationality and Protection in the Mandates," in *Britain and the World*, 16 (2023): 168–91.

25 D. Gilmour, *The Long Recessional. The Imperial Life of Rudyard Kipling* (London, 2002, 2003 edn.), p. 297.

26 K.A. Sandford and B. Stoddart, *The Imperial Game. Cricket, Culture and Society* (Manchester, 1998).

27 B.R. Tomlinson, *The Political Economy of the Raj, 1914–1947: the Economics of Decolonization in India* (London, 1979).

28 S. Clarkson, *Uncle Sam and US Globalization, Neoconservatism, and the Canadian State* (Toronto, 2002), p. 20.

29 R. Bickers, *Britain in China. Community, Culture and Colonialism, 1900–49* (Manchester, 1999); S.K. Fung, *The Diplomacy of Imperial Retreat: Britain's South China Policy, 1924–1931* (Oxford, 1991).

30 R. Hyam, *The Failure of South African Expansion 1908–1948* (London, 1972).

31 A.T. Maitrii, *The Return of the Galon King: History, Law, and Rebellion in Colonial Burma* (Athens, OH, 2011).

32 M. Kolinsky, *Britain's War in the Middle East: Strategy and Diplomacy, 1936–42* (New York, 1999); N. Shepherd, *Ploughing Sand: British Rule in Palestine, 1917–1948* (Piscataway, New Jersey, 2000).
33 T.C. Holt, *The Problem of Freedom: Race, Labor, and Politics in Jamaica and Britain, 1932–1938* (Baltimore, MD, 1992).
34 W. Reid, *Fighting Retreat: Churchill and India* (London, 2024).
35 A. Muldoon, *Empire, Politics and the Creation of the 1935 India Act: Last Act of the Raj* (Farnham, 2009).
36 P. Chowdhry, *Colonial India and the Making of Empire Cinema: Image, Ideology and Identity* (Manchester, 2000).
37 Chiefs of Staff Sub-Committee, "Appreciation of the Situation in the Event of War Against Germany," 14 Sept. 1938, NA. Cabinet Office papers 24/278, pp. 345–59.
38 E. Gibbon, *The History of the Decline and Fall of the Roman Empire*, ed. J.B. Bury (7 vols., London, 1897–1901), IV, 166.
39 A. Jackson, *Persian Gulf Command: A History of the Second World Warin Iran and Iraq* (New Haven, CT, 2018).
40 B.J.C. McKercher, *Transition of Power: Britain's Loss of Global Pre-eminence to the United States, 1930–1945* (Cambridge, 1999).
41 P. Orders, *Britain, Australia, New Zealand and the Expansion of American Power in the South-West Pacific, 1941–46* (Basingstoke, 2002).
42 M. Crowley and S. Dawson (eds.), *Home Fronts: Britain and the Empire at War, 1939–45* (Woodbridge, 2017).
43 Quote, N. Smith, *American Empire. Roosevelt's Geographer and the Prelude to Globalization* (Berkeley, CA, 2003), p. 360.
44 M. Hauner, *India in Axis Strategy: Germany, Japan and Indian Nationalists in the Second World War* (Stuttgart, 1981).
45 Wavell to Field Marshal Brooke, Chief of the Imperial General Staff, 4 July 1944, Kings College, London, Liddell Hart Archive (hereafter KCL. LH), Alanbrooke papers 6/4/12.
46 A. Jackson, *Botswana 1939–1945: An African Country at War* (Oxford, 1999).
47 F. Houghton, "'Alien Seamen' or 'Imperial Family': Race, Belonging and British Sailors of Colour in the Royal Navy, 1939–47," in *EHR*, (2022): 1429–61.
48 See, eg. Admiral Sir Geoffrey Layton, Commander-in-Chief of Ceylon, to First Sea Lord, 13 Sept., Lord Louis Mountbatten to Layton, 15 Sept. 1944, BL. Add. 74796; and N.A.M. Rodger, *The Price of Victory. A Naval History of Britain 1815–1945* (London, 2024), p. 613.
49 M.H. Murfett, "Old Habits Die Hard: The Return of British Warships to Chinese Waters after the Second World War," in Murfett and J.B. Hattendorf (eds.), *The Limitations of Military Power* (London, 1990), pp. 203–17.

50 Manchester, John Rylands Library, Auchinleck papers, nos. 1136, 1143, 1155.

51 P.J. Brobst, "Sir Olaf Caroe and the Question of British Grand Design," in *Commonwealth and Comparative Politics*, 36 (1998): 95.

52 A. Husain, *Mapping the End of Empire: American and British Strategic Visions in the Postwar World* (Cambridge, MA, 2014).

53 F. McKenzie, *Redefining the Bonds of Commonwealth 1939–1948* (Basingstoke, 2002); G. Krozewski, *Money and the End of Empire. British International Economic Policy and the Colonies, 1947–58* (Basingstoke, 2001).

54 N. Westcott, *Imperialism and Development: The East African Groundnut Scheme and its Legacy* (Woodbridge, 2020).

55 C. Harvie, "The Moment of British Nationalism, 1939–1970," in *Political Quarterly*, 71 (2000): 328–40.

56 A. Heinonen, "A Tonic to the Empire? The 1951 Festival of Britain and the Empire-Commonwealth," in *Britain and the World*, 8 (2015): 76–99.

57 D. Edgerton, "The Nationalisation of British History: Historians, Nationalism and the Myths of 1940," in *EHR*, 136 (2021): 950–85.

58 A. Sutton, *The Political Economy of Imperial Relations: Britain, the Sterling Area and Malaya, 1945–1960* (Basingstoke, 2015).

59 J.J. Seah, "Singapore, Hong Kong, and the Royal Navy's War in Korea, *c.* 1950–1953," in *Journal of Military History*, 83 (2019): 1213–34.

60 J. Mohamed, "Imperial Policies and Nationalism in the Decolonization of Somaliland, 1954–1960," in *EHR*, 117 (2002): 1177.

61 S. Onslow, "'Battlelines for Suez': The Abadan Crisis of 1951 and the Formation of the Suez Group," in *Contemporary British History*, 17, 2 (1008): 1–28; M. Beloff, "The Crisis and its Consequences for the British Conservative Party,". in W.R. Louis and R. Owen (eds), *Suez 1956: The Crisis and its Consequences* (Oxford, 1991), pp. 319–34; S. Ball, *The Guardsmen: Harold Macmillan, Three Friends and the World They Made* (London, 2005).

62 A. MacInnes, *A History of Scotland* (London, 2019), p. 169.

63 Liaison Committee, 5 July 1963.

64 Standing Committee, 28 Oct. 1959.

65 *Annual Report 1957–58*, pp. 2–3.

66 Standing Committee papers, 21 Jan. 1965.

67 S.C. Smith, *Kuwait, 1950–1965: Britain, the al-Sabah, and Oil* (Oxford, 1999); N. Ashton, "Britain and the Kuwaiti Crisis, 1961," in *Diplomacy and Statecraft*, 9 (1998): 163–81.

68 M. Jones, "A Decision Delayed: Britain's Withdrawal from South East Asia Reconsidered, 1961–8," in *EHR*, 117 (2002): 569–95.

69 A. Jackson, *Buildings of Empire* (Oxford, 2013).

70 R. Fox, M. Cronin and B. O'Conchubhair (eds.), *Routledge International Handbook of Irish Studies* (Abingdon, 2021).

71 I. Patel, *We're Here Because You Were There: Immigration and the End of Empire* (London, 2020); P. Panayi, *Migrant City: A New History of London* (New Haven, CT, 2020).

72 E. Mercau, *The Falklands War: An Imperial History* (Cambridge, 2019).

Chapter 8 Endnotes

1 For highly critical accounts, D. Hicks, *The Brutish Museums. The Benin Bronzes, Colonial Violence and Cultural Restitution* (London, 2020), P. Docherty, *Blood and Bronze: The British Empire and the Sack of Benin* (London, 2021) and B. Phillips, *LOOT: Britain and the Benin Bronzes* (London, 2022).

2 For a less tendentious account of a related topic, A. Jackson and D. Tomkins, *Illustrating Empire – A Visual History of British Imperialism* (Oxford, 2011).

3 I.F.W. Beckett (ed.), *Army, Empire and Cinema: British Imperial Conflict on Screen* (Exeter, 2025); C. Fowler, *Our Island Stories. Country Walks through Colonial Britain* (London, 2024), emphasizes slavery.

4 H. Adi (ed.), *Black British History: New Perspectives* (London, 2019).

5 See, for example, *University of Oxford. Access and participation plan 2025–26 to 2028–29* (Oxford, 2024), "Intervention Strategy 6: Race Equality Actions" section, https://academic.admin.ox.ac.uk/sitefiles/university-of-oxford-app-2025–26–v1–10007774.pdf.

6 R. Waters, *Thinking Black: Britain, 1964–1985* (Oakland, CA, 2019).

7 S. Seth, *Difference and Disease: Medicine, Race, and the Eighteenth-Century British Empire* (Cambridge, 2018).

8 For contrasting views, K. Niemietz, *Imperial Measurement* (London, 2024); W. Hutton opinion piece in *Guardian*, 5 May 2024, R. Tombs, opinion piece in *Spectator*, 20 Ap. 2024.

9 P. Stamatov, *The Origins of Global Humanitarianism: Religion, Empire, Advocacy* (Cambridge, 2013).

10 D. Kennedy, *The Imperial History Wars: Debating the British Empire* (London, 2018).

11 R.G.S. Cooper, *The Anglo-Maratha Campaigns and the Contest for India : The Struggle for Control of the South Asian Military Economy* (Cambridge, 2004).

12 W. Dalrymple, *The Golden Road: How Ancient India Transformed the World* (London, 2004).

13 See, for example, D. Veevers, *The Great Defiance: How the World Took on the British Empire* (London, 2023).

14 L. Benton, *They Called It Peace: Worlds of Imperial Violence* (Princeton, NJ, 2024).
15 Benton and L. Ford, *Rage for Order: The British Empire and the Origins of International Law, 1800–1850* (Cambridge, MA, 2016).
16 See also N. Robins, *The Corporation that Changed the World: How the East India Company Shaped the Modern Multinational* (2nd ed., London, 2012); "The Londoner," in *Evening Standard*, 9 June 2020.
17 S. Ward (ed.), *Embers of Empire in Brexit Britain* (London, 2019).
18 J.H. Bentley (ed.), *The Oxford Handbook of World History* (Oxford, 2011).
19 J. Miller, *Way of Death: Merchant Capitalism and the Angolan Slave Trade, 1730–1830* (London, 1988).
20 For very different approaches, N. Biggar, *Colonialism: A Moral Reckoning* (London, 2023) and A. Lester, "The British Empire in the Culture War: Nigel Biggar's *Colonialism: A Moral Reckoning*," in *Journal of Imperial and Commonwealth History*, 51 (2023): 763–95, and (ed.), *The Truth About Empire: Real Histories of British Colonialism* (London, 2024).
21 H. Butterfield, *The Whig Interpretation of History* (New York, 1965).
22 See, for example, K. Yusoff, *Geologic Life* (London, 2024).
23 J. Schindler and D. Dorling, "The Empire Was Celebrated as A Great Thing," in *Der Spiegel On-line, 31st May 2019,* https://www.spiegel.de/international/europe/oxford-professor-on-brexit-s-colonial-roots-a-1270238.html.
24 S. Haggerty, A. Webster and N. White (eds.), *The Empire in One City? Liverpool's Inconvenient Imperial Past* (Manchester, 2008); J. Belchem, *Before the "Windrush": Race Relations in Twentieth-Century Liverpool* (Liverpool, 2014).
25 Statement by Sir Keir Starmer and Pravind Jugnauth, Prime Minister of Mauritius, 3 Oct. 2024.
26 See, for example, R. Gildea, *Empires of the Mind: The Colonial Past and the Politics of the Present* (Cambridge, 2019).
27 J.M. Black, *Contesting History. Narratives of Public History* (London, 2014) and *Clio's Battles. Historiography in Practice* (Bloomington, IN, 2015).

Chapter 9 Endnotes

1 *Daily Telegraph*, 7 Aug. 1945.
2 J. Black, *Beyond the Military Revolution: War in the Seventeenth Century World* (Basingstoke, 2011).
3 J.G. Sharman, *Empires of the Weak: The Real Story of European Expansion and the Creation of the New World* (Princeton, NJ, 2019).

4 M. Thomas and R. Toye, *Arguing about Empire: Imperial Rhetoric in Britain and France, 1882–1956* (Oxford, 2017).

5 J. Peacey (ed.), *Making the British Empire, 1660–1800* (Manchester, 2022).

6 K. Burk, *The Lion and the Eagle: The Interactions of the British and American Empires, 1783–1972* (London, 2018).

7 A.G. Hopkins, *American Empire: A Global History* (Princeton, NJ, 2018); S. Wertheim, *Tomorrow, the World: The Birth of U.S. Global Supremacy* (Cambridge, MA, 2020).

8 G. Lundestad, "Empire by Invitation? The United States and Western Europe, 1945–1952," in *Journal of Peace Research*, 23 1986): 263–77.

9 E.M.T. Powell, *Egypt, Great Britain, and the Mastery of the Sudan* (Berkeley, CA, 2003), quote p. 219.

10 J. Saha, *Law, Disorder and the Colonial State: Corruption in Burma c.1900* (Basingstoke, 2013); R. Kroeze, P. Dalmau and F. Monier (ed.), *Corruption, Empire and Colonialism in the Modern Era: A Global Perspective* (Cambridge, 2021).

Index